THE MEANING OF

JUNGKOOK

THE TRIUMPH OF BTS AND THE MAKING
OF A GLOBAL POP SUPERSTAR

MONICA KIM

SIMON & SCHUSTER

NEW YORK   AMSTERDAM/ANTWERP   LONDON   TORONTO
SYDNEY/MELBOURNE   NEW DELHI

Simon & Schuster
1230 Avenue of the Americas
New York, NY 10020

First Simon & Schuster hardcover edition June 2025

SIMON & SCHUSTER and colophon are registered trademarks of Simon & Schuster, LLC

Interior design by Ruth Lee-Mui

Manufactured in the United States of America

1   3   5   7   9   10   8   6   4   2

Library of Congress Cataloging-in-Publication Data has been applied for.

ISBN 978-1-6680-8276-8
ISBN 978-1-6680-8278-2 (ebook)

CONTENTS

WHAT IS IT ABOUT JUNGKOOK?

Forty seconds. It took forty seconds, by fan and media accounts, to sell out the tickets for Jungkook's solo debut. Jeon Jungkook—surname Jeon, first name Jungkook, professionally styled Jung Kook, but more commonly spelled Jungkook—the "sold-out king," as he's affectionately called, is the center and youngest member of BTS. Short for Bangtan Sonyeondan, or Bulletproof Boy Scouts, the South Korean boy group is the country's most celebrated pop-cultural export to date, hailed as a spiritual successor to the Beatles. An outlier in the K-pop industry, BTS possessed a rare Cinderella story that saw them go from an underdog act, playing for a crowd of 5,000 across three days at AX-Korea in 2014, to performing two sold-out nights at London's Wembley Stadium in 2019 for 120,000 screaming fans.

BTS has shattered many records. At various times they have: held the most viewed YouTube video in twenty-four hours, been the fastest to reach one million followers on TikTok and the first Korean act to debut at number one on the Billboard 200, been the most streamed group on Spotify, the most followed group on Instagram, had the most Twitter (now X) engagements, and been the first Asian act to perform at Wembley and sell out the Rose Bowl in Pasadena. In 2019, they became the first band since the Beatles to score three number-one albums on the Billboard 200 in a single year. They have been on the cover of *Rolling Stone* and *Variety*, plus *Time* magazine on three separate occasions. ARMY, the official name of their fan base, who number in the tens of millions by unofficial counts, are known for their passion and devotion, racking up more than twenty Guinness World Records for the group through sales and streams. Strictly by the numbers, BTS has become the biggest K-pop group in the world. Though often compared to era-defining acts like the Beatles or One Direction, BTS holds the distinction of being the first all-Asian boy band to reach such great heights without any native English speakers.

The thought of any artists breaking out of their cultural and linguistic restrictions to introduce seven distinctly Korean names—Kim Namjoon, Kim Seokjin, Min Yoongi, Jung Hoseok, Park Jimin, Kim Taehyung, Jeon Jungkook—into the mainstream was unfathomable, something that I and many others of the Asian diaspora considered a pipe dream. The success of BTS and their dominance through the late 2010s and early 2020s is undeniable.

After reaching the top as a member of BTS, Jungkook was set to embark on a new endeavor as a Korean solo artist, aiming to break through an even higher ceiling to singular global pop stardom. He made his opening move in July 2023, as a sweltering heat wave simmered over New York City. Unlike his debut with BTS under the fledgling record label Big Hit Entertainment, Jungkook's second debut was supported by the might of HYBE, a billion-dollar entertainment company with a dedicated US division run by Scooter Braun, former manager of Justin Bieber, Ariana Grande, and Demi Lovato. Jungkook chose "Seven (feat. Latto)," a three-minute, four-second song sung not in Korean but in English. The performance was not on a Korean music show like *Inkigayo* or *Music Bank* but on *Good Morning America*. Jungkook was the first K-pop solo artist invited to kick off the program's Summer Concert Series with a three-song set in Central Park. Demand was so high that free-ticketing platform 1iota opened the raffle for tickets at 12:00 p.m. EST and closed it down before one minute had passed.

The concert was scheduled for Friday morning, and the line of ticket holders began to form on Monday at Seventy-Second Street, stretching down Fifth Avenue and hugging the low stone wall that encircled the park. Seeking shelter beneath the towering elm trees, their deep green leaves providing ample shade, the fans came with rolling shopping carts and blue IKEA Frakta bags, from which they withdrew collapsible camping chairs and inflatable sofas and pool rafts in shades of pink and silver and blue. Fleece blankets for comfort and warmth, despite the nearly ninety-degree days, were shared between clusters of friends who took turns waiting, cycling between hotel rooms and health clubs to shower and rest, co-opting the Apple Store bathroom on Madison Avenue as an outpost. ARMY was as organized as a local militia.

By Thursday afternoon, more than seven hundred people stood in line, according to fans who checked in at the entrance; by nightfall, close to two thousand, and by dawn of Friday morning, the line reportedly wound its way twelve city blocks down to Sixtieth Street, wrapping back into the park along East Drive. By sunrise, Jungkook, who had flown in from Seoul two days prior, made his way to Rumsey Playfield. Still nursing a stubborn sore throat that had stuck around for several weeks, he was worried how the performance would go, and the storm clouds overhead, threatening heavy rain and thunder, increased his troubles. Dressed in simple light-wash jeans and a white tank with two thin silver chains, a black zip-up worn on top, Jungkook gripped the railing, bouncing slightly on the heels of his Balenciaga sneakers, looking tense.

Jungkook was scheduled to perform at eight a.m., but not long after seven, the storm warning had become a reality, and the impending lightning made it impossible to proceed. The *Good Morning America* team made the call to cut the rehearsal short and move up and prerecord the sound check to air instead, a contingency plan that caught Jungkook off guard. Fans were quickly ushered past the barricades, clutching their phones and pink plush dolls of Cooky, the adorable muscular bunny that Jungkook had created as a cartoon avatar of himself for BTS's collaboration with Japanese messaging app LINE. Backstage he laughed in disbelief, as the hairstylist fussed over his bangs. For the performance, his stylist exchanged his hoodie for a studded white Givenchy top.

Despite the last-minute change in schedule, Jungkook didn't seem too bothered. Ascending the stairs, Jungkook flashed the camera an easygoing smile, the light catching on a hoop pierced through his bottom lip. The first strains of "Euphoria," a solo from the BTS compilation album *Love Yourself: Answer*, began, the camera closing in on the ARMY logo printed on Jungkook's custom in-ear monitors. When he walked down the bleachers, fans stretched their hands toward him and he gave a few high fives, their recipients gazing giddily at the palms he had briefly touched.

Over the course of nine minutes, Jungkook performed three songs, including the first live performance of "Seven." The music video had dropped at midnight and, according to *Good Morning America*, gained eighteen million views on YouTube by the time of the recording. He sang in his smooth tenor, moving with a light step, a modern-day Fred Astaire had Astaire learned hip-hop. Backed by a live band and with four dancers beside him, Jungkook serenaded the crowd of men and women, who had been screaming and barking for the last half hour. They pumped their fists and crossed their thumbs and index fingers into little hearts, chanting his name. The fans were experiencing unfettered joy, something that BTS had always offered. Now Jungkook was providing it alone here: communal, unbridled happiness. When he sang a solo rendition of "Dynamite," BTS's first English-language single, Jungkook held the microphone out to the crowd to sing together, as raindrops began to fall. When the concert aired, broadcast-friendly tweets scrolled along the bottom of the screen:

"he was born to perform & Rock on Stage Superstar Jungkook."

"Jungkook has the most beautiful smile!! How do you not instantly fall in love with him??"

"OH JUNGKOOK YOU WILL ALWAYS BE THE MAIN CHARACTER"

"Our Boy is a Born Star . . . So So So Proud of him . . . Feeling Emotional R8 now7"

Not long after he wrapped, the skies opened and the downpour began, as if they, too, had waited for the performance to go on, quenching the crowd that had waited days for what felt like a historic event. "Seven" would become the fastest song to reach one billion streams on Spotify. Jungkook went on to set the first-day sales record for a K-pop soloist, according to Korean music chart Hanteo, debuted at number one on the Billboard Hot 100, and number three on the Official UK Singles Chart, making the then-highest charting UK debut for a Korean solo artist. He made history, and it all started there with ARMY. From the hundreds of fans who attended BTS's first public showcase back in 2013 to those who tuned in to Jungkook's YouTube vlogs, which he began recording as a teenage trainee. This was the latest episode on their shared journey. They championed Jungkook. They loved him. They had watched him grow over the years, mesmerized by his talent, addicted to his music, and now they stood with him as he began the next chapter. Braving the sweltering heat and sleepless nights on the sidewalk, fans witnessed Jungkook's first steps on the road from K-pop to main pop stardom.

Four months later, when Jungkook released his solo album, *Golden*, he became the first K-pop soloist to have three of his singles—"Seven," "3D," and "Standing Next to You"—hit the top ten of the Billboard Hot 100. *Golden* set the record for longest-charting album on the Billboard 200 from a Korean solo artist, surpassing every bar and expectation that had been set for him. In the span of only eight months, Jungkook once again achieved the unthinkable. An Eastern male singer backed by the Western entertainment industry, applauded by not only ARMY but the laymen who caught him on network TV, Jungkook broke through the foreign trappings of K-pop and set the stage for his ascendance as a global pop superstar.

"The name's Jungkook. The scale's nationwide." That was the first time I heard the name Jungkook when, in June 2013, BTS debuted on the weekly music show *M Countdown* with a performance of "We Are Bulletproof Pt.2," which opened with Jungkook delivering that playful boast. I thought it was charming how the young artist, then fifteen years old, introduced himself with the braggadocio pun (Jungkook and *jeonguk*, the entire nation), but never imagined the name Jungkook would surpass the national scale to be known around the world. It should have been impossible. Back then, long before I covered K-pop for publications like American *Vogue*, before I moved from New York to Seoul and spent one summer working for a record label, I was a K-pop fan like any other. But rather than a fan devoted to any one group, I considered myself more a scholar, who studied the inner workings of the industry with fascination.

When I speak of K-pop, I am not speaking of Korean pop music, which encompasses everything from ballads to rock. I am speaking of the idol system, which was adapted from Japan and developed around fandom culture. As South Korea's most visible cultural product, K-pop was an illuminating means of learning about the country's global reputation, its role and relative position in the world. A child of immigrants, I derived particular interest from watching the way Korean artists were received overseas, as they became a proxy for understanding the way I was received. Observing the constant clash of cultures, taste, and values, the different ways of engaging with the artists and their work, was as engrossing as the earworm songs and hypnotic performances I had enjoyed since the days of H.O.T. and Shinhwa—the first generation of K-pop stars—whose VHS tapes my mother rented from the local Korean market. After I fell into groups like SHINee as a teen, I became absorbed by the wealth of content increasingly available on YouTube.

From my vantage point in the US, I watched so many artists spark for an instant, each one taking a small step forward, laying stones to cross a river without being able to glimpse the opposite shore. In 2007, Rain topped *Time* magazine's Time 100 reader poll; the solo singer received the first-place vote two more times and appeared on *The Colbert Report* and Hollywood's live-action *Speed Racer*. Wonder Girls opened for the Jonas Brothers World Tour 2009. "Gee" by Girls' Generation went viral, to the point where it was played in the dining hall at my American college campus. In 2012, I heard Psy's "Gangnam Style" everywhere, from a greasy club in Midtown to a tiny trattoria in Rome. Before "Gangnam Style," the first YouTube video to ever hit one then two billion views, the average American, in my personal experience, had such a limited view of Korea that the go-to cultural reference was *M*A*S*H*, a seventies TV series about US soldiers in the Korean War.

That was no longer the case. Each artist made a blip, ripples large and small, before returning home to successful careers, largely forgotten by the West. When BTS began trending overseas, I thought it would be another flash in the pan, another "Gangnam Style" moment of virality. I was delightfully wrong. Every time I thought BTS had hit a wall, that the Sisyphean boulder would tumble downhill, they found a way to push forward. Ten years after their debut, their international feats continue to surprise me.

Among the seven members, Jungkook, with his dimples and easy smile, was the name and face that popped most readily in the Western cultural consciousness. He was mentioned by name, for example, on a 2021 episode of *The Simpsons* ("everyone in BTS, except for Jungkook, he's too pretty for my taste."). By 2024 he'd topped the inaugural Billboard K-Pop Artist 100 list. It is not as simple as declaring him the most popular member. All seven members have their own dedicated fandoms. All seven members have made a unique contribution to the group's success. The edict in K-pop fandom is to love and support every member. Anything counter to that is particularly foreign to BTS, whose found-family dynamic has stood the test of time, nor is it what Jungkook himself, always humble and shy, seemed to want, being dedicated to the group and to ARMY. Yet beyond raw statistics, superstars possess a more ineffable quality that draws public attention; in that regard, Jungkook has been the pick of the general populace. As early as 2017, when BTS performed at the American Music Awards, Jungkook drew comparisons to Justin Timberlake and Harry Styles as the potential "breakout" star with the strongest solo prospects. Again and again, people came calling for him: singer-songwriter Charlie Puth, who requested Jungkook for his song "Left and Right" in 2022. The 2022 FIFA World Cup, where he was invited to perform the song "Dreamers" at the opening ceremony in Qatar. Calvin Klein, who appointed him a global brand ambassador in 2023.

Five years after the American Music Awards, after BTS had transcended their genre to become a cultural phenomenon, the seven members gathered for Festa 2022, their anniversary celebration, and announced a pause on group releases that stunned the public and sent HYBE stocks down by nearly 28 percent. In hindsight, the announcement made perfect sense. Widely referred to as Chapter 2, this new phase would allow each member, for the first time in nine years, to fully pursue their own personal projects, before enlisting in the military to complete the service mandated by South Korean law, which would essentially place a dead stop on their careers. Each could make the music he wanted, not restrained by the needs of the group or the company. They could even take a break if they so wished, which Jungkook did for almost five months.

From that moment, their musical paths began to diverge, just a little. In brief: J-Hope released the hip-hop album *Jack in the Box* and performed at Lollapalooza 2022, the first Korean artist to headline a major US festival. Jin released an upbeat pop-rock single called "The Astronaut," cowritten with Coldplay, and flew seventy-two hours round-trip to Argentina to perform at the band's Buenos Aires show; the eldest, he began military service first, paving the way for the rest of the group. Grappling with creative burnout, RM released the sonically eclectic studio album *Indigo* with a trip to NPR's Tiny Desk concert series, collaborating with a range of artists like Erykah Badu and Youjeen of nineties Korean rock band Cherry Filter, and, in a nod to his artistic inclinations, filmed a twelve-minute concert special at Dia Beacon in Upstate New York. Jimin dropped *Face*, a pop and R&B studio album sung in Korean and English, breaking a slew of records including the first

K-pop solo artist to top the Billboard Hot 100. Under the alias Agust D, which he first used in 2016, Suga released the rap album *D-Day* and went on the Suga Agust D Tour, which became the highest-grossing US tour by an Asian soloist. V took the time to slowly work on the sort of music he liked, not pure pop but a more R&B and jazz-influenced work called *Layover*, which was another record-breaker on release.

As each chose to express himself in his own way, anticipation began to build for Jungkook, nicknamed the golden *maknae* (*maknae* meaning youngest) by RM during their trainee days, who appeared to possess the greatest global ambitions. Those became clear when he released *Golden*: eleven pure pop tracks, sung entirely in English.

By the end of his debut, which featured remixes with artists like Usher and Justin Timberlake and songwriting credits by Shawn Mendes and Ed Sheeran and Diplo, Jungkook seemed to possess a new aura. As a guest on *Suchwita*, the YouTube series hosted by Suga, Jungkook presented his first solo output and received the ultimate recognition from his beloved bandmate. "The moment I saw the cover [of *Golden*], I thought, ah, a true pop star," Suga said. "Now an Asian pop star has finally appeared." His words felt like a coronation, as he declared what many others had been thinking for years.

An Asian pop star, embraced by the West—how did Jungkook achieve the impossible? There are a dozen company heads still gnashing their teeth over this very question, wondering how a boy named Jeon Jungkook from Busan, picked up by a small and struggling music label, became an international sensation. In truth, the potential had always been there. I will never forget the first time I saw him in the flesh. In 2016, when I was still a young editor at American *Vogue*, I had spent a year making an impassioned plea to cover BTS for the website and magazine. At the time, the mainstream media regarded idols as a passing curiosity. Compared to Western pop stars, K-pop stars' public images appeared more meticulously crafted to present a manufactured fantasy that the average American found difficult to digest. But BTS seemed different. With their raw visuals and insightful lyrics and the unfiltered flow of content on social media platforms like YouTube and Twitter, BTS felt more authentic—and appealed to the West. At the center of that group stood Jungkook, who, even in those early days, had the makings of an it boy. While working for *Vogue* and then as a stylist, I have met more celebrities than I can recall. But the moment Jungkook walked into the room will always remain in my mind.

It was November 2017, and the boys were occupying the tenth floor of the JW Marriott in Los Angeles, a long stone's throw from the Staples Center, where they had performed for the American Music Awards. I remember I was helping a stylist unpack the steel-toed cowboy boots that she had called in from Raf Simons's Calvin Klein, from whom she had spent several days coaxing the samples. We were working with a skeleton crew, just me, the shoot producer, and the stylist, who had flown in from New York for the project. BTS's previous interview was running over schedule, and we were nervous about meeting our own strict timetable. I was anxious about the tensions between Big Hit and *Vogue*, who spoke different languages in more ways than one. I'd pushed for this feature, and I was counting on it to succeed. As I was checking on the seven iced Americanos the label had requested, Jungkook walked into the room without any warning and stood still for a moment, eyes wide, like a deer caught in headlights. In later years, I heard from friends in the industry that HYBE, the K-pop conglomerate that Big Hit would become, instituted some of the strictest policies among labels. Shoot locations were scouted and vetted by HYBE employees, and phones were either confiscated or their camera lenses covered by blue stickers that said "shooting forbidden" in Korean (the latter was my experience covering a HYBE group for the March 2023 issue of *Vogue*). Interaction with the members was strictly controlled, NDAs signed. But not in 2017.

There was something about Jungkook in that moment that stuck with me. The wide-eyed look in his eyes, as he politely bowed to us and darted away; the way he sang softly to himself in the makeup chair; his ever-present smile, despite the jet lag. He possessed the rare brand of charisma that came through without effort. It was a natural charisma that couldn't be curated or controlled by a label's heavy hand. Despite his center position, he did not draw unnecessary attention to himself. He still seemed a bit shy and deferential to the other members, who were like his older brothers, who fussed over him as they adjusted the collar of his denim shirt. Yet when it came time to dance the chorus of "DNA," which they performed thrice across the city, Jungkook took the lead, humming the melody as he stood at the front. As he moved with ease, he became magnetic, enchanting the film crew of K-pop agnostics. "I'm obsessed," one said to me in a hushed voice, as Jungkook walked past unaware.

When I first considered the rise of Jungkook, I hoped to pinpoint what gave him such exceptional crossover appeal—in the eyes of not only ARMY but the everyman and higher powers, the record labels and publications that gravitated toward him. Jungkook spent only eight months performing as a soloist and, in that short span of time, he broke new ground for Asian artists. Despite his shaky grasp of English, he worked hard enough that it did not matter. I spent months dissecting his dance practices, absorbing livestreams and live performances, making him my dinnertime companion. With his face on my tablet screen, as we ate the same red-hot Buldak noodles, I would come to understand on an intrinsic level what it's like to be his fan. There is an unquantifiable magic at work, an ephemeral charm that belongs to Jungkook alone.

The truth is that Jungkook's success is a culmination of many forces. There is the triumph of BTS, who are inextricably linked to his story; without BTS and the six other members who practically raised him, per his own admission, there is no Jungkook. There are the technological advancements, the rise of social media platforms, and the globalization of pop culture. ARMY is an international force of fans who are among the most internet-savvy in the world and generate limitless content. There is Covid-19, the global pandemic that shut down the world in 2020 and stirred a collective need for the intimacy, joy, and optimism that artists like Jungkook could provide. Of course, there are his artistic talents. His sumptuous voice and his dancing style, which can be traced back to Michael Jackson, the king of dance. His good looks, which meet the conventional Korean standards of beauty but are subverted by his tattoos and piercings. His kindness and humility, which remained even after his rise to stardom. Then there are the larger driving forces that pushed K-pop forward, the historical backdrop and the cultural nuances that made BTS and Jungkook, in particular, palatable to both the East and West.

The complex factors that led to the making of Jungkook are intertwined and impossible to replicate; there is no manual to creating a global pop star. Yet examining these different aspects provides a richer understanding and appreciation for the artist and what he has accomplished in such a short amount of time—and what he can achieve going forward. This is a celebration of Jungkook, as it explores his cultural lineage, his musical influences, K-pop history, and all that he and BTS have achieved together and apart. It is a look at the deeper meaning behind his success. The making of Jungkook, the golden *maknae*, and Jungkook, the pop superstar, is a story about overcoming the odds. Through his triumphs, he challenged the status quo. And he's not even done yet. Not even close.

CHAPTER 1

HIS UNDERDOG STORY

The BTS story began with a classic exposition, containing the bones of a hero's journey: seven boys from the "countryside" move to the unforgiving city to chase after their dreams. It is a timeless trope for good reason, and the relatable underdog story became the group's narrative backbone, part and parcel of their universal attraction.

Gwacheon and Ilsan, satellite cities to the south and northwest of Seoul in the province of Gyeonggi. Daegu, the erstwhile "Apple City," a textile hub and commercial center to the southeast. Gwangju, the political hotbed to the southwest, where the student uprising and subsequent massacre of 1980 marked a pivotal moment in South Korea's road to democracy. Geochang, a county in South Gyeongsang Province. And Busan, the port city on the southeast side, known for its sand and pebble beaches and rugged coastline. These are the hometowns of the seven members of BTS. Ilsan and Gwacheon are a mere half-hour drive from central Seoul, without traffic, like Long Island from Manhattan. Busan, the second-largest city in Korea still dwarfed by Seoul, is certainly not backcountry. Even Korean Americans, if they did not grow up in Korea, will find it difficult to grasp the vast gaps that exist between Seoul and every other city.

Seoul is more than the capital of South Korea. It is the metaphorical heart and cultural epicenter. Like Chicago is to Illinois, New York City to New York State, the city has become synonymous with the greater area around it. So much of Korean commerce and creativity, business and politics, is concentrated in 234 square miles of earth. Compared to other capitals, however, Seoul takes its centricity to an extreme. In 2024, the city was home to about 9.6 million residents, nearly 20 percent of the total population, with more than 40,000 people residing per square mile. It is extraordinarily dense. (For reference, New York City was estimated to have about 29,303 residents per square mile in 2020). According to a 2024 report by the Bank of Korea, the percentage of the population living in the greater capital area (50.6 percent) was the largest among the twenty-six countries of the Organisation for Economic Co-operation and Development (OECD).

To live in Seoul is to wage daily war, locked in ceaseless competition with those around you. Fighting day in and day out to carve a space of your own: for parking, a seat at the café, acceptance to a top university, a good job. Those born of privilege have it easier. Those who aren't suffer, and those who are able to win these battles earn the right to reside in the city where everything happens. Being a "Seoul *saram*," which literally translates to a "Seoul person," is a mark of prestige. As in other metropolitan cities, there is a distinct sense of snobbery. Take the existence of the *chaebol*, which are family-run conglomerates supported by the government, immortalized for their wealth and glamorized in Korean TV dramas like *The Heirs*. Their pervasive influence extends to general attitudes: Seoulites tend to be obsessed with brand names and clout to a degree that rivals the upper crust of Manhattan and the glitterati of Los Angeles. The model of imported car you drive, the prestigious name on your college degree, the logo of the handbag slung from your shoulder, the *Fortune* Global 500 company where you work—these function as shortcuts, allowing you to assign the correct level of respect in an instant, saving time in encoding your social interactions. The pursuit of brand names as signifiers of value is not exclusive to Korean culture, but Koreans, known for needing things done quickly, appreciate the ability to assess a person's importance at a single glance.

It feeds into the elitism that is born from that hypercompetitive mindset. This elitism extends to the K-pop industry, where SM Entertainment, YG Entertainment, and JYP Entertainment—known as the Big Three—dominated the industry when BTS debuted in 2013. After finding success as a composer at JYP, Bang Si-hyuk founded his own record label, Big Hit Entertainment, in 2005, but the Big Three had originated in the mid-nineties. With such a head start, the Big Three had amassed financial resources, stacked talent rosters, and cultivated relationships. Connections with brands and sponsors, with media and broadcast companies that guaranteed airtime and publicity, even for their rookie groups. Surrounded by these Seoul elites, BTS fought the battle to exist there.

That said, the members of BTS are far from the only idols to come from disparate parts of the country. Before K-pop stars were international figures with lucrative brand deals and cultural capital, idol music was generally regarded as a low form of entertainment by the Korean public due to its lack of originality and perceived youth marketing, focused on fan service. Many of the trainees came from smaller cities and others from struggling families, hoping to make enough money to give them a comfortable life. Seventeen's Seungkwan is the pride of Jeju, Red Velvet's Irene came from Daegu, Suzy is from Gwangju.

Consider the prevalent attitudes toward *satoori*, which refers to the regional dialects that exist across South Korea. Often compared to accents, like a Southern twang or a Midwestern roundness, *satoori* can range from the subtle twist of a vowel—an "eh" instead of an "ah," "oo" over "oh"—evoking rurality, to something so thick, it is nigh unintelligible. In parts of Jeju Island, even natives struggle to understand each other. I've found that Seoulites tend to view *satoori* with a degree of condescension. On dating shows like *Single's Inferno*, contestants with *satoori* are generally less popular. Celebrities with *satoori* are often called to speak with it on variety shows, to the hosts' overt fascination. Overseas fans are also charmed by *satoori*, unable to grasp the linguistic nuances, but resonating with the melodic lilt and softness that resemble the rural dialects in their own homelands.

At entertainment agencies, idol trainees are given lessons to correct their *satoori*, learning to speak in the standard Gyeonggi or Seoul dialect, similar to the way that actors and news anchors in the US are coached to speak with a nondescript standard American accent or how Received Pronunciation (RP) in British English maintains a lofty status. Winter of the SM Entertainment girl group Aespa once spoke about this training on an episode of the popular variety show *Knowing Bros*. Panelists noted that Winter, a native of Yangsan in Gyeongsang Province, seemed to pass as a Seoulite because she didn't have *satoori*. "I mostly fixed it when I was a trainee," she commented. In November 2013, Wonwoo of Seventeen, who was born in Changwon, filmed an evaluation as a trainee for Pledis Entertainment. He introduced himself with a shy smile, before being interrupted by a female staffer, who scolded him. "What did we say we'd do if you use *satoori* . . ." she said, her voice trailing off.

In 2011, RM, J-Hope, and Suga were three Big Hit trainees poised to debut as BTS. They released a song called "Paldogangsan," nicknamed "Satoori Rap." Suga with his Gyeongsang dialect from the east, J-Hope with his Jeolla dialect from the west, riffed back and forth, letting their *satoori* run free. The song was a clever commentary on the perceived superiority of Gyeonggi or Seoul dialect. "What is he saying?" the chorus repeats in Gyeongsang *satoori*. At the end, RM chimes in with his Seoul speech, making the point that it's all the same language. *Satoori* illustrates the regional divisions in Korean society, which is often depicted overseas as homogenous and harmonious. Before moving to Seoul, my grandfather hailed from Chungcheong Province, sandwiched between Gyeonggi and Jeolla; he could identify the provenance of a cod fillet pancake, native to Chungcheong, with a single bite. When my grandmother, a woman from Seoul, went down to Chungcheong to meet her future mother-in-law, she received a disapproving shake of the head and a cutting remark that a Seoul woman was coddled by city life.

What set BTS apart was the way they embraced their roots. Whereas other idols were polished to gemstones, like paupers made into princes, BTS remained rough, which suited the hip-hop concept encouraged by Big Hit. "Paldogangsan" pushed back against prejudices toward *satoori*. It was a sensation on Naver portals that made the *SBS Eight O'Clock News*, as Koreans marveled over the rare use of *satoori* in popular music. It even went on to inspire a variety show called *Are We Strangers*, which aimed to improve communication between Koreans from different provinces. "Paldogangsan" caught the attention of a young V, who said on the *New Yang Nam Show* that it was because of that song that he went to the Big Hit audition. BTS stood out because they wore their outsider status as a badge of honor. They were proud of where they came from and refused to scrub themselves of their origins, instead celebrating them. The group rerecorded "Paldogangsan" for the 2013 album *O!RUL8,2?* In 2015, they revisited their hometown pride with the song "Ma City," a loving ode to the smaller places from where they came.

Jungkook's *satoori* peeks out often, especially when he's with Jimin, who also grew up in Busan, or V, who came from the same Gyeongsang Province. His *satoori* is one of his charms. Busan *satoori* is typically low-toned and masculine, associated with the Busan gangsters portrayed in movies like *Nameless Gangster* or *Wish*. As he's grown older, Jungkook does at times employ the deep and slightly slurred speech of a Busan man, his words running together in a loose and carefree way. But the *satoori* that Jungkook uses most often is distinctly cute. He speaks with a soft drawl with the slightest lilt. When he ends a sentence with "dae-ee" instead of "dah," it summons a simple train of thought: cute, cute, so cute. There is a clip from a November 2016 Jungkook livestream that illustrates this. *"Sa-too-ri?"* he said, as he sipped milk from a paper carton, the pitch of his voice angling up with each syllable. "Everyone, I don't use *satoori* anymore, right? Right . . . I don't use *satoori* now." He continued to insist he didn't use *satoori*, while his speech contained the subtle inflections of Gyeongsang. "Cause nowadays I think I really use Seoul-speak. Right?" he said, seeking his fans' affirmation and not finding it. ". . . You mean I'm using it?" he said, truly unaware. It was a part of him, and he'd never be able to let it go, no matter how high his career ascended, how elite he became.

Before founding his own label, Bang Si-hyuk was a respected composer and producer who worked with JYP Entertainment founder Park Jin-young and groups like g.o.d and 2AM, but Big Hit Entertainment was still a minnow in a pond with three whales. The Big Three were household names. Big Hit was nothing. The company was financially strapped due to the public's poor reception of Glam, a girl group that debuted in 2012 and was co-run with the small label Source Music. In this sense, Jungkook and the members of BTS were underdogs from the beginning, but their disadvantages became their strengths. To this day, the characterization works to their advantage. Much of *Beyond the Story: 10-Year Record of BTS*, the official book, positions Big Hit as a David going against the Goliaths of the industry, armed with naught but a slingshot. As the first full male idol project from a relatively unknown label, BTS was nearly a *nugu* group, a term that Western fans have adopted to refer to artists that are lesser known, their name prompting the response *"nugu?"* the Korean word for "who." Of the dozens of groups that debut each year, only a handful find success. BTS did win the Best New Artist award at the 2013 Melon Music Awards, among other notable rookie titles, but there was little competition among new boy groups at the time, by Big Hit's account, due to the dominance of the Big Three.

In the K-pop industry, I have heard Bang Si-hyuk described as the world's luckiest man, who walked into a shop at the exact right day and time and bought a winning lottery ticket by selecting seven numbers in the correct order. He'd be the first to admit that luck was on his side—the industry's inability to replicate the BTS phenomenon seems to suggest that it cannot be repeated with any amount of funding. But crucially, what Bang could not provide in money, he compensated for in artistic freedom.

This liberal approach applied to not only BTS's music but their promotional strategies. In *Beyond the Story*, writer Kang Myeongseok makes a point to call out EXO, a record-setting boy group that debuted in 2012 from SM Entertainment and, throughout the mid- to late-2010s, was considered a rival to BTS. EXO was the establishment pick to the up-and-comer BTS. The fandom wars were among the worst I've ever seen. Kang himself draws a direct line between the two, saying that in the one hundred days leading up to EXO's debut, SM dropped twenty-three teaser videos to introduce the members and their story lore, building the world of "Exo Planet." In "EXO Teaser 1_KAI (1)," uploaded to YouTube in December 2011, Kai emerged from a vintage car on a stage set of a foggy street, then began dancing in shallow water, the resulting waves pushed around in slow motion. Each video was a polished production, showcasing the twelve boys in different formations. BTS launched the *Bangtan Blog* on Tistory in December 2012, six months before their debut, with an entry by RM that didn't receive its first comment, according to Kang, until three days after it was posted.

Kang talks about the blog, a Twitter account, a fancafe, and, importantly, the YouTube channel BANGTANTV, which was launched with a series of vlogs called Bangtan Logs. BTS released forty-nine vlogs, each titled with the date and the member's name, in the lead-up to their debut. The Bangtan Logs were seemingly shot without supervision. For years, even tweets were posted by the members directly, which was nearly unheard of in the industry. On December 22, 2012, Jin introduced himself with an unposed selfie and a simple greeting, promising to tweet often. The next day he posted, without fanfare, a second grainy selfie captioned "my lower lip is charming.jpg" that was neither filtered nor polished.

"We heard that there are companies that wouldn't allow their artists to use SNS, but we can use it freely," the members said in a 2014 interview with *The Bridges* magazine. Companies kept notoriously tight leashes on their rookie idols, fearing PR scandals. In contrast, Bang Si-hyuk let BTS express themselves, not blinking an eye when they uploaded a song called "A Typical Trainee's Christmas." The music video opened with footage of Bang promoting Hit It the Second Audition,

Big Hit's audition program, before the boys launched into a diss track that skewered him for making them work through the holidays and not buying them *hwesik* or company meal. The rap was intercut with memes like "Dramatic Chipmunk" and footage of BTS members working in the studio and spinning through the streets. "What we want is one group dinner," Suga rapped coyly. "Our company, our boss, I don't like any of you," RM said on the extended track. "I miss my mom."

The Bangtan Logs read like diary entries, as brief as a minute or two. Sometimes they were mundane, the perfunctory small talk you might share with a friend or family member over dinner. Other times the boys spoke about their struggles. In the first Bangtan Log, "130107 RAP MONSTER," RM revealed a piece of Bang's criticism. The boss had said that he wouldn't be as good as the major or underground rappers, motivating RM to work harder. In "1301112 Jin," Jin said that the boss had commented on his weight gain. There were moments of vulnerability and insecurity, alongside scenes of unrehearsed silliness. In "130225 RAP MONSTER (Feat. SUGA)," RM turned on "Kiss the Rain," a soft and contemplative piece by the pianist Yiruma, before Suga entered the room, singing "The Imperial March" from *Star Wars* with an acoustic guitar. In "130227 J Hope & Jungkook," J-Hope showed off his new pants by swiveling his hips like a gate on a hinge.

These clips were the public's introduction to BTS, and the refreshing intimacy and unedited nature of their interactions carried on after their debut in the famous Bangtan Bombs. Much like the Logs, the Bangtan Bombs were short videos that provided a behind-the-scenes glimpse of their lives. But where the Logs allowed for introspection, the Bangtan Bombs captured chaotic, off-the-cuff moments that were random and playful. The first Bangtan Bomb, "130617 VJ Jungkook," showed Jungkook messing around with a handheld camcorder in the dressing room for thirty-four seconds. In October 2013, Jungkook sang a comedic trot (a Korean music genre) rendition of "N.O," before joining Suga, Jin, V, and J-Hope in an operatic version of the track. In February 2015, V began practicing a dance set to Run DMC's "It's Tricky," which the group performed at the 2014 KBS Song Festival, each member falling into line one by one like windup toy soldiers. There are dozens of clips of the boys breaking into random song and dance in greenrooms and conference rooms: Jungkook and V lip-synching to Linkin Park's "Given Up" while Jimin and J-Hope polish off their lunch boxes; in Chippewa Woods park near Chicago, Jungkook held a portable Bluetooth speaker and a selfie stick, shooting the boys tossing their heads and crab-walking to "Show Me Your Bba Sae."

These snapshots provided an unposed glimpse of each member, the scraps coming together over time to create a mosaic portrait of surprising depth. The Bangtan Bombs mimicked the way a relationship in the real world is built, getting to know someone not in pure biographical data points but in the smaller day-to-day moments. They were light and cheerful, and seeing the boys having fun made fans forget their own worries too. That casual approach to social media made BTS so unique in an industry as cutthroat as K-pop. Ultimately, the Bombs showed a brotherhood that transcended a professional bond. And they exemplified what BTS has always given to their fans: joy.

Not much is known about Jungkook's early life. He was born in Busan by the sea, where he grew up with his father, mother, and older brother in Mandeok-dong, a neighborhood known for squared houses with tiled roofs that resemble Lego blocks in hues of red and orange, green and blue. He speaks fondly of his family—how his father dressed up as Santa Claus for Christmas and snuck into Jungkook's room, his fake Santa beard brushing across his son's face. How his mother took him to the playground in the evenings to exercise, tossing a basketball around, and his grandmother lovingly raised the two baby chicks a young Jungkook had purchased for 500 won apiece. Fans assume he grew up in a typical household, not very rich or very poor. But unlike the average Korean family, Jungkook's mother and father raised him with a surprising amount of freedom. They did not fuss over his grades, letting him do what he liked, and scolded him only when he erred, like the time he cheated on a spelling test. So Jungkook considers his early childhood a happy time, free from the unnecessary pressure that most Korean parents do place on their children. "I'm really grateful for that. To my parents," he said on a livestream. "They let me do what I really wanted to do."

I wonder whether Jungkook's parents knew of his dream to be a global pop star, which according to Bang Si-hyuk, had always been his ambition. Before BTS, the top groups from the Big Three were geared toward Asian tastes, and music labels marketed idols to the Korean, Japanese, and Chinese fans who craved them, later branching into Southeast Asia. Months spent courting an uninterested Western audience meant months spent neglecting the industry back home, which moved at such a rapid pace that a top artist could become a relic of the past within a year, if they failed to release music at the same quarterly frequency as everyone else. So, it remained better to focus on the East and reap easy gains. The idea of an Asian pop group truly making it in America was fantastical. Even the top K-pop group was the greatest underdog in America.

The perception of South Korea in the Western cultural consciousness can be roughly defined by a split into two eras: pre– and post– "Gangnam Style." Psy's 2012 single was a cultural reset in the truest sense of the phrase. It wasn't just the hypnotic EDM-style beat, the imitable cowboy shuffle step that predated TikTok dance challenges, the viral YouTube video that was the first to hit one billion views.

The lyrics shone a direct spotlight on Gangnam, the area south of the Han River in Seoul known for its nouveau riche. What had once been fields for rice and mulberry trees was now wide streets lined with corporate offices. The glittering Galleria department store was stocked with Chanel hand cream and Louis Vuitton bags. "Gangnam Style" sounded an alarm, calling attention to how far the once impoverished country had come since the Korean War.

I remember the day "Gangnam Style" came out in 2012. One of my friends from college, who shared a fondness for K-pop, was visiting town and, as we were catching up, decided to pull up the video on YouTube, which we watched with great interest. Afterward, we went out to brunch, joyfully imitating Psy's lasso dance as we walked down the sidewalk toward Central Park, not then knowing how iconic it would become. A few months later, there was a sudden influx of curiosity about South Korea in the media. One day, my boss, an editor at Condé Nast, approached me in the cafeteria with a copy of *The New Yorker* in hand, creased open to a feature about K-pop that had been published in its October 8, 2012, issue. He was fascinated by the details, wanting to know if it was true, if K-pop really was as the writer had described. Having not read the week's issue, thinking back to the stack of unread *New Yorkers* piling up by my bedside, the corners turning yellow, I glanced over the headline on the page, which read "Factory Girls." I could quickly surmise the man's premise, the idea that K-pop stars are manufactured. "Oh sure," I had mindlessly agreed, "the training system is pretty intense."

Back then, in publishing circles, a feature in *The New Yorker* provided the ultimate cachet. The fact that *The New Yorker* had written about South Korea, about K-pop, opened doors. Suddenly my bosses were interested in where I had come from, asking questions that I, at the time, had trouble answering. Over the years, coverage of Korean culture would slowly increase in Western publications, to the point where articles about "K-culture" are now staple foods in the media diet. When I am commissioned by publications, eight times out of ten it has to do with our skincare, our food, our fashion. That *New Yorker* feature provided a key starting point, and I always considered it with respect. When I sat down to write this book, however, I went back to revisit the piece that had been so influential in the publishing sphere and was shocked by how things had changed in the span of a decade.

Of SHINee, the author wrote, "The boys were fun to watch—heavily made-up moussed male androgynes doing strenuous rhythmic dances. But . . . the degree of artistic styling is much more Lady Gaga than Justin Bieber. Perhaps there is an audience of ten-to-twelve-year-old girls who could relate to these guys, but there's a yawning cultural divide between One Direction, say, and SHINee." Among his many choice observations, one stands out as particularly rich in irony: "But I'm going to go out on a limb and say that there is no way that a K-pop boy group will make it big in the States."

It's easy to dismiss his remarks as those of a man from a different time. But he made a few observations that help explain why K-pop artists have always been underdogs, historically difficult to translate to Western audiences, despite the many attempts to precede and succeed those of BTS. "Factory Girls" was an impactful headline that set the tone of the conversation. In countries like Korea and Japan and China, K-pop stars are idealized as paragons by nature of the original idol system. They are meant to be perfect. Idols represent a fantasy; they are in the business of selling dreams, providing an escape from reality.

Not always, but often: their songs are saccharine earworms that thrive off repetition, permitting the most mindless enjoyment; their dance is hypnotic. They are attractive in an unworldly way, their jawlines sharper than their synchronized steps. If you ignore the hours of personal interaction they provide in livestreams and variety shows, then they might seem robotic or scripted. They have teams behind them, an army of producers, managers, songwriters, stylists, hair and makeup artists, marketing and planning teams, directors, photographers, and executives, involved in their making. Pop stars in America, the land of individualism, are not all that different; rarely do they retain full creative control of their output and image. Yet the idea that K-pop stars are more highly manufactured persists. As the article in *The New Yorker* stated, "I found myself wondering why overproduced, derivative pop music, performed by second-tier singers, would appeal to a mass American audience, who can hear better performers doing more original material right here at home?"

I wondered what had been so badly lost in translation, or if it was simply their Asian-ness that seemed insurmountable at the time. The image of factory boys and girls, of idols as robots, manufactured and dehumanized, played into long-held stereotypes about Asians in America. Conscious or subconscious, the perception of the "other" still lingers. The "forever foreigner," the "perpetual foreigner," a term that can be traced back to a 2002 article by law professor Frank H. Wu, refers to a key element of the Asian American experience: the fact that Asian features mark you as foreign, no matter your birthplace. Asia is treated as a monolith, billions of men and women who look the same, act the same, sound the same, as though they came off an assembly line. They are fake, or they can't be trusted. When applied to K-pop, "perpetual foreigner syndrome" meant that idols struggled to show the individuality valued by the Western audience. Back then it seemed impossible to conquer this unwillingness to engage with something different.

Ironically, BTS debuted only eight months after *The New Yorker* article was published, and from the outset, they were seen as different from other K-pop stars. The core concept behind BTS, as discussed by Bang Si-hyuk and Big Hit and the boys, boiled down to one mission: to talk with those their own age, as friends and peers, unpacking the joys and pains of their present lives. In their own words, that notion clashed with the existing nature of idols as paragons. "Actually, talking with your peers about what you're feeling at the moment [and] claiming to be an unreachable idol can be quite contradictory, depending on how you look at it," RM explained on the SBS documentary show *Archive-K*. I vividly remember they were marketed that way by word-of-mouth fan channels in the West, who praised their authenticity and relatability and the depth of their lyrics. "They're more real," I was told on several occasions by K-pop fans and music journalists who had watched the group's journey, in those Logs and Bombs, and seen BTS's desire to overcome every obstacle in their path. There are other underdog groups from small companies who have succeeded despite the odds in K-pop—Infinite from Woollim Entertainment, Seventeen from Pledis Entertainment, Ateez from KQ Entertainment, for example. But BTS had an underdog story that captivated the public's imagination at the perfect moment.

BTS and Big Hit know that they had timing on their side. Twitter provided an efficient vehicle for fandom and the globalization of content. ARMY was more interconnected and ready to go to bat for their favorites. Those with short attention spans, like mine, craved the rapid and digestible content that BTS so readily provided. BTS was in the right place at the right time, sharing their authentic selves when people were searching for a newcomer to cheer for. Practically outcasts at their debut, given their outmoded styling and small company, Jungkook and his group mates shared their daily battles and moments of happiness. On February 12, 2013, one of the members tweeted that they had gained more than a thousand followers after a month and a half and were thrilled to receive even a little interest. "It became really natural," said J-Hope on *Archive-K*. "Has this sort of communication become a daily routine? And as we did it, we became closer to our fans." BTS offered an unheard-of level of access and intimacy that gained a foothold in Korea and among international fans, who saw BTS as not just idols but seven boys trying their best, despite the odds stacked against them.

Everyone loves an underdog, and the underdog effect—the psychological desire to support the disadvantaged, the unlikely winner—has been well-documented. Some studies suggest it has to do with human empathy, others with an attempt to reconcile with perceived unfairness, enacting what small justice we can. Suffice it to say the underdog narrative has been effectively leveraged by creators and companies to engender attachment. In America, where the myth of equal opportunity persists, people adore a working-class hero who overcomes the odds.

BTS has often been compared to One Direction, the British-Irish boy band formed on *X Factor* in 2010 that was the biggest group in the world until Zayn Malik departed in March 2015, with the group entering a hiatus five months later. In their early days, the boys sat huddled in a dimly lit stairwell and filmed video diaries to keep their fans updated week by week, sharing their progress and a glimpse of their growing chemistry. Niall Horan from County Westmeath in Ireland, Zayn Malik from West Yorkshire, Liam Payne from West Midlands, Harry Styles from Cheshire, and Louis Tomlinson from South Yorkshire: five boys from humble beginnings, "from normal working-class families," as Malik described them in *One Direction: This Is Us*. Another set of underdogs, bolstered by the fans that fell for them after forging a real connection. In that same documentary, the boys spoke of their desire to eschew the common provisions of pop. "We tried to stay away from the typical boy band thing," said Malik. "We're normal people doing this abnormal job," Horan said. And that thread was carried forward by BTS, which was a dark-horse pick in Korea, let alone the Western pop world.

In Korea, which was heavily influenced by American culture after the Korean War, the same fable of hard work being rewarded has significant sway. There is a relentless drive to pursue new heights. Hard work and long hours, pushing your body and mind to the limit: these are the elements of the underdog story that resonate with the widest audience.

In 2015, BTS attended the Idol Star Athletics Championships (ISAC), an annual reality program where artists compete in sporting events like archery and soccer—the idol Olympics. BTS was still rising in Korea, and the commentators barely acknowledged them during the finals of the 400-meter relay, expecting B1A4 or Teen Top to win. Jungkook was assigned the anchor position, and by the time J-Hope reached him, it seemed that B1A4 had secured victory. Then the announcers' mouths fell open as Jungkook came from behind, sprinting so fast he outstripped the other runners by yards. "This is like real life," a top comment read. "Nobody expected BTS to succeed but they did! So proud of these boys." It was a perfect microcosm of their story that delights fans to this day.

It's easier to show than tell: go through the Bangtan Logs, the Bangtan Bombs, their earnest tweets and blog entries. See a fifteen-year-old Jungkook, removed from his family, dark circles beneath his eyes, tired and lonely, and any person with an ounce of empathy would feel the need to protect him. See the older members watching over the younger ones, like a found family, as they tug violently on your heartstrings. As you consume their content, it stirs the same emotional core as observing a down-on-his-luck hero in a TV series, except with much higher stakes—a real boy with his real future on the line, whom you can support with your own power. For ARMY, those protective instincts were further heightened by the intense cyberbullying—from members of the public and fans of rival groups—that occurred as BTS began to gain more success (2015 to 2017 is named a particularly difficult period in the official biography). They were plagued by accusations of *sajaegi*, or chart manipulation; anti-fans tried to trend these hashtags on Twitter and ARMY fought to overwrite them.

My mind drifts to "the burger incident." In 2016, before BTS had won their first Daesang (a top prize at a Korean music awards show), Jungkook made a solo appearance on *Flower Crew*, a variety travel show for celebrities and MCs. In one episode, Jungkook arrived with hamburgers and soft drinks that he had bought for the cast. Comedian Jo Se-ho said they looked like leftovers and refused to accept them. Over time, the moment was twisted and mythologized, and the context was lost and only the shell of the interaction remained: the image of Jungkook being disrespected by a public figure, his face falling as his humble offering was refused. Following the online outrage, Jo issued an apology, but the damage was done. The moment triggered a visceral reaction among ARMY, who were reminded of all the online hate the group had endured by that point in time. In 2021, BTS appeared on a special episode of the show *You Quiz on the Block*, where Jo was a cohost, which felt like a full-circle moment. It was proof of how far Jungkook and BTS had come, the triumphant return of the Davids who had slain the industry's Goliaths and could enjoy their spoils.

BTS's success has made an estimated $32.6 billion contribution to the South Korean economy over one decade, according to the Hyundai Research Institute, reportedly comparable to the contributions of Korean Air. They have had brand deals with Samsung, Louis Vuitton, the NBA. Approximately eight hundred thousand foreign tourists visit the country each year due to them and spend an estimated five trillion won, or more than $3 billion. In 2023, the Korea Post made special commemorative stamps to celebrate BTS's ten-year anniversary and sold some 1.5 million. Yet despite their fairy-tale arc, BTS never seemed to change all that much. On *You Quiz on the Block*, Jungkook, who appeared to be on good terms with Jo, gave the man a warm embrace, which fans received with pride. It was proof that despite the heights he had reached, Jungkook had not lost the kind and warmhearted spirit of the boy who had started at the bottom. He'd remain a lovable underdog till the end.

CHAPTER 2

HIS WORK ETHIC

Jungkook is good at everything, or so the story goes. Type the phrase "Jungkook good at everything" into any social media platform and you'll find a procession of clips and threads that list in short succession all the things that Jungkook is good at: dancing, singing, rapping, painting, cooking, boxing, running, swimming, snowboarding, modeling, archery, gaming, filmmaking, designing. It is an impressive catalog, a result of what his fans have seen him do over the years: Jungkook scraping a paintbrush over a canvas, dicing a green onion in perfectly even chunks, ducking beneath a right hook, performing an effortless backspin. Each moment accumulated and contributed to his reputation as a genius, the golden *maknae* of BTS. *This* is central to his story. Jungkook might have been talented from birth, but what sets him apart—what led to the genius tag—is the way he works hard to be the best he can be. He has a singular drive that stands out, even among the highly driven field of K-pop stars.

In May 2013, one month before their debut, RM and Jungkook recorded a Bangtan Log, chatting about their first music video shoot. RM, then eighteen, asked Jungkook, then fifteen, what he wanted to show their fans. When Jungkook said that he planned to rap and sing and dance, RM called him an all-rounder. "Not to the point of being an all-rounder . . ." Jungkook began to protest, but RM interjected, "a golden *maknae*," making a soft pun between the words *manneung* (well-rounded) and *maknae* (youngest).

The sobriquet has followed Jungkook ever since, clinging to him like a coat of gilding. A YouTube video from 2018 titled "BTS Jungkook Is Good at Everything - Golden Maknae Moments" has earned more than nineteen million views and features seven minutes and fifty-eight seconds of feats. Jungkook sprinting to a gold-medal finish, Jungkook plucking a bouquet of pink roses from a crane machine, Jungkook winning several arm-wrestling matches. During an interview on *The Tonight Show Starring Jimmy Fallon* in 2021, Fallon asked, "Jungkook, you are known for being great at everything. This is the rumor. You're great at singing, you're great at dancing, you're perfect at video games. Is there anything you're not good at?" Jungkook smiled and shook his head, saying there were plenty of things he could not do well.

"He's like top-tier out of just like the whole industry, like he's good at everything," said Bang Chan, the multitalented leader of Stray Kids, on a livestream. "I mean, he's the same age, but I've looked up to him ever since I was a trainee, as well. You have to admit, he's good at everything."

Jungkook's own bandmates call him a genius with regularity, taking great pride in his gifts. For Jungkook, V once recorded and shared a message, thanking him for donating his talents to BTS and not anywhere else. "I think because of you, our group was able to go this far," V said, to which the other members murmured in agreement. V called Jungkook the most talented person he had ever seen. But Jungkook himself disagrees. "I don't think I'm a genius. I've never thought of myself as a genius," he said with a timid laugh in the documentary *Jung Kook: I Am Still.* "I just know the areas I lack in, so in part, I try to hide what I'm lacking as much as I can. I strive to be better too. I'm not always good, you know."

For all Jungkook's natural talents, he has always worked hard to improve them. His formative years were spent away from home doing nothing but that. The idol training system is one of the most distinguishing facets of the K-pop industry. The first variant was designed in the 1960s by Johnny Kitagawa, known as the founder of the J-pop idol system. Kitagawa scouted fresh talent, allegedly recruiting boys as young as ten, then housed the trainees in dormitories as they underwent years of boot-camp-style lessons for singing and dancing and acting. Idols were molded from an impressionable age, and turned into perfect stars that dominated the charts. In the 2010s, he was recognized by the Guinness World Records for producing the most number-one singles and artists. Kitagawa's legacy was marred by accusations of sexual abuse that spanned decades, and the Guinness World Records removed his distinctions in 2023.

Lee Soo-man, founder of SM Entertainment, adapted this style of training in South Korea. In typical Korean fashion, the blueprint was replicated by other K-pop companies and perfected through a yearslong process of trial and error. Ironically, given how much of the West maligns K-pop stars for being "manufactured" and "factory made," one inspiration for the idol trainee system was Detroit's Motown Records, whose founder Berry Gordy applied the factory-line process of the city's automobile industry to music production. In 1964, Motown established an Artist Personal Development Department led by Maxine Powell, a finishing school instructor who spent hours teaching artists like Diana Ross and Marvin Gaye how to present a refined image to the public. "This department would groom and polish them so that they could appear in number one places around the country and even before the king and queen," Powell said in an interview with WGBH radio station.

The standard of performance demanded of J-idols, a more domestic industry focused on fan service and charisma, is different from the one later adopted by K-idols. By the time the average K-idol debuts, they will have spent years in training, undergoing regular evaluations to assess their progress (Jihyo of Twice, for example, entered JYP Entertainment at age eight and trained for ten years). They are expected to perform formidable choreography, while singing and rapping deftly. They'll learn Korean, English, Japanese, or Chinese from language tutors, for starters, and have staff dedicated to their well-rounded development. When I worked at a K-pop label, spending late nights and early mornings, 10 a.m. to 5 a.m., arranging trunks of clothes in a basement, I often found myself alone with the trainees, aspiring idols who sign a contract with a company to prepare for a potential debut. They were never guaranteed to debut. Yet they committed years of their lives in the hopes that they might. Sometimes they'd have a lesson with one of the dancers or receive English instruction from their tutor in a room no larger than a storage closet. Often, they'd sneak into the dance practice room alone, running through the steps for their next evaluation. The ones still enrolled in school had fewer hours to rehearse, and I sometimes heard them fretting about falling behind.

Nowadays, the curriculum encompasses even more subjects. Rookies practice eclectic talents to display on variety shows, such as performing impressions of cartoon characters, Korean celebrities, or even the sound of a vibrating phone. Variety shows are a type of reality talk program, where MCs and stars participate in games and comedy skits, giving idols a chance to showcase their personalities. Seventeen, the Pledis Entertainment boy group with thirteen members, received gag comedy lessons, which helped them become the "variety kings" of their generation. Members of Ive, a girl group under Starship Entertainment, took selfie and TikTok lessons, learning the art of the viral post. Hours are spent honing every possible skill, trick, and talent to help them stand out from the crowd—from the dozens of other trainees, competing for a debut spot.

Real blood, sweat, and tears go into the making of an idol, an excruciating slough of sleepless nights and sacrifice. As I've said before, a tireless work ethic is deeply ingrained in the Korean mindset, from the moment a child enters the school system (think: Suneung, the infamous college entrance exam that lasts eight hours). The highly educated populace is forced to compete for limited opportunities (according to the government organization Statistics Korea, more than 1.26 million people aged fifteen to twenty-nine were unemployed in 2023, and 52.86 percent of them were college graduates), and working hard becomes as natural as breathing. There was a viral photograph taken during the summer monsoon in 2022, when severe flooding swept the streets of Seoul with murky brown water. An office worker in a suit emerged from his sedan, which was partially submerged, and was reclined on the windshield, looking at his phone indifferently. Friends speculated he might have been responding to emails. I have no doubt he was—come hell or high water, Koreans don't stop working.

The process doesn't end once an idol has debuted. More than ten years after "No More Dream," the members of BTS still practice relentlessly for their performances, despite having six number-one songs on the Billboard Hot 100. Jungkook, who became a trainee at age thirteen, has spent nearly half his life in this grind, which means that, when he crossed over into the Western pop sphere, he came prepared in a way that surprised collaborators like Charlie Puth and producer

Andrew Watt, who were unfamiliar with the Korean standard. There are a few moments from the course of his career that provide a glimpse at his incredible work ethic, developed with BTS, that prepared him for his arduous solo debut. The first shows what Jungkook sacrificed in exchange for the ability to achieve his dreams; the second, the way in which he grows and improves himself through effort; and the final two moments examine the love for ARMY that drives him.

February 8, 2013. Jungkook, age fifteen, a trainee four months before his debut. Jungkook leaned toward the camcorder propped up at the corner of the desk, the public's first close and personal glimpse of the teenage boy who would become, over the course of a decade, an international pop star. He examined the fish-eye lens, his first words to his fans spilling forth: "2013 February eighth. Jungkook's daily log."

Only two years had passed since Jungkook moved from his family home in Busan, the coastal city two hours south by bullet train, to cram into a two-room dormitory with up to nine teenage boys training at Big Hit Entertainment. The dormitory was tucked on a side street in Nonhyeon-dong, Gangnam, a no-frills apartment complex, somewhere between 534 to 605 square feet. The dorm was on a quiet residential block near a convenience store. Sometimes, he would go there to buy a cup of instant ramen noodles and scarf them as he cried because he missed his mother. Unable to eat nice dishes, he would buy a single banana milk after practice as a treat when he was really craving it.

The convenience store, the swing set at Hakdong Park, the bicycle paths along the Han River: these spots offered the future BTS members a reprieve from their grueling schedules. Once the group had been whittled down to seven members, the trainees were moved, one month before their debut, to the third-floor Nonhyeon-dong apartment immortalized in *"I-sa* (Moving On)," released in 2015 on *The Most Beautiful Moment in Life Pt.1.* Dubbed the Blue House—since the doors, the bathroom, and the veranda were all painted a bright shade of cobalt—all seven boys slept in a single bedroom with three sets of bunk beds. Jungkook, the youngest, slept on a twin-size mattress. At the time, he was five foot seven but still growing. Seven teenage boys shared one bathroom, and Jungkook, shy as he was, waited to shower until everyone else had fallen asleep. Jin, the oldest, drove the boys in his Mini Cooper, dropping Jungkook off at Singu Middle School, ten minutes from the river.

Jungkook recorded that first Bangtan Log on the day of his middle school graduation. He wore a white collared shirt with a slim necktie and a wool winter coat, his thick black hair neatly swept to the left. The ceremony was attended by a smattering of photographers from BTS's first fansites (fan-run websites dedicated to a favorite idol), who were intrigued by the group's pre-debut social media presence and showed up to document the moment. Jungkook was seen smiling for the cameras, holding up his diploma in its clear file folder, with bouquets of chrysanthemums in his arms. Jungkook's parents were not in attendance. Instead, Jin, Suga, and Jimin came, posing proudly with their youngest.

Hours after the ceremony ended, the foursome had returned to Nonhyeon-dong to resume their training. Bang Si-hyuk rented a practice space beneath a restaurant called Yoojung Sikdang because he was unable to accommodate rehearsals in the Cheonggu Building, the five-floor office where Big Hit was headquartered. In one of four basement studios, the boys danced and sang as the smell of grilled pork wafted above. On an average day, the boys woke up around 10 a.m., eating a scant breakfast of salad or bread or grilled chicken breast, before heading to the studio, where they would practice until 10 p.m. or so.

In the two months before their debut, the rehearsals stretched twelve to fourteen hours. Vocal lessons were provided by Kim Sung-eun, who trained Jin, V, and Jungkook for more than one year. Performance director Son Sungdeuk taught dance. J-Hope and Jimin, trained and naturally gifted dancers, provided additional assistance by guiding the newbies. J-Hope, with his remarkable talent, would go on to become the team's dance leader. Years later, Jungkook reflected on this difficult period of all-nighters and strict diets. "Hardship was an expectation at the time," he said. "I wouldn't be able to do it again if someone asked me to."

Not long before he sat down for the Log, Jungkook had recorded his first dance video, a cover of a routine choreographed by Kyle Hanagami. It was the fruition of two years of practice, captured in the minute-long short, rehearsed hundreds of times. In the squeaking and slapping of his sneakers, snaking across the floor in time with the beat, fans could see Jungkook's skill, which he would need to execute BTS's sharp, synchronized dance, each boy matching the others.

That night, after another late dance practice, Jungkook walked alone to the Bangtan Room, a small studio with a Maschine MIDI pad on the desk and an ASR-10 synthesizer, where the boys filmed their vlogs and made music. He still wore the winter coat from his graduation with the hood up, its black fur trim shrouding his face like a grim halo. Without makeup, fans could glimpse a faint shadow around his eyes. He spoke in soft tones with frequent pauses.

"Mm . . ." He glanced off camera, looking unsure of himself. "Today I finally graduated. I thought I'd be really happy about it but, in reality . . . having graduated, I don't feel all that great." He looked down and nodded to himself several times, as if wrestling with his thoughts. "Yeah. And right now, it's . . . 11:39 p.m. I came here to have dance lessons but . . . it'll be *seollal* [Korean New Year] soon so . . . I want to go soon . . . back home. I want to see my mom." He laughed softly to himself. "And I want to see my dad. Everyone will be waiting for me . . ."

There were no guarantees that these years of sacrifice would amount to anything. BTS was reportedly one of 36 boy groups to debut that year, hoping to catch the public's eye, and Jungkook one of 163 male hopefuls, vying to be a star. Yet despite that, Jungkook's words did not feel like complaints. They were musings, a show of vulnerability from a teenage boy, unsure of his future and the weight of what he had given up. In closing, he smiled for the camera, as if resolving to carry on. Even as a child, he possessed uncommonly strong resolve. Despite the stress, suffering, and sacrifice, he worked through those hardships for himself and for BTS. One day, he would reap the results of his efforts and come to understand what he lost and gained along the way. Until then, he'd have to manage the uncertainty and control only what he could: his work ethic. He'd keep practicing and keep sacrificing to make his dreams come true.

July 2012. Jungkook, age fourteen. In a baseball cap and sunglasses, a travel pillow around his neck, the boy flashed a peace sign after boarding the twelve-hour economy-class trip from Seoul to Los Angeles. It was the first flight in his life, he confessed in a *Bangtan Blog* post published shortly before his debut. Traveling only with Son Sungdeuk, who chose Jungkook as the most promising trainee, he looked surprisingly bright-eyed when he emerged from Tom Bradley International Terminal at LAX wearing a charcoal-gray tee and black shorts and carrying a red backpack and just enough clothing to last him for his roughly monthlong stay. As they drove to their accommodation, Jungkook was captivated by the scenery, the lush greenery and blue sky, so different from the gray cityscape of Seoul. They pulled the car over to take a photograph. Jungkook posed in the middle of a street, towering palm trees on either side.

After dropping off their luggage, he went straight to dance lessons. On the first day, Jungkook took two or three classes at Movement Lifestyle in North Hollywood, founded by Shaun Evaristo. Evaristo had choreographed for the K-pop group BigBang, whom the members of BTS idolized. The first lesson wasn't as difficult as Jungkook anticipated. But during the second lesson, perhaps struck by jet lag, Jungkook experienced a "mental breakdown," as he wrote in his blog. He was unable to understand the instructor's words and found the choreography much more demanding. In a practice video, Son and Jungkook reviewed a difficult snippet that featured a series of pop-and-lock movements and finger-tutting to "Pull My Hair" by Joe. At the end of the sequence, Jungkook smiled timidly at Son. He was considering his many missteps and thinking about how to improve.

For the next few weeks, Jungkook woke up and went to the Korean restaurant closest to their lodging, ordering spicy noodle soup with a side of yellow pickled radish or other Korean dishes that staved off any homesickness and gave him the energy to rehearse at the studio for hours. Once or twice a week, he went to a coin laundromat, washing and drying his clothes. On weekends, Jungkook went to the beach. He ate corn dogs and lo mein. Instructed by Bang Si-hyuk to let Jungkook enjoy himself and experience new things, Son took him to the Getty Center, where he would have seen a curation of Gustav Klimt drawings on loan from Vienna and black-and-white portraiture by Herb Ritts. Before leaving, Jungkook struck a one-handed handstand that he called "the Nike" on the travertine stone steps and again on the manicured lawn.

He bought a skateboard for the first time and started to ride it, coasting down the NoHo sidewalk in front of the Movement Lifestyle building. He watched the sun set on the beach, sinking into the Pacific. The day before he flew home, Jungkook went to the Lobster on Santa Monica Pier, overlooking the ocean, and ate lobster for the first time, though he proudly pronounced that, for a boy from Busan, snow crab remained the best. He confessed that after his month in L.A., he wanted to become a professional dancer instead of an idol.

According to Son and the other members of BTS, a change came over Jungkook. He had grown confidence and a drive to push himself to a world-class level. "He gained the eyes of a tiger," Son described in a YouTube interview. Jungkook began improving at an incredible rate, reinforcing the public perception that he was a genius. But at the heart of it all was practice, effort, and a desire for self-improvement. Over the years, Jungkook would continue to mature by chasing new challenges and acquiring new skills, as though his personal growth helped him to understand the love and trust he was being given. "I'm not someone with very high self-esteem," he said in a 2023 interview with *Weverse Magazine*. "I might not know why all those people love me, but I always remember they appreciate me. So, I started to think, what's the point of all those people appreciating me and supporting me if I don't have confidence? I think that's why I've been changing a bit."

March 2017. Jungkook, age nineteen. Santiago, Chile, was the first overseas stop on the Wings Tour, the group's second worldwide tour, to promote the eponymous album. The lead single, "Blood Sweat & Tears," was BTS's first to hit number one on the domestic Circle Chart, formerly known as the Gaon Chart, and broke the record for fastest K-pop video to pass ten million views on YouTube. Expectations were high for the Wings Tour. The group's last large-scale tour was the Red Bullet Tour in 2014, which traversed seven cities across Asia before receiving an extension to cover twelve more cities in 2015, including New York and Los Angeles. Back then the members worried about having enough songs to fill the set list, their inexperience and lack of company resources preventing them from giving their best.

Wings was different. In 2016, BTS won their first Daesang, the top prize at an end-of-year Korean music awards show, receiving the validation they had spent three years working toward. There were more than five hundred thousand preorders for *Wings* in the first week, which was three times more than the preorders for their 2015 EP *The Most Beautiful Moment in Life Pt.2*. Every element of the live show was thoughtfully considered to reflect what the boys had achieved and how far they had come, as individuals and as a group. The set list featured twenty-eight songs, including an encore and solo stages for each member.

They scheduled two shows in Chile, and the group flew thirty to thirty-two hours to reach that first stop with a layover in the US. More than a hundred fans waited at the airport, standing in neat rows as the boys passed through arrivals. As the members boarded their white passenger van, pulling away from the airport, some of the fans began running after the car. Jungkook sat in the back in a black sweatshirt, hood up, a bright smile on his face, as he practiced his English; when they arrived at the hotel, he flashed an easy peace sign at the cameraman documenting the trip. They went to eat Korean BBQ that first night, and Jungkook performed an exaggerated cover of Jimin's "Lie" to the others' delight. BTS was in high spirits.

Both shows took place at the Movistar Arena in downtown Santiago, which can seat up to seventeen thousand fans, who performed dance covers outside the venue and waved their pickets (fan-made hand fans with their favorite member's face) for the cameras. Inside, they raised a sea of ARMY Bombs, the official fan light sticks, shining in the dark.

The first night was going as planned and rehearsed. The screams from the crowd reached the dressing room, surprising the boys with their intensity. In return, they resolved to deliver a show worthy of ARMY's fervor. Partway through the concert, Jungkook walked backstage and slumped onto a sofa, breathing heavily, sweat beading along his neck. He drank water, trying to regain his strength, as staff tended to him. RM watched in shock, having never seen Jungkook openly tire before. In that moment, he realized that the flawless *maknae* at the center of BTS was as human and fragile as the rest of them. For his part, Jungkook tried to live up to his golden reputation and pushed his body to its breaking point.

His condition worsened the second night. Between sections, Jungkook walked offstage, bent over, and staff massaged him and tried to cool him down. His eyes were closed and shirt removed, as someone stretched his neck, back and forth; he appeared barely conscious, the in-ear microphone still sounding off. Medics held a can of oxygen to his mouth, supporting the back of his neck, prompting him to breathe. The other members watched Jungkook with fear and worry. He sat there, low on the ground in the dark behind the curtain, head bowed, until the cue played, and he walked onstage and performed, as if nothing were the matter. ARMY had come to see him, and the members were counting on him.

His solo stage, "Begin," started with Jungkook singing steadily, as he performed agile twists and bends. By the time the group performed "Fire," an extraordinarily fast-paced track that leaves the members breathless under the best conditions, Jungkook was struggling. In the quiet lull before the final dance break, he stumbled for a moment, his hand touching the floor to keep himself from falling. He betrayed only one moment of weakness, one rare misstep, before he gathered the strength to perform the last forty-five strenuous seconds.

After they took their final bow, Jungkook staggered backstage into a room, where he was laid down on an exercise mat, his eyes closed. Medics gathered around him, putting the canned oxygen to his mouth, as he appeared to drift in and out of consciousness. Suga went to the bathroom and cried in secret, worried about Jungkook's condition.

A gel ice pack was held to Jungkook's forehead, and there were two cans of oxygen on the floor to his left, while Jimin remained near his side. He began to respond when a staff member knelt to remove his socks. Jungkook shook his foot gently, not wanting to be barefoot. Eventually, he recovered enough to join the other members in the greenroom, all of them relieved that their youngest was okay. They marveled at the fact that he had been able to finish the concert, showing the best performance he could for the Chilean ARMY.

"I was in bad condition. My body felt it, my head felt it, but I performed with only one thought in my mind: I won't be able to see [these fans] for a long time," Jungkook said. There lies the reason behind Jungkook's punishing work ethic: his devotion to his fans and the desire to repay the love he has been given.

Summer 2021. Jungkook, twenty-three, on the cusp of twenty-four. The once struggling BTS was now a household name, a group that had broken every barrier in their path to become a cultural phenomenon. Their success had transcended the national and become global. The year 2021 was monumental: BTS passed eleven billion streams on Melon, setting a record for the online Korean music platform. The Dynamite Trilogy encompassed their sixth era, focused on their first full English-language singles, each song ushering new fans into the fold. "Permission to Dance," "Dynamite," and "Butter" hit numbers five, two, and one on the Billboard charts in the US, while five of their tracks debuted at number one on the Billboard Hot 100 that year.

"Dynamite" was the first K-pop song to be nominated for a Grammy Award. RM, Jimin, V, and Jungkook gathered to watch the nomination announcement together, and when BTS flashed on the screen alongside names like Lady Gaga, Ariana Grande, Dua Lipa, Justin Bieber, and Taylor Swift, the foursome was stunned and elated.

"So, it really is possible," Jimin said in awe.

When "Butter" dropped in May, it received more than eleven million Spotify streams in a single day, while its music video broke four Guinness World Records for YouTube views. "Butter" would earn BTS their second Grammy nomination for Best Pop Duo/Group Performance. By any measure, they had become the most famous boy band in the world, but the members refused to rest on their laurels.

In August, BTS shared a remix of "Butter" featuring Megan Thee Stallion, which also hit the top spot on the Billboard chart. Over the summer, J-Hope, Jimin, and Jungkook of 3J, the group's original "dance line" (a term that refers to the strongest dancers in a K-pop group), began preparing a special dance break over the featured verse. The idea was suggested by J-Hope, the dance leader, who texted Jimin and Jungkook. It was the first gathering of 3J for practice in four years, by Jimin's recollection, and they wanted to showcase the powerful synchronized dance they had not done in some time.

The thirty-second dance break was choreographed by Nick Joseph and filmed in one of the HYBE practice rooms with neon purple tube lighting along the edge of the floor. The trio danced through the sequence once, as J-Hope monitored the rehearsal with Son Sungdeuk. Dressed in loose sweats and sneakers, they performed another run-through, their perfectionism already beginning to seep through the cracks.

The three of them sat down to monitor the footage, reviewing each frame, before returning to shoot another pass—then another and another and another, each time fussing over the finer details. Between takes they stopped to break down the more difficult segments, matching their movements in the mirror to check their coordination, their feet shuffling and stepping left and right, back and forth. Examining the monitor, the sweat still clinging to their bangs, the three kept prompting each other to go for one more "real final take."

Each version was performed and filmed and reviewed with smiles. Well aware of their acute perfectionism, 3J could only laugh good-naturedly at the lengths they were willing to go. So, they filmed it again. And monitored it again. And were dissatisfied again and could only laugh at themselves again. On the umpteenth attempt, the subtitles on the video read: "On behalf of Jungkook, who has regrets, the members who will do one last real-real-real final take."

They danced once more and monitored the footage once more. Turned to the crew, bowed politely, and wrapped. For most artists, that would have been a remarkable testament to their dedication to their craft and a colossal effort for thirty seconds on film. That last real-real-real final take would have been the end of it. But BTS is an extraordinary group by any measure, and Jungkook and Jimin, as guided by J-Hope for more than eight years, shared a drive to always do better, to push themselves to the limit for the sake of ARMY. BTS has always taken ARMY's devotion seriously. Their fans' long hours spent streaming and supporting each member's projects, their money spent on album sales and concert tickets and merchandise, are returned through BTS's commitment to world-class performances.

And so, the 3J trio changed into fresh white outfits and returned to try one more time, even after the official shooting schedule had wrapped. They filmed a take, then went back to review it, Jungkook rehearsing the hand movements alongside the footage.

"Shall we go?" J-Hope asked with a wide smile.

"Let's go!" Jungkook cheered, as Jimin sat there looking exhausted, with a small smile that said he was used to this sort of thing by now.

Joseph, the choreographer, who had been observing the shoot, stepped in to walk the boys through a particularly troublesome section of shuffle steps and kicks, giving them a reassuring thumbs-up that they did, indeed, have it. Jungkook continued to redo the footsteps in the mirror, as J-Hope provided guidance. They filmed another. Another. Again. Again. Another. Another. Until the day had blurred into an amorphous blob of attempts.

Once again, they monitored the footage. After a slight pause, Jimin began, "I really hate this and normally don't do it . . . but one real final take?"

The crew broke into laughter, resolving to do it for Jimin. The trio stood in front of the camera, energized for their final take—which they messed up immediately to their delirious glee. Then they shot one last take. When they sat down to monitor it, they seemed happy at last. Clapping his hands, Jungkook went to hug and thank the choreographer, bowing politely to all the staff who stayed late.

"We took two takes to film this video," J-Hope said at the end with a knowing smile.

The result: a video of one minute and eight seconds, shared on BANGTANTV on September 9. It has received more than seventy-eight million views to date. The behind-the-scenes footage, published about one month later, revealed how much effort 3J had put into such a brief but beautiful moment. To put so many hours into a thirty-second dance break, it's clear how much Jungkook and BTS have brought to everything else they do.

CHAPTER 3

THE WAY HE SINGS

In the 2023 documentary web series *BTS Monuments: Beyond the Star*, Bang Si-hyuk, the founder of Big Hit Entertainment and chairman of HYBE, sat down to share his first impression of each BTS member. When it came to Jungkook, a thoughtful expression crossed his face, as he noted the vast potential that he saw despite Jungkook's troubling lack of self-confidence. Fans could almost see the memory flashing back in his mind's eye, knowing the image that must have come forward: teenage Jungkook, his eyes trained on the floor, so shy and uncertain of his voice that he was unable to perform at company evaluations, and instead fidgeted in place for fifteen minutes. The other members have recalled the way that Jungkook could not sing on command, so anxious that he dissolved into tears. It would take thirty minutes of pleading from his *hyungs*, or brothers (a term used by younger Korean males toward older ones, connoting a closeness not bound by the familial), to coax a single song from his lips.

Jungkook is said to possess perfect pitch, though some have contested that he has relative pitch (the ability to recall notes in relation to each other) and not absolute pitch (the ability to identify them independently). Moreover, Jungkook's innate knowledge of music is impressive. On episode 150 of the variety show *Run BTS!*, Jungkook matched a sequence of seven notes, rung on a row of rainbow bells, in short succession, moments after hearing them once, leaving his fellow BTS members in awe. Though he explained that he didn't know the note names, he was quickly able to pluck the first fa from the air. Charlie Puth shared in several interviews that he believes Jungkook has the same gift as him. "He's a low-key prodigy. He has perfect pitch and can recall any note on the spot, which I found very impressive," Puth told *Rolling Stone*. "The only artists that have ever sent me perfect vocals or recorded perfect vocals in front of me are Jungkook, Boyz II Men, and James Taylor," Puth elaborated in an interview with Buzz-Feed.

Jungkook's recorded vocal range spans somewhere from a G2 to a B♭5, covering three octaves. He sings in a delicate tenor with a rich timbre that lingers in the ears. Light, clear, sweet, smooth: there are entire Twitter accounts dedicated solely to his voice, with thousands of followers each. Even for K-pop fandom, notoriously adulatory about every inch of their idols, this represents an astonishing appreciation.

His ability to seamlessly blend his chest voice and head voice, shifting into a falsetto in a loose and natural way. His remarkable stability and stamina and breath support, which let him stay clean and clear and on pitch even as he dances feverishly. His vocal agility, the way he can dart through runs and ad libs, accurately hitting each note. His phrasing—the way he shapes and expresses each passage, where he places his breaths—is gorgeous, delicate, with an intuitive understanding of rhythm. By the time he made his solo debut, Jungkook had become a singer admired by millions with a distinctive voice and skills praised by producers around the world. Coldplay's Chris Martin was openly awed after watching Jungkook in the recording booth for

"My Universe." Cirkut, who coproduced "Seven" with Andrew Watt, commented on Jungkook's versatility, calling him a vocal chameleon with power and a beautiful falsetto, who could mold his tone to fit any genre. Watt, the Grammy-winning producer known for his work with Justin Bieber and Post Malone, was also impressed by Jungkook's range. Kang Hyo-won, the music producer known as Pdogg who worked with Bang to create BTS, considers Jungkook a natural genius. "What caught our eye is, should I say his power? The power that Jungkook's voice has, that's how it all began," Pdogg said in the documentary *Jung Kook: I Am Still*. "He is faster than anyone at picking up on a song's mood [and] he's really good at making the song his own."

What strikes me the most is his vocal color. It is warm and mellow, like honey or butter, but with an airiness that is light as foam or froth. There's a brightness with a slight huskiness, a breathy quality supported by power. I find his falsetto remarkable, the notes floating, feather-like whispers. Like dandelion fluff. His voice has an addictive quality that is hard even for professionals to describe. In a separate chat with SiriusXM, Puth simply put it: "I honestly just love his voice."

Jungkook is unlike the prototypical Korean pop vocalists, who undergo formal vocal training and are praised for their powerful, Broadway-style belting ability—not that one is better than the other. The first generation of idols included boy groups like H.O.T. and Shinhwa, whose initial songs leaned more on rap and hip-hop sounds that were novel to Korean audiences at the time. TVXQ, a five-member boy group that debuted at the end of 2003, bridged the first and second generations. They had voices that rang in exquisite harmonies, arching up to showstopping high notes. TVXQ heralded an industry shift, gaining an unprecedented following in countries like Japan and China, setting the Guinness World Record for the largest official fan club in 2008 (more than eight hundred thousand members) and the most photographed celebrities in 2009 (about five hundred million times). One of the biggest groups of their era, TVXQ brought K-pop to a new level, displaying its potential for international success.

TVXQ's influence extended to later groups like Super Junior and SHINee of the second generation. Even BigBang, best remembered for their hip-hop records, maintained two strong singers in their roster, who were easily able to sing several octaves. By the time BTS debuted, K-pop had reached its third generation. EXO had three main vocalists, who put a focus on impressive power and technique, and BTOB became one of the most beloved acts in the country due to their unmatched vocal talent. Loud, bright, resonant voices, almost operatic in training: by and large, those singers were praised and spotlit on popular Korean shows like *I Can See Your Voice*, a program where judges tried to identify real singers over tone-deaf lip-synchers; *Hidden Singer*, where the audience had to separate the celebrity from five imitators by ear; and *Immortal Songs*, which featured showstopping reinterpretations of classic compositions.

In contrast, Jungkook's voice stood out for its more subtle qualities that, in hindsight, suited a Western sensibility. His lighter, nuanced style bears more in common with Justin Bieber, to whom he is often compared, than it does to top Korean idol singers. Pdogg has described him as the epitome of pop. Over the years, Jungkook has curated playlists for ARMY of songs in a similar pop and R&B vein, sung by Troye Sivan, Kehlani, Frank Ocean, and other soulful vocalists, alongside alternative Korean singers like Dean and Zion.T. Voices that are mellow, digestible, drinkable. Again, not better; just a different flavor. "I think he's the only one in Korea who can pull off pop like this," Suga said on the episode of *Suchwita* where Jungkook presented his single "Standing Next to You." "Who'd hear this song and think it was sung by a Korean?" In a conversation with Kim Jong-wan of the alt-rock band Nell, Suga revealed that HYBE had asked him to stop using Jungkook to record his demo tracks, as his style seemed to subconsciously pressure the singer to follow in his lead.

If Korean tastes dictate a certain vocal style, how did Jungkook come to sing in a way that exemplifies Western pop? In his unique, now trademark style? To find the sound that suited him best, Jungkook drew inspiration from not only Western artists he admired but Korean artists that had charted untrod paths before him, as well as his own inner strength and determination.

"Ay-yo, finally! Is this what you've been waiting for?"

August 2009. A young man, twenty-one, appears on-screen. The camera pans up his body. Black pants, black tank, black gloves. A platinum-blond cut, swept to one side, and shield sunglasses à la Lady Gaga, whose chart-topping single, "Just Dance," had been released one year earlier. The man in the video wears frosted lip gloss, as he sings with heavy Auto-Tune to a synth-pop beat that draws the ire of Sony Music, due to its resemblance to "Right Round" by Flo Rida, who later features on a remix. The song, "Heartbreaker," is the solo debut of the artist known as G-Dragon, a member of the Korean hip-hop-style idol group BigBang and one of two influential Korean artists without whom we would not have Jungkook as he is now.

I remember 2009 as one of the most consequential years in K-pop history, commanded by the Big Three of JYP, SM, and YG Entertainments. From JYP, Wonder Girls became the first Korean act to chart on the Billboard Hot 100 with their retro dance-pop single "Nobody," and were summoned to open for the Jonas Brothers, an American band of three brothers, on the North American leg of their world tour. SM Entertainment's Girls' Generation had released the song and MV for "Gee," which became an early viral hit on YouTube, as my classmates were transfixed by the nine dark-haired girls shuffling back and forth, heel-toe heel-toe, in intricate formations, dressed in matching neon shorts and white heeled sneaker-boots. My American friends observed this cohesion with fascination, so different from the divas of America whose individuality was their hallmark—the Beyoncés and Gagas of the time.

Not all the landmarks were positive. Three members of TVXQ, who had just swept East Asia with the single "Mirotic" and become the top K-pop act of the time, filed a lawsuit against SM, citing the exploitative thirteen-year "slave contracts," as they were called, and alleging long hours and unfair pay distribution. They claimed the company held an unreasonable amount of power over their careers, stifling their professional and creative aspirations. A watershed moment that shocked the public, their subsequent split with SM revealed the underbelly of K-pop, leading the Korea Fair Trade Commission to standardize entertainment contracts to not exceed seven years. For many fans, it was the first crack in the facade, a high-profile glimpse of the ugly reality on which the dreamlike idol industry was built.

Amid all this, G-Dragon, the stage name of Kwon Ji-yong, or GD as he's known to fans, was attempting to establish himself as an artist who broke the mold. He defied the uniformity common in K-pop groups. He bleached his hair and tattooed his body. "Heartbreaker" featured heavy Auto-Tune, a pitch modulation software that Kanye West famously brought into the mainstream with his 2008 album *808s & Heartbreak*, which upon release was initially divisive but is widely considered one of the most influential records in rap. GD's single presented a departure from the powerful belting seen from groups like TVXQ, whose vocalist Changmin slid from a high C#5 to an E5 in "Mirotic" to raucous applause. Even for a member of the iconoclastic BigBang, a group with hip-hop roots, G-Dragon and "Heartbreaker" made a bold choice in experimenting with an unconventional look and sound that took more cues from international artists (i.e., Lady Gaga and Kanye West) than his peers. This was a different tack for idols going solo and enabled future idols to think outside the box.

After "Heartbreaker," he began to wear more designer brands, becoming a Chanel ambassador in 2016, and collaborated with foreign artists, like the aforementioned Flo Rida. Unlike other Korean idols, whose companies took careful measures to ensure relative group harmony, GD went against the grain with his visible ambition and desire for individual success. As an idol-producer, responsible for much of BigBang's discography, his work was considered novel at the time. He was not a replaceable idol in a company-made group but an aspiring artist in his own right; this forthrightness would inspire the next generation of idols to branch out. The most compelling feature of GD was his overwhelming confidence, that propensity for individualism and "swag" copped from the hip-hop artists that BigBang would approximate. For a Korean like Jungkook, who had grown up within the narrow confines of the country, someone like GD opened a window to the world. GD promoted a fantasy of freedom and creativity, let loose from the strictures of a society that demanded rigor and conformity.

So it was "Heartbreaker" that called out to Jungkook, who was only eleven years old when the song was released, a precocious child who, by his own account, was prone to dream. In an interview included on the *2015 BTS Live* 花樣年華 *on Stage* DVD, he ran through a list of his childhood aspirations: to be Haku, the male lead from the Studio Ghibli animated film *Spirited Away*, because the character was good-looking and could turn into a dragon; to be a professional player of KartRider, a Korean online multiplayer racing game he became obsessed with after his parents bought him a computer in third or fourth grade; to be a professional badminton player, inspired by Lee Yong-dae, who won gold at the 2008 Beijing Olympics for mixed doubles; and then, lastly, to be a singer, a dream that began after he heard "Heartbreaker" and nurtured his admiration for GD.

The influence of GD and BigBang on Jungkook and BTS was substantial. "It wouldn't be an exaggeration to say that [BigBang] made BTS," Suga said on *Suchwita*, while interviewing BigBang's Taeyang. Debuted in 2006, BigBang brought the concept of "hip-hop idols" to the fore and were known for taking creative control over their musical output. T.O.P had been an underground rapper before becoming an idol, which lent his work more credence than other idol-trained rappers. BigBang and YG Entertainment always took pride in their more Western approach; in conversation with a former YG director, I was told how "free, open, and Americanized" the company was compared to its rivals. They allowed each member, like GD, to develop their own individual character and pushed the boundaries with their music and fashion, which made them more intriguing to Western fans and media—a blueprint that was the precursor to BTS.

In 2011, BigBang won the MTV Europe Music Award for Best Worldwide Act, beating Britney Spears. Their 2012 EP *Alive* was the first K-pop album to chart on the Billboard 200. As a K-pop group, they felt more connected to the world, in touch with trends from overseas that they exposed to Korean audiences, like tattoos and pastel hair dye. They employed collaborators like New Zealander Parris Goebel, known for her work with Justin Bieber and Rihanna. Goebel choreographed "Bang Bang Bang," which became a national sensation. Despite several scandals that marred their legacy, BigBang's influence cannot be denied. Through their subversive music and style and their desire to maintain artistic control, BigBang offered an alternative model for BTS and many other groups of the third and fourth generations, who found ways to stand out from the growing competition. In their early years, BTS openly stated their admiration for BigBang, even calling them role models at their debut showcase. "They are incredibly inspiring and influential people," RM explained in a radio interview later that month. "And in the same way that BigBang has their own style of music, we as BTS want to make our own style of music."

Each member drew different inspiration from their role models. Jimin admired Taeyang's expressive vocals and stage presence; he was featured on Taeyang's comeback single "Vibe" in 2023. Suga followed GD as a producer and songwriter, becoming a full member of the Korea Music Copyright Association (KOMCA) in 2018. KOMCA is a nonprofit copyright collective that manages musical works in South Korea. Musical copyright owners such as composers, producers, and arrangers are granted associate membership and promoted to full membership once they have produced a substantial amount of work. RM and J-Hope joined Suga as full members in 2020, and Jungkook was promoted to a full member in 2024.

GD may have inspired Jungkook in one especially crucial way. GD, who is not the strongest vocalist, found ways to use his voice as an instrument, singing and rapping with an unconventional raspy tone that was immediately recognizable, turning a weakness into a strength. Jungkook, whose voice similarly did not fit the K-pop standard, may have gained the courage to set himself apart in the way his idol had done.

Opposite of GD, we have Lee Ji-eun, best known as IU, the female vocalist whose wholesome public image earned her the title of "nation's little sister." As of 2024, IU is the artist with the most number-one songs in Korea, according to the Circle Chart, and is the most streamed female artist on Melon, the country's top streaming service. Not only beloved by the general public, IU is a favorite of hip-hop artists, having collaborated with musicians like GD, Jay Park, Zico, Zion.T, and Suga. IU was the first artist whose CD Jungkook bought with his own money. He has often been caught singing her songs—sitting in a computer chair, crooning "Ending Scene" into a microphone, bathed in rainbow light; "Through the Night" on a VLIVE livestream in his hotel room; "Sogyeokdong," which he sang lightly backstage. His members treated his singing like background noise. IU, whose career trajectory transcended that of the idol singer to model that of a widely respected and beloved vocalist, also provided a model for Jungkook to follow.

It bears repeating that idol music is not the genre most listened to or most favored by the average person in South Korea. Among the general public, the office workers and aunts and uncles that I have always known, ballad singers are the ones who command great respect. The history of pop music in South Korea is still short. The first song, fully recorded and produced in South Korea, was the national anthem in August 1947, only two years after Korea was liberated from Japanese colonial rule. Melon contains data from as far back as 1955, only two years after the Korean Armistice Agreement brought a ceasefire to the Korean War. Popular music became an outlet for emotional expression, and singing, a tradition dating back to seventeenth-century *pansori*, rooted itself more deeply in the culture. Singing remains a much-loved national pastime by way of *noraebang* or karaoke-style singing rooms. There are high-end *noraebang* with cinema screens, leather sofas, and swirling disco lights in soundproof rooms rented by the hour, and there are coin *noraebang*, quick and casual booths where you slip a 500 won coin into the slot for a song. Singing provides a form of cathartic release, an escape from the long hours and low pay, the soul-crushing hierarchy that characterizes Korean work culture.

The first time that Koreans were tracked alongside global artists on Melon was 1964. Poring over the charts of the top songs from each decade, one can see certain trends emerge:

From the 1950s, "Love Is a Many-Splendored Thing" by the Four Aces.

From the 1960s, "Yesterday" by the Beatles and "Before Fall Comes" by Iyeongsuk.

From the 1970s, "Bridge Over Troubled Water" by Simon & Garfunkel and "Under an Umbrella in Autumn Rain" by Choi Heon.

From the 1980s, "Take My Breath Away" by Berlin and "My Love Too Far to Have Near" by Lee Kwangjo.

From the 1990s, "The Power of Love" by Céline Dion and "My Love By My Side" by Kim Hyunsik.

From the 2000s, "I'm Yours" by Jason Mraz and "Gee" by Girls' Generation.

From the 2010s, "I'm Not the Only One" by Sam Smith and "Cherry Blossom Ending" by Busker Busker.

These love songs and power ballads, belted in the tens of thousands of *noraebang* that popped up across the country from the early nineties, represent the prevailing tastes of the public. Songs whose deep lows and powerful highs allow Koreans to release the pent-up stress and anger and resentment that defines the national character. Kim Gun Mo, a singer active during the nineties, held the title for most albums sold in the country for twenty-four years, until BTS would snatch the record in 2019 with *Map of the Soul: Persona*. Western artists like Ed Sheeran and Sam Smith, known for their strong voices and yearning melodies, are superstars in South Korea. Domestically, vocalists like SG Wannabe, Lee Seung Gi, and more recent singers from the late 2010s like Lim Young-woong are lauded for their heart-wrenching performances.

IU's debut single fell neatly into this mold. "Lost Child," sung by the then-fifteen-year-old, was about the bitter end of a relationship. For her debut performance on *Show! Music Core*, she appeared onstage backed by a string octet, standing straight in a black shift dress with sheer cape sleeves. She looked a bit stiff, the mature staging and strong vocals at odds with her youthful appearance. Reception was mixed, and IU later called the first album a failure, but the ballad went on to become a cult hit that resonated with fans like Jungkook, who chose the song when he auditioned to become a singer.

Superstar K is an audition program series in the style of *American Idol*. Started in 2009, *Superstar K* was at the peak of its popularity when Jungkook decided to audition in 2011. The final round of the first season featured two renditions of "Calling," a song composed by Bang Si-hyuk, who had launched Big Hit in 2005. As the winner, Seo In-guk released "Calling" as his debut single, and would go on to become a successful singer and actor. The second season, *Superstar K2*, earned an 18.1 percent rating during its live finale, setting the record for a cable show. More than 130,000 text message votes were sent by viewers, choosing Huh Gak, a ventilator fan repairman, who had been forced to drop out of middle school due to his family's financial circumstances. Talent that had been overlooked, an underdog whose journey would unfold on-screen, with a powerful rags-to-riches story, was the secret to success, in some way foreshadowing the advent of BTS.

The third season, *Superstar K3*, aired in 2011, and one of the preliminary rounds took place in April in Jungkook's hometown. Thousands lined up outside the Busan Exhibition and Convention Center at dawn, of the nearly two million that reportedly auditioned in cities like New York and Beijing and Osaka, and filed, one by one, into rectangular audition booths, covered with *Superstar K* advertisements, to perform for judges. Hopeful and all of thirteen years old, Jungkook auditioned. Like millions of others, his tapes never even made it onto the broadcast.

Only years later was the footage found and his "origin story" re-created, unearthed from a pile of two thousand preliminary auditions: A thirteen-year-old boy, wearing a white long-sleeve Evisu shirt and black jacket, a backpack slung over his shoulder, steps into the audition booth, setting the bag on the floor and handing a sheet to the judges. Asked to remove his jacket and reveal his number, B-71, he introduces himself quietly, nearly drowned out by a neighboring contestant. His hands clasped in front of him, he begins to sing "Lost Child," his voice soft and sweet in tone, unlike the belting all around him. When called to sing again, he chooses "This Song" by 2AM, a group comanaged by JYP Entertainment and Big Hit.

Jungkook did not proceed to the next round, but he left with seven business cards from agencies, pressed into his hands by scouts who saw potential in the boy with the mellow voice: JYP (which managed the groups Wonder Girls, 2AM, and 2PM), TS Entertainment (Secret, B.A.P), Starship (Sistar), Woollim (Infinite, Epik High), Cube Entertainment (4Minute, Beast), FNC Entertainment (F.T. Island, CN-BLUE), and Big Hit. And from the pile of famous companies, he chose Big Hit, which had the least number of successful groups to their name but did have several promising trainees. Jungkook has often said in interviews that it was pre-debut videos of RM that impressed him, because he evinced the GD style of cool that the young Jungkook idolized. In *Beyond the Story*, the official BTS book, he added that his father had suggested Big Hit based on founder Bang Si-hyuk's appearances on *Star Audition*, another popular music program.

At age thirteen, Jungkook packed his bags and headed two hours by KTX train northwest to Seoul, dragging his things down a narrow side street near Hakdong Park to the third-floor apartment on an unremarkable street, Nonhyeon-ro 149-gil, where RM, Suga, J-Hope, and a handful of other trainees were already living. At the time, the dorm was what J-Hope described as "a den of rap." BTS originally planned to debut as a crew of rappers and producers. The arrival of Jungkook heralded a shift from a hip-hop crew to an idol group that could rap and sing and dance. Yet how to turn a group of rap obsessives into idols, especially in Korea, a country so enamored with vocalists? The burden fell to the "vocal line," as the singers of an idol group are called: Jin, Jimin, V, and Jungkook, who, despite being the youngest of the seven, was assigned the role of "main vocalist," meaning he was responsible for the most challenging parts.

For K-idols, that role is a matter of pride. Main vocalists are called to demonstrate their skills on variety shows through high-note battles, each singer ascending the scale to demonstrate their prowess, or asked to perform the golden *noraebang* standard "Tears" by So Chan-whee, belting up to a G5. The main vocalist represents the talent of the entire group. MR-removed videos, which purport to edit out the backing vocals and instrumentals to leave only live singing, are immensely popular. Although the validity of MR-removed videos is questionable, fans often use them as proof that their favorite singers are talented ("they eat CDs for breakfast!") or talentless hacks. On weekly music shows, the winners perform live encore stages, which are not prerecorded; they have become a public test as idols demonstrate their singing chops on the spot and are eviscerated online if they fail.

In raising a group of hip-hop idols, Big Hit initially placed more emphasis on their dance and rap abilities over formal vocal instruction. Their debut single album *2 Cool 4 Skool* predominantly featured rap, and given their priorities, the public maintained low expectations for their singing; in fact, the group's "vocal line" received criticism for years. Jungkook, only fifteen when he debuted, faced immense pressure, along with Jimin, V, and Jin. They have spoken of hearing the other artists through their in-ear monitors while waiting backstage at weekly music shows and perceiving a skill gap that felt as wide as the ocean. On June 13, 2013, when the group first appeared on the program *M Countdown*, they would have heard songs like "A.D.T.O.Y" by 2PM, their voices flowing directly into their ears. The sextet, which had five years of experience as idols, was promoting their third studio album, *Grown*, and had recently performed at the Tokyo Dome for more than 110,000 fans over two days. Their steady performance intimidated the rookie group, particularly Jungkook, who felt responsibility as the main vocalist and began to feel self-doubt creeping in. "I realized after I debuted," Jungkook reflected in a 2021 interview on *You Quiz on the Block*, "I was the main vocalist of BTS, but the main vocalists of other groups sang so well, danced so well, they were cool and good-looking . . . What am I? Is it right for me to stand here as the main vocalist of this group?"

Days into his career, Jungkook faced a crisis of confidence, while BTS grappled with their general inexperience. As a result of the criticism, each member resumed training with a focus on their vocal performance skills: running in place for ten to twenty seconds before singing their parts to build stamina, using oxygen-depriving elevation training masks to build lung capacity. As the main vocalist, Jungkook began singing with more fervor than anyone else. He may have taken solace in his role model IU, who also debuted at fifteen and spent years toiling to gain the industry's respect; her single "Good Day" launched her to national acclaim years after "Lost Child," and her delayed success gave her a greater appreciation for what she had achieved. "I thought the only person who could change the way things were was myself," Jungkook said. "From that moment, I got rid of the notion of vocal training time. In the car, as I showered, of the twenty-four hours every day, every moment that I could possibly sing, I sang no matter what."

From the moment he woke up, in the car between rehearsals and shoots, in the makeup chair, in the greenroom, he would sing to himself, warming up his vocal cords and refining his techniques. He sang so often that he was scolded. To this day, he still sings to himself in cars and on livestreams, with friends and with family, wherever he goes. Beyond improving his range and other fundamentals, Jungkook made a concerted effort to develop his musical interpretation, the ability to express a song's character, for which IU was well-known. If GD inspired Jungkook to embrace the uniqueness of his voice, which differed from what the country was used to and broke expectations, IU might have shown him the universal truth: that music is popular because of its power to convey and process emotion, and in singing, that is what matters most.

In 2016, Jungkook undertook the challenge of appearing on *King of Mask Singer*. By then it appeared that he had found his footing. Having passed round one with a tremulous rendition of "I'm in Love" by Ra.D, Jungkook began the second-round semifinals still dressed in a white fencing uniform with the Korean flag on his left chest, a silver mask over his head. He began to sing "If You" by BigBang, his delicate voice drifting through the air.

Jungkook lost the round to his competitor but drew the audience in with his melodic rendition of the ballad, which was written by his hero GD, who also lacked a classical belting voice and whose music allowed more space for lightness and sensitivity. The panel described Jungkook's singing as sweet, his voice as distinct, mysterious, dreamlike; they said he possessed the ability to imbue even heavy songs with a delicate feeling, a sweeping nostalgia and sentimentality, reminiscent of his other role model, IU. "That voice can really pierce through one's heart, but because of that I can't say that he's an idol singer," one panelist remarked. "I mean, if he is an idol singer, it would be shocking." They were indeed shocked once Jungkook removed his mask.

"You don't usually sing like this in [BTS], do you?" one asked.

"I'm still lacking a lot vocally, so," Jungkook began, but was swiftly interrupted by a wave of protest.

"I was shocked that you're [nineteen] years old," the panelist continued, referring to the emotions Jungkook was able to imbue in his singing. How could someone so young possess the depth of experience to convey the feeling of heartbreak, of yearning, in such a poignant way?

Frankly, I wasn't surprised. Beneath the gloss and sheen, Seoul, where Jungkook moved alone at a young age, is a vicious city. I find it more fast-paced and merciless than Manhattan, where I lived and worked for a decade. Manhattan feels like a suburban escape whenever I return to visit, so imagine what Seoul might have felt like for Jungkook, coming from the coastal city of Busan. In the entertainment industry across all levels, it is survival of the fittest. Aspiring artists across disciplines are encouraged to tear their competition down, sleepless nights are de rigueur, and suffering is worn like a badge of honor. In Manhattan, my coworkers raced to leave the office as soon as they could; in Seoul, they waged passive-aggressive battles over who could stay the longest, who was making the greatest sacrifice. It's hard, unthinkably hard. It must have been even harder for Jungkook and the other members of BTS, who spent years being passed over, looked down on, and ignored. Yet suffering is rich in experience. Years of sweat and tears, shed by Jungkook, shaped him into a singer able to convey tragedy, hope, longing, and heartache in a way that only he can.

Though he was eliminated from the competition, Jungkook's appearance represented a turning point in public opinion about his singing, as well as of BTS. From that moment on, he continued to improve, alongside his older brothers, growing with each new song. Both

Jungkook and Suga agreed that it was from "Dynamite," the group's first full English-language single released in 2020, that he reached a new level; Suga has said that Jungkook's live singing now sounds like it has been run through Auto-Tune. Thanks to hours and hours of practice, his range, stability, tone, breath control, and phrasing developed to a point of perfection with his own flavor. Jungkook had become a world-class singer, capable of handling pop and R&B as well as any Western artist, as he showed on his solo album *Golden*. Still, even now he's not satisfied. In a 2022 interview for *Weverse Magazine*, writer Kang Myeongseok asked Jungkook what singing meant to him. Jungkook replied that he wanted his name to become shorthand for singing. "I keep thinking, how freeing and fun would it be to get up on stage and be able to sing the perfect song?" he said. "Completely worry free, just like in my imagination."

When I consider what makes Jungkook's singing special, I do return to that cover of "If You," a song of longing, each note imbued with an almost aching tenderness. The way he skirts between notes, holding and breaking at the right moments, stirs my heart. "Even without subtitles or translations, I think BTS's hopes and dreams are evident within their music and videos," said Adele, an ARMY who works with the fan-run translating group BTS-Trans. "Their heart behind the music is what naturally captures audiences." In the early days of BTS, Jungkook bore the challenge of conveying the meaning of their songs to those who didn't speak the language. It didn't matter whether or not you spoke a lick of Korean. Without knowing a word, you could feel every ounce of what he was feeling. Through his moving voice, he continues to convey the soul of music in a way that's universal.

CHAPTER 4

THE WAY HE MOVES

The first glimpse of Jungkook on BANGTANTV is a dance practice uploaded four months before his debut. Just over one minute long, the short opens on Jungkook, fifteen years old, standing at the back of a sparse basement studio with fluorescent overhead lights. He dances to "Save Your Goodbye" by Mike Posner, performing a routine that choreographer Kyle Hanagami had created and uploaded to YouTube two years prior. Though he had no formal dance training before entering Big Hit, Jungkook had been handpicked by Son Sungdeuk, the company's performance director, to spend about one month practicing at the Movement Lifestyle studio in Burbank, California, where renowned dancers like Hanagami taught classes. The camera is set up on the ground, providing a full view of the room and highlighting Jungkook's practiced movements, the eight-count pattern clearly ringing in his head. Though he is young, still inexperienced and growing, there is an uncommon beauty to the fluid moments when his arms float and snap into place like stalks in the wind, matching each beat precisely.

Alongside singing, dancing is a core skill more fundamental to

K-pop than Western pop. Since Western pop is sung in the universal language of English, it reaches a wider audience. For Korean artists, dance provides a mode of communication that does not need translation; many international fans, or I-fans for short, are first drawn to K-pop by the spectacular dances that surpass the average pop star performance in difficulty. Body waves and isolations are considered basics, as seen in the dance fundamentals routine rehearsed by trainees at JYP Entertainment, which is known for its strong dance program. To compete with Western stars, K-idols are expected to clear a higher bar, developing a skill set closer to a professional dancer.

I find that dance practice videos, like Jungkook's "Save Your Goodbye" cover, are the best way to appreciate an idol's skills. Dance practice videos are posted by every company for every single's release. They are an essential marketing tool with the average view count of a BTS practice numbering in the millions—their "MIC Drop" rehearsal has about 131 million more views than the actual 2017 MAMA Awards performance. I prefer their simplicity and pared-back production. Without visual flourishes, I can get a better sense of the choreography and each performer's abilities. I like seeing them dressed in casual clothes and the different rooms in which they rehearse.

For example, one can glean a lot about Big Hit from Jungkook's first dance practice. In 2013, the practice room was a rented studio at the bottom of a stairwell beneath a restaurant known for its black pork dishes, stir-frys, and stews. Jungkook wore a snapback hat that said "Dope" and a Channel sweatshirt, a knockoff of Chanel found in Seoul flea markets. In his movements there was tension: his shoulders were tight and his unblinking eyes fixed on the camera lens, as if desperate to perfect each step and prove his worth. By 2021, the era of the Big Three labels of SM Entertainment, YG Entertainment, and JYP Entertainment had given way to the Big Four, with HYBE reaping the successes of BTS. Big Hit Entertainment rebranded to BigHit Music, a HYBE sub-label, and moved into a nineteen-story, multimillion-dollar headquarters in Yongsan. Two years after that—a full decade after Jungkook's "Save Your Goodbye" cover was uploaded—Jungkook filmed the practice video for "Standing Next to You," the third single off *Golden*, in a sprawling dance rehearsal space with a basketball hoop in frame. Chicly dressed in black leather pants and a classic white tee, he moved with confidence, flocked by six backup dancers. Compared to the humble circumstances of "Save Your Goodbye," the world-class "Standing Next to You" showed that Jungkook had made it. He was a superstar, backed by one of the most powerful entertainment companies in the country. Seeing these two practice videos, back-to-back, marks the passage of time, throwing the weight of what BTS accomplished in sharpest relief.

H.O.T., considered the first K-idol group ever, debuted in 1996 from SM Entertainment. Launched in 1989 as SM Studio and rebranded in 1995, SM was founded by Lee Soo-man, who is often called the King of K-pop, though the Godfather of K-pop feels more apt. The pioneering Lee modeled his strict training methods after Japan's idol industry, setting up the fully in-house K-idol system now known around the world. Through complete control of artist development, he created a polished product. The results spoke volumes: H.O.T.'s second album sold more than a million copies in ten days per an unofficial sales tally. In 1998, Lee introduced his second boy group, Shinhwa. With Shinhwa, SM's approach to dance gravitated away from the loose and free hip-hop bounces and weight shifts that typified early K-pop performance toward the commercial pop choreography seen today. There was an emphasis on technical prowess and precision; the synchronized chair dance seen in Shinhwa's "Wild Eyes," for instance, raised the bar.

Lee went on to produce many of the most successful groups in K-pop history: TVXQ, Super Junior, SHINee, Girls' Generation, EXO—whose collective revenue kept SM at the top of the Big Three for years. SM Entertainment was the first entertainment company to go public in Korea in 2000. Though he left SM in 2023 after a series of internal corporate disputes, Lee's legacy still reverberates today with groups like NCT, the seventh major boy group created under his direction, reportedly selling more than forty million albums by 2024.

With each generation, K-pop artists have elevated the level of choreographed dance expected by fans and peers. Within SM alone, the chronological record of dance practice videos captures the stylistic shifts over time. Allegedly the established video format—the fixed-camera single take filmed in the company practice space—did not appear until the early 2000s, after SM accidentally posted footage of an "Only One" dance practice by Shinhwa. Fans went wild for the unvarnished look at their behind-the-scenes rehearsal, a precursor to the candid vlog-style content that contributed to the rise of BTS. It was an astonishing success. Not long after, dance practice videos became an industry mainstay and integral to a song's promotional run.

In the early days, SM's practice room wall featured a white cloud backdrop that fans of past generations, like me, remember fondly. Among the videos that stick out most in my mind: SHINee's "Lucifer," which incorporated technical styles like tutting and showcased the fluid and graceful moves of Taemin, one of the industry's greatest dancers. In "Lucifer," Taemin's Breton striped shirt bends like a piece of op art. With more than twenty-six million views, the video's longevity is astounding and shows how dance practice videos became a way for fans to further appreciate the artists. "officially a decade later and we're still talking about taemin's shirt," read a top comment. "me: tries to focus on other members / taemin's shirt: how about no," wrote another. I enjoyed SHINee's "Everybody," a physically demanding piece full of leaps and backbends, which, for some reason, was shot with a fish-eye lens; it has more than fourteen million views. Super Junior's "Sexy Free & Single" was remarkable for the way the ten members moved like schools of fish swimming in synchronized circles. Ten members seemed like so many at a time when most K-pop groups consisted of three to six, though that was only the beginning for SM, whose twelve-member boy group EXO formed a human tree in the leaked dance practice for "Wolf," and who had the eighteen members of NCT in 2018 perform "Black on Black" together.

But what began as an unembellished format became a way to highlight a group's choreography and tease fans. Companies began to release multiple versions with entertaining twists, such as "Part Switch Ver.," where members swap positions, and "Eye Contact Ver." The "Halloween Ver.," where idols don costumes, is a yearly treat; BTS's 2017 Halloween dance practice of "Go Go," where they dressed as Snow White and the Seven Dwarfs, has more than 246 million views. They began to stylize even basic dance practices. Outfits were curated by the visual team, even when they called for a basic T-shirt and athletic pants (the backup dancers were styled too); professional hair and makeup was a given, and a DP or director of photography was brought in to work the camera, sometimes employing a dolly to get the perfect, steady zoom in and out. Stylistically, my reigning favorite is EXO's "Monster," which has more than seventy-six million views as of this writing. Backlit to form moody shadows, the boys are dressed simply, the lighting and saturation levels adjusted to perfection. The camera moves forward and back, far enough to show the full choreography, but close enough to highlight the members' facial expressions. It is transfixing, but I do miss the simplicity of that humble cloud wall of the past.

• • •

When it comes to K-pop's infiltration of the Western market, the showstopping music videos provide the cleanest entry point. The industry indulges in a level of multimillion-dollar visual spectacle that no longer exists in the West the way it did from the eighties through the aughts, when music videos were the primary means of captivating fans. For pop stars like Michael Jackson and Janet Jackson, Britney Spears and Jennifer Lopez, dance was the centerpiece of the music video. Yet the days of Michael and Janet's $7 million "Scream" are long gone. With a few exceptions, the marketing budget is directed toward shorts and dance challenges that are significantly cheaper to make and more likely to go viral, abetting digital streaming over physical record sales. "There was an era that existed in the North American music industry, this mentality of investing in the visuals of a song," said Val "Ms. Vee" Ho, a dancer and choreographer specializing in hip-hop and street dance, who became the first to teach hip-hop at Juilliard. "Now it's shifted over there to K-pop."

In a way, K-pop calls back to the golden age of pop visuals that many, like me and Ms. Vee, grew up watching. Dance, the core element of a performance, has intrinsic appeal. As such, K-pop labels made a point to create these incredible dances and the dancers to execute them. "They have the resources to do all that stuff," Ms. Vee said of the reason why Korean dancers may seem to outshine their peers. "They have resources to pay a choreographer, a director . . . they are supported." The typical K-idol group is expected to execute highly complex choreography that fuses different styles together, built on the foundations of hip-hop. "If you don't have a strong hip-hop foundation, you can't make [K-pop choreography] look good," said Ms. Vee. "Underneath the commercial-ness of the choreography, they're using a lot of technique that's not super obvious unless you know the dance."

Although BigBang is often called BTS's direct predecessor, I find more spiritual similarities between BTS and Infinite, who debuted in 2010 with Woollim Entertainment. Both groups started with seven members and modest beginnings. Despite coming from smaller labels outside the Big Three, Infinite and BTS managed to rise to the top of their respective eras by bucking industry standards. For Infinite, it was their disciplined approach to dance. When an average Korean thinks of K-pop, it is *kalgunmu* that comes to mind. *Kalgunmu*, pronounced kahl-goon-moo, literally translates to "knife group dance," referring to the synchronized dance steps of a boy or girl group moving with an eponymous knifelike sharpness that evokes militaristic precision. It is the polar opposite of contemporary Western pop dance. The idea of synchronized dance in a pop group itself is not new. Western groups from the Jackson Five to NSYNC have been dancing in sync for decades. But it is the level of synchronicity that has become representative of K-pop. Infinite is credited with bringing *kalgunmu* to the forefront; the term was popularized to describe the absolute perfection of their dance.

I have a soft spot for Infinite, whose dance practice videos are among the greatest of all time. I could spend hours talking about "The Chaser," "Be Mine," or "Come Back Again." The most exemplary is "BTD (Before the Dawn)," the second track off their second EP in 2011, whose performance featured the Scorpion, a version of a Rise Up incorporated by former member Hoya. In a circular formation, the boys lay on their stomachs before propelling themselves back up to their feet in unison, like a flower's petals unfolding in reverse. It remains one of the greatest moments in K-pop dance history. Their dance was always mesmerizing. Infinite's weight shifts snapped crisply to the beat. Heavy drops and buoyant lifts, the clean lines and geometric shapes created by the bend of a knee or flick of the wrist not once but seven times in a row. There is something so satisfying about watching seven dancers with such complete body control that the seven can move as one. As hypnotic as watching a pendulum swing, *kalgunmu* seems to defy the limits of human ability, like seeing synchronized swimmers plunge through water at the Olympics. It is a feat of art and athleticism.

Kalgunmu requires one thing: practice. Hours and hours of it, countless repetitions, until each movement, each beat is engraved into your mind and muscle memory. It is dedication, the desire to push yourself to the utmost, a character trait that I see embedded throughout Korea. Only after moving to Seoul and working at a traditional corporate office did I, a Korean American, taste a fraction of the soul-crushing stress and heavy expectations that Korean-born Koreans, indoctrinated since birth, find as normal as the air they breathe. Koreans in these industries, stuck within social hierarchies, will push themselves past the breaking point to please their superiors. There's never enough time. Work-life balance is a myth, and sleep is for the weak. One day, after pulling a thirty-six-hour shift to meet a deadline with drastic last-minute changes, a depressingly regular occurrence, my boss turned to me and said, with a delirious smile on her face, "Doesn't it feel incredible when you achieve something that should have been impossible to do?" It is this insane drive, the pressure to succeed, to break the limits—of time, of your body, and of your mind— that is a striking characteristic of Korean society. And it is that drive that informs *kalgunmu*.

It requires skill, yes, but more than skill, it is diligence and "thousands and thousands and thousands of repetitions to really master," Ms. Vee said. That was the original purpose of these dance practice videos—for the dancers, their instructors and choreographers, and even the company heads to watch and fuss over each misstep. According to Jin, Bang Si-hyuk would pore over the footage frame by frame, until even the boys' finger placements were in sync. As trainees, BTS rehearsed up to fourteen hours a day, some days dancing for twelve hours. The BTS "dance line," composed of the members who handle the key parts, includes J-Hope, Jimin, and Jungkook, with the addition of V in 2018. But according to Ms. Vee, every member of BTS is an exceptional dancer. "Specific to them, it's really great choreography," she said. "They're doing it so clean, it's so crispy . . . all of them are good at what they do." *Kalgunmu* requires a commitment to the collective, staying in sync and working together to create something greater than any individual effort. The resulting display of harmony and martyrdom is mesmerizing.

Kalgunmu is a skill that can be bought not with money but with enough time and effort. It demands the sort of hunger and drive that only underdogs tend to possess. My first introduction to Seventeen was their "Very Nice" dance practice, which went viral (more than twenty-nine million views) for the stunning *kalgunmu* of its thirteen members. I can only imagine the conditions under which those boys spent years training in the "Melona room," as fans called it, some of which have been alluded to in interviews and captured in pre-debut videos that I find too painful to watch. "All the bad memories of my life are from that time," Seventeen's Mingyu said in a YouTube interview. "I couldn't sleep, you know. I would practice until four in the morning, then take the subway to school and sleep there . . . I would head back to the studio for more practice during lunchtime. Often, I'd nod off on the subway ride there, then spend the entire day practicing. At night, it was back to the dorm, and straight off to school again. That was my routine every single day." The sharpness of their moves is a testament to their sacrifice, the same way BTS poured everything they had into their dance.

I don't think it's a coincidence that boy groups from smaller companies—to name a few, Infinite (Woollim), BTS (Big Hit), Seventeen (Pledis), and Ateez (KQ)—gained early attention for their synchronized dance. None of these labels had the resources to compete with the Big Three in terms of marketing and production, and so they pushed their idols' abilities as far as they could. RM uploaded a video in January 2013, five months before his debut, at 3:30 a.m., remarking that the day's work wrapped up earlier than expected. At the time, RM was jokingly nicknamed "dance prodigy" by the Big Hit staff due to his lack of skills. By the time of their debut, he was able to keep up with J-Hope and Jimin, widely considered two of the best dancers in K-pop. As Big Hit performance director Son Sungdeuk would later say in a BBC Radio interview, "Not everyone is a great dancer, but they practice hard to become one."

I first saw BTS perform live during the "Fire" era, and I remember being impressed by their energy and stage presence, which felt as passionate as their rookie debut. "I'm a thousand percent confident it's all the practice that they have to do," said Ms. Vee. "I'm sure it's so grueling. It looks like ten hours a day of rehearsals. There's an importance placed on unison and no one sticking out too much."

Yet that is an inherent weakness in *kalgunmu*. It lacks individuality. *Kalgunmu*, with its focus on perfect unison, asks each dancer to adjust their individual skill level to match the group. The stronger dancers must minimize their moves, the weaker dancers must rise to the challenge, and this equality disguises flaws in the members' dancing. "Sticking only with *kalgunmu* never helps you improve your dance ability," said Hoya, in an interview with *The Dong-A Ilbo*. There is no room for expression or creativity in the movement. It is about presenting this surreal construction—the more members, the more impressive.

It is the embodiment of harmony, placing the needs of the group above the individual, a collectivist mindset with roots in Confucianism that found expression in a mode of modern K-pop dance—one reason why *kalgunmu* is so fascinating, on a subconscious level, to Western audiences. The idea of sacrificing the self for the whole, conceptualized in the span of a pop song, is so interesting and strange. I have heard non-K-pop fans in America, my former coworkers among them, describe it as almost unsettling, calling to mind the spectacle of the 2008 Beijing Olympics opening ceremony where 2,008 drummers beat perfectly in sync. Yet among East Asian viewers, *kalgunmu* more often stirs respect, as proof of how hard the young idols have worked. Their sacrifice is admired.

Synchronicity possesses its own beauty but can feel soulless. By nature, dance is expressive. It resonates most when you can connect with the performer, when their movements are fluid and alive, not necessarily strict and precise. Compared to solo artists, K-pop-style synchronized groups struggle to find their foothold with the Western general public. Freedom, individuality, and artistic expression are more valued. There is the pervasive Western perception that K-pop idols are manufactured, lacking individuality and personality—the racially charged statement that they all look the same, move the same, sound the same. *Kalgunmu* implicitly reinforces these stereotypes because it ultimately places a limitation on personal artistry. It is one reason why Infinite, the group most associated with *kalgunmu*, began to put it aside in their later years. As Hoya told *Dong-A*, "We used to create the image of *kalgunmu*, even though each member has a different body type and their own feeling. It is not the time for us to conceal our own style anymore." In the same interview, his fellow member Dongwoo said, "We were not able to show our styles," while Woohyun added, "My dance has improved a lot after stopping *kalgunmu*."

BTS debuted with their single "No More Dream" on the weekly

music show *M Countdown*, performing choreography they had practiced for nearly two straight months, according to Jin. There was something rough and earnest in the way the members' bounces and shimmies matched up with the lyrics, which questioned the conformity of Korean culture. The "killing part" occurred when Jimin, lifted up by Jungkook, ran across the backs of the other five members. Unlike the *kalgunmu* of Infinite, BTS's dance, while in sync, was still unpolished, relying on the members' individual energies to connect with the audience. It marked a return to the hip-hop spirit captured by Seo Taiji and Boys, one of the first K-pop groups, who were also protesting the restrictive nature of nineties South Korea. As Bangtan Sonyeondan (BTS), they debuted with a clear goal: to share the dreams and frustrations of their youth. You can almost feel the hunger, the desperation, in each step.

When Jungkook began his solo career, he decided to release an English pop record. It called for a different approach to dance, for him to let loose a little. Among his technical skills, Jungkook possesses an innate musicality—matching his movements to the song's rhythms—that he can dial up or down, depending on the situation. It is his groove, the sharp yet relaxed way he moves his body, that makes his dancing so pleasant to watch, even when compared with dancers that possess greater technical skills. For his solo work, he dialed up his groove, according to Ms. Vee, who noted his ability to pay homage to Michael Jackson, one of the greatest dancers of all time, with the Jacksonian tribute "Standing Next to You," choreographed by Keone Madrid. When I showed her a series of Jungkook's dance practices, charting a course from "Save Your Goodbye" to *Golden*, she was impressed by the evolution. "In ['Standing Next to You'], you could tell he was settled in—not just in the choreography and the dancing, but settled in himself too," she said. "That dance requires clear confidence in its execution. It's very clean. You can tell it was rehearsed hundreds and hundreds of times. When it's BTS, they're all killing it. They're very much in unison and you can feel the group dynamic. When he's doing his solo stuff, he's got a lot of swag. That stuck out more."

Choreographer Brian Puspos, who danced backup for Jungkook on "Standing Next to You," described the routine as physically taxing, filled with references to Michael Jackson's minute movements that were challenging in their subtlety—the way Jungkook stands and gestures in front of the mic stand. "We already knew Jungkook was a high-level performer, but we were literally impressed," Puspos said in a video for online dance studio STEEZY, where he reviewed the song's practice footage with director Clay Boonthanakit. They admired Jungkook's stability and body control, and well as his ability to handle the polyrhythms (simultaneous contrasting rhythms) and match the energy of high-level professionals like Puspos.

"You know what's crazy, that's not even, like, he's like Gear 3 right now," Puspos added, making a reference to the techniques of Monkey D. Luffy, the protagonist of the manga series *One Piece*. "When he goes to like Gear 5, we're all over here like, bro, we have to pull up." At the two-minute-forty-five-second mark, as he enters the song's final dance break, Jungkook's thin silver necklace catches on his ear. As he rolls his arms up, without missing a beat, he rips the chain off his neck and tosses it to the side, so swiftly that it goes nearly unnoticed.

"Standing Next to You" is a tour de force performance, but I find myself equally captivated by his light and breezy dance cover of "Perfect Night" by Le Sserafim with four of the girl group's members behind him. Just as Jungkook is known for his ability to sing across musical genres, he can express a range of dance styles, including those of a girl group. The way he sways his hips and snaps his arms, moving lithely in frame, is so effective, he could easily pass as their center. "It feels like he directly output the feeling the choreographer wanted to express," read a top Korean comment. "This doesn't seem like it's from memorizing the choreography, but just listening to the music and outputting it with your body. Matching the beat exactly, the natural flow of the rhythm . . . isn't he really a genius?" read another.

Clean and confident, settled in his own body: these qualities have exemplified Jungkook's solo career thus far, traits that resonate with a Western audience. Yet, when called on, Jungkook can capably return and meld into the group, happily giving up his ego to not stand out. It's not easy to manage both the self-sacrificial art of *kalgunmu* and the free-spirited expression of Western pop dance. But the ability to do both is one that all the greatest K-pop dancers, like Jungkook, possess. There are two facets of Korean culture that I find most fascinating: the tendency toward repression and the gift for unfiltered expression. I can see both halves reflected in his dance, such a conductive medium for emotion.

In April 2022, BTS flew to Las Vegas to perform "Butter," their second English-language single, at the 64th Grammy Awards. The James Bond–inspired stage was a true group effort. Each member contributed to the choreography and kept their arms at matching 45-degree angles. Even once they reached the MGM Grand Garden Arena, where the ceremony took place, they dissected and reassembled the routine, huddled together to review the rehearsal footage. J-Hope instructed the others to relax and groove, a slight departure from *kalgunmu*, to better fit their global star status. Jungkook fell into formation—as the center, an integral member, but not sticking out any more than he should.

Seven months later, Jungkook was asked to perform at the opening ceremony of the 2022 FIFA World Cup in Qatar. Though he was invited alone by organizers, he went as Jungkook of BTS, considering it a transitory phase between his group and solo work. The Qatar World Cup was marked by controversy due to the labor abuses, accusations of corruption, and the country's record of human rights abuses, echoing the horrors committed by the Korean government in the lead-up to the 1988 Seoul Olympics. Jungkook's performance was met with disappointment by some ARMY, who'd hoped he would boycott the event on moral grounds, and pride by others, who were excited that he would become the first Asian artist to perform the official World Cup anthem.

"Dreamers," the World Cup song produced by RedOne, was already a hit, surprising even those who had requested Jungkook sing it. "It's the first time a World Cup song ever in the history, that does over a hundred countries, at number one in the first day," RedOne said in an interview with AP News. "We're just starting, and the video is doing crazy, like almost twenty million in almost two days' time. It's unbelievable." About one year later, the music video surpassed two hundred million views.

That November, Jungkook arrived in Qatar a few days ahead of the ceremony. The night before the dress rehearsal, he received the choreography video, thinking that he needed to move with the backup dancers, and stayed up until six in the morning learning the steps. He continued to practice at every spare moment. In the greenroom, in the car, on the way to the stadium, his eyes closed in visualization, Jungkook began considering ways to improve the stage. He reworked sections of the choreography, providing detailed notes on blocking to the team, and added a dance break. The next day, he went to the rehearsal space to observe the dancers and practiced with intense focus; at night in his hotel room, he washed up and went through the formation shifts, running through the routine alone until sunrise.

His first solo performance made history and was seen by millions of people around the world—around five billion people engaged with the 2022 World Cup, according to FIFA—many of whom met Jungkook for the first time. In front of a crowd of some sixty-seven thousand people, plus millions of at-home viewers, Jungkook stood on his own as an artist, bouncing and grooving before the camera with a natural "swag," as Ms. Vee would put it. His live vocals remained strong and stable as he moved across the stage, meeting Qatari singer Fahad Al Kubaisi on the center platform in a moment of unity.

"It was one of the most beautiful experiences I've had, working with this wonderful artist with a presence, charisma and multiple talents all his own," Al Kubaisi later said in an interview with *Esquire Middle East*. Al Kubaisi added that he had expected FIFA to choose an American or European singer, but that "honestly, there was no better choice." Jungkook performed in the same style and at the same level as any Western pop star, smiling and playing to the crowd and camera, evoking lightness and joy in a different way than he had at the Grammys. Clinical perfection and liberated expression. In my eyes, one is not more right than the other. There is beauty in both, and the ability to seamlessly shift between the two is one thing that makes Jungkook quite special.

CHAPTER 5

THE WAY HE LOOKS

Jungkook is pretty. Like, really pretty. An official Calvin Klein model and global ambassador by age twenty-five, seven months before he released *Golden*, Jungkook has a classic handsomeness that crosses cultural lines. Clean-cut yet rugged, good boy yet bad. In 2024, Calvin Klein displayed his image on the seventy-five-foot billboard on Houston Street in Manhattan—for more than fifteen years, "the most iconic billboard in the world," according to *GQ*—and he looked as timeless as the advertisements from the nineties, when most brands did not feature an Asian man as a standard of beauty. Modeling for CK, Jungkook has clear and shining skin; his black hair is long and curls gently against his shoulders in one image, or coiffed neatly behind his ears in another. You can glimpse the tattoos peeking from the cuff of his sleeve, a double hoop jabbed through his lower lip, and rows of silver hoops lining his ears.

The official press release for his appointment as global brand ambassador for Calvin Klein Jeans and Calvin Klein Underwear announced that he was "one of the world's most popular artists; he possesses a rare ability to connect with international audiences through both his music and his style." The brand was lucky to get him: according to Launchmetrics, which tracks fashion industry performance, Jungkook's fall 2023 campaign for Calvin Klein Jeans generated $13.4 million in media impact value in forty-eight hours, making him their top-performing ambassador. From my time consulting in the industry, I know of at least three top fashion houses that fought hard to get him but were turned away.

Jungkook debuted at fifteen years old, the same age as Justin Bieber when he released "Baby." He stirred a protective instinct in older fans because he was handsome for his age, but also innocent and sweet. To them, he was an adorable baby brother who deserved the world. A 2017 YouTube compilation titled "Jungkook is still a baby . . ." has more than fourteen million views with comments like, "No matter how old he gets, he will always be a baby that we must protect." Consider his *dongmulsang*, a popular practice in Korean fan culture that compares celebrities' facial characteristics to animals, such as a cat face for sharp eyes that go up at the outer corners. Jungkook has been linked to a deer, due to his round doe-like eyes. He has a habit of looking surprised or dazed in a charming way, like a deer in headlights, inspiring the meme "Jungshook." He is also associated with a rabbit. His incisors are slightly larger than his canines, affectionately called bunny teeth by fans, and when he smiles, his eyes curl up into half-moons. When it came time to design his BT21 character, a mascot in collaboration with the Japanese messaging app LINE, he came up with Cooky, a "pinkish tough bunny" with one floppy ear and a mischievous grin. A cute yet tough bunny is how the other members see him even now. In episode 129 of the online variety series *Run BTS!* from February 2021, the group played a three-on-four tennis match. When Jungkook hit the net on his serve, he cutely called out that he'd made a mistake. He was allowed to serve again. Jimin laughed good-naturedly and asked why it was a mistake when Jungkook mis-served, but when others did, they lost a point.

"Why?" Suga asked, his racquet on his shoulder. "Because Jungkook is cute."

"If you don't like it, be reborn as the youngest," Jin added, rolling up his sleeve.

As Jungkook grew up, though, his looks drew a new level of attention, as he spent hours at the gym boxing and lifting weights to hone his physique. In 2021, rapper Jessi was asked on the talk show *Jessi's Showterview* about her ideal type.

"Lately there's a guy who I've been thinking, wow, he's so cool," she said, reluctant to reveal his identity for fear of upsetting his fans. "A member of BTS . . . recently this guy has become more manly."

"Jungkook!" her cohost Jo Jung Shik said without a moment's hesitation, to her surprise.

"Long ago, I shot an advertisement with BTS," Jessi added. "Back then he was a baby. I was a baby then too. But now he's become a man."

In January 2024, a fan posted a three-second clip of Jungkook walking backstage shirtless on Twitter and earned more than 2.9 million views, 44,000 reposts, and 128,000 likes. In 2019, he was named the winner of TC Candler's "The 100 Most Handsome Faces of 2019," a popular YouTube series that fans take quite seriously, despite the unserious nature of the video (Jungkook placed first over Swedish YouTuber PewDiePie). In 2020, he was named *People* magazine's "Sexiest International Man" after winning the annual online poll, sandwiched between Prince Harry ("Sexiest Royal") and Joe Jonas ("Sexiest New Dad") in the November 30 print issue. He returned in the magazine's "Sexy at Every Age" feature in the 2022 Sexiest Man Alive issue, representing age twenty-five. Even his look-alikes have gone viral. In 2022, a

YouTuber named Dex was catapulted to fame on the dating show *Single's Inferno* largely thanks to his initial resemblance to Jungkook, with his slightly wavy mullet and sleeve of ink on his right arm. Dex is now a star in his own right, a host of *Single's Inferno* and his own show, *Dex's Fridge Interview*. He won male Rookie of the Year at the 2023 MBC Entertainment Awards. His shift from dating show contestant to bona fide celebrity—unprecedented in South Korea—speaks to the power Jungkook can provide. A Japanese woman named Hirai Saya, who married Korean actor Shim Hyung-tak, became a trending topic for looking exactly like a teenage Jungkook in a long wig. Even Jungkook acknowledged the similarity on a Weverse livestream with a laugh.

Unlike the typical *kkotminam*, or flower boys—a term that emerged in the nineties to refer to beautiful men, often depicted in media targeted toward women—Jungkook possesses a broader charm like a modern-day David Bowie, who was able to navigate the masculine and feminine. When BTS made *Vanity Fair*'s 2019 Best-Dressed List, Jungkook defined great style as "Wearing anything you like, regardless of gender." For many Americans, Jungkook may have been their first introduction to the K-pop world. He is groomed in a way that most Western male celebrities, with their untamed facial hair or sun-damaged skin, are not. Jungkook has no stubble. Pore-less skin or the appearance of it, thanks to the magic of foundation and powder. Shaded brows, eyeliner to enhance his eyes. Full lips. Not a hair out of place or a wrinkle in sight, and a well-built body. Jungkook is more clean-cut than his Western peers because he also meets a different standard of beauty—Korean.

Stars like Jungkook have made massive strides in altering the Western perception of East Asian men, who have historically been viewed as undesirable and lacking sexual appeal. As far back as the 1800s, when Chinese immigrants entered the US en masse to provide cheap labor, Asian American men have been subject to emasculating stereotypes, aimed at diminishing their power and preserving the status quo. In the *Hangover* movies, from 2009 to 2013, actor Ken Jeong's portrayal of Mr. Chow and his near-nonexistent manhood made him the butt of the joke. In contrast, the thirst tweets about Jungkook show how he and other Korean stars have shattered those racist notions: tweets like "I'm losing my mind IM LOSING MY MIND rolling on the floor kicking my feet screaming crying" and "Father master daddy sir lord" are among the tamer responses to that three-second shirtless clip. Hearing hundreds of men and women, barking in unison at one of his live shows, will quickly dispel misconceptions of how sexy Asian men can be.

There is a phenomenon that I've witnessed several times, a sort of thousand-yard stare that occurs when a person begins to contemplate Jungkook's attractiveness. In an interview with SiriusXM, Charlie Puth, when asked about collaborating with Jungkook, said, completely unprompted, "They're all very talented. I don't listen to a whole lot of BTS but now I am and, uh, Jungkook is a very attractive human . . . No but like he's, I was like, wow." He said, eyes cast downward, as if reliving it, "I was like, hey now." Dancer Brian Puspos had a similar moment while watching Jungkook's "Standing Next to You" practice video. He was commenting on the razor-sharp executions when, after watching a short section of circular hip thrusts performed by Jungkook in black leather pants, Puspos said, unprompted, "He is so hot," before turning to the camera, eyes round, as if he had voiced an intrusive thought by mistake. A friend recently messaged me to say she might be coming to Seoul with her husband, who wanted to get a nose job to look more like Jungkook, who he called "the best-looking one in BTS."

Jungkook is handsome, but nearly all male idols are handsome. What I find compelling is the way that his looks have dismantled standards in the East and the West. In Korea, where he was born and raised, the beauty standard is the world's most extreme, both difficult to achieve and crucial to success. Until 2019, job applications required a photograph alongside your résumé across industries, regardless of whether or not your looks were relevant to the work. A "blind hiring" bill passed the national assembly, but visual standards persist. The average Korean puts great care into their appearance—the third-largest market in the world for online beauty sales in 2023, according to Euromonitor—and makeup for men is not stigmatized. Your looks are commented on with great frequency, the feedback brutally honest yet delivered in a blasé way, as if one is observing the daily weather. "You got prettier" or "You gained weight" are quotidian greetings among friends and family, coworkers and receptionists. When coupled with the cultural pressure to conform, it's difficult to push back against expectations.

Though tastes have evolved over time, beauty standards are entrenched: a small face, indicated by its size relative to that of a human fist; large eyes with double eyelids; a high nose bridge; a shapely forehead; the V-line, a sharp jaw and chin ending in a neat point; *aegyo-sal*, or the pockets of fat underneath the eyes associated with youth; skin so bright and gleaming, pale and pore-less, as though it has never seen the sun. Body proportions are important: broad shoulders and a slim waist for men, ultra-thin with no more than a slight S-line for women. There is pressure to meet these beauty standards regardless of what you do. Whenever I meet a new dermatologist, I leave with insecurities I could not have fathomed. I never worried once about my "flat forehead," until a doctor asked if I'd like to add dermal fillers to round it out.

There is substantial cultural context behind these strict beauty ideals, factors like the dog-eat-dog society immortalized in works such as *Squid Game*. In the way that students are pushed to their academic limits to attend the best universities and achieve financial stability, beauty opens a pathway to a successful career, a loving marriage, a happy life. I also argue that it has to do with the value placed on hard work. Some are born beautiful, but to maintain beauty of the highest degree—to the standard demanded by the K-pop industry—requires Herculean effort. Years ago, I went to visit Jenny House, a beauty shop frequented by celebrities, and sat in the chair for three hours, as the makeup artist and stylist perfected my "daily makeup," the kind a star would receive every day while doing promotions. I was seated next to two male idols and a female star, who had been there since dawn. The men were fast asleep in their chairs. When I visit my friend Park Eunkyung of Unistella, the cult nail artist known for her work with Blackpink, it's another hour or two of painstaking labor to receive an exquisite manicure, as she swirls paint and applies layers of gossamer paper or glass beads. No wonder press-on nails have become the industry staple. You could spend your whole life trying to be beautiful.

In America, I went to the dermatologist only once I became a beauty editor, and even then, maybe once or twice a year to deal with specific skin issues. In Korea, I started going at least once a month for regular checkups and upkeep, per my friends' and family's advice. Due to the overwhelming demand for skincare treatment, appointments are easy to book and relatively affordable. Idols make weekly visits for lasers and facials. Once, a former idol friend of mine, seeing me in rough condition, sent me to an underground spa she visited for body treatments. I spent two to three hours on the table, being massaged and moisturized, bathed and pinched and suctioned to tautness. Though I'd never looked better, it was mentally exhausting to spend so much time, paying someone to pick and pore over every inch of my body. I never went again.

Hours are spent each week at the gym with a personal trainer or a Pilates instructor, along with a punishing diet of skinless grilled chicken breast (Jin called it the "eternal ingredient" in a pre-debut blog post) and boiled eggs to maintain that hard-earned physique. K-pop stars are expected to maintain an extremely low weight that matches up to fashion industry standards and summarily praised for their hard work. In 2013, IU revealed the now-infamous diet she used to lose about eleven pounds in five days, subsisting on an apple, two sweet potatoes or bananas, and a protein shake each day. She later disclosed that an audience member called her a pig at her debut, and she began to struggle with eating disorders and poor body image. BigBang's T.O.P was initially turned away by YG Entertainment founder Yang Hyun-suk for being too chubby; after losing about forty-four pounds in forty days, he returned and was accepted.

The constant upkeep is not enough. A few years ago, I was on set for the album jacket shoot of a top K-pop star who, in person, was absolutely stunning, practically a walking doll. Despite the two hours of hair and makeup and manicure, I still watched as the photographer, in real time, used the Liquify tool to adjust her perfect proportions, bringing down the slope of her shoulders to create an even flatter line and nipping in her waist, taking this naturally perfect human to an inhuman level of perfection. In the West, it's the same. Working in fashion and media, I've seen images and video retouched like you wouldn't believe. But nothing shocked me more than that photoshoot. I'd never seen someone start from the highest point of perfection and still not be good enough.

There's the pressure to be perfect, then coupled with the need to conform that pervades the culture. With a long history of oppressive governments, conformist policies have been historically used to suppress individual rights and control citizens. In 1973, President Park Chung-Hee introduced the Minor Offenses Act, which limited the length of men's hair and the shortness of women's skirts, associating them with hippie counterculture; that year, approximately twelve thousand men had their hair cut against their will by the police. The scars from that era have not yet healed. There is an uncanny feeling that sits in the air, like a low-hanging cloud of pressure that pushes people toward the same point. Koreans have long promoted the idea of unity, of assimilating for the sake of harmony and a high-functioning society, by enforcing strict policies in schools. "The angled stone shall meet the mason's chisel" is a Korean proverb, similar to Japan's "the nail that sticks out gets hammered down," which are both antithetical to America's "the squeaky wheel gets the grease." In 2018, the Seoul Metropolitan Office of Education moved to abolish hair-length regulations at schools, a holdover from the Japanese imperial era and Korea's dictatorships. Though an initial ordinance was passed in 2012, it proved difficult to implement. Even Westerners who stay here too long can find themselves bending to the will of the majority. Everything is much easier here when you fit in: when you dress the same, look the same, act the same. For years, I bleached my hair, but when I moved to Seoul, I found it much simpler to go back to black. Cabdrivers no longer questioned me, cashiers gave me the best service, my aunts and uncles praised the way I looked. That is another thing that makes Jungkook so remarkable: the ways in which he has broken with expectations, maintaining his charm without caving to the standard.

Every member of a K-pop group has a designated role. There's the leader, the *maknae*, and the center, as well as dancer, singer, and rapper, divided into different levels of responsibility. The most unusual role is called "the visual," which refers to the member with the most broadly eye-catching appearance, who, even as a noncelebrity, would turn heads as they walked down the street. The visual raises awareness of a new K-pop group, luring fans like a siren that brings sailors to a shipwreck. The visual has a specific role in cultivating fandom. The term emerged around the mid-aughts and was reserved for the member that best fit Korean beauty standards. Companies sought the sort of clean and wholesome good looks that would pop on an advertisement. Becoming a soju model remains a holy grail booking. It's a sign that you're as crisp and refreshing as the national spirit.

Historically, my favorite member has always been the visual; coming from the fashion industry, I have always appreciated a pretty face, in the way one might admire a model on the runway or a piece of fine art in a museum. I'm sure it's the same for others. I loved L, from Infinite; Minho from SHINee, who upstaged Melania Trump at the 2018 PyeongChang Olympics; Jaejoong from TVXQ, the original *manjjitnam*, which is a shortened slang for a man ripped from a *manhwa*, or comic page. Jaejoong was so surreally beautiful that he became the source of a rumor twisted into a running fan joke: after his contract dispute and departure, SM Entertainment founder Lee Soo-man was so haunted by the loss that he spent years developing a series of "Jaejoong clones" in the SM basement, young idols who bear a striking resemblance to the original beauty. When many think of the platonic ideal of a visual, the first name that comes to mind is Cha Eun-woo of Astro, who became one of the country's most popular stars despite coming from a smaller agency. Eun-woo fits the Korean beauty standard so well, his nicknames include "face genius." A viral TikTok video from Dr. Charles S. Lee, a Beverly Hills plastic surgeon who frequently evaluates celebrities, said: "I noticed that this man's face is perfect. His horizontal thirds are perfect. His vertical fifths are perfect. And his profile is perfect. I searched through his childhood photos and this man was just born perfect. Any more people born like this and I'm going to be out of business."

The visual of BTS is Jin, who went viral at the 2017 Billboard Music Awards as the "third one from the left," before the group became a household name. (Internationally, fans dubbed Jin, V, and Jungkook the "Bermuda line," a term that emerged to refer to a trio whose good looks will confound you like the titular triangle.) Cheekily nicknamed "Worldwide Handsome," Jin, with his porcelain skin and cherry-shaped lips, is good-looking in the same bright and refreshing way as Cha Eun-woo is. Jin has always been praised for his looks by BTS members and the Big Hit staff. He once shared that he was discovered on the street in middle school by SM Entertainment and received a callback, which he didn't attend. When he was eighteen years old and in his first year at university, he was allegedly discovered by a Big Hit casting director who spotted him getting off the bus. Handsome, kind, earnest, possessing a wholesome and good nature, Jin embodies the qualities that the general public admires.

At first Jungkook, described as a shy and hardworking kid, appeared to follow in his footsteps, and the visual team at Big Hit tended to give him more natural styling, even during darker concepts, positioning him as the boy next door. But even back then Jungkook possessed a more open mind than most Koreans. When he was sixteen years old, filming the reality show *BTS American Hustle Life* in L.A., he sat in front of the camera and spoke of all the things he wanted to do when he grew up. He wanted to get a tattoo, he said. Alarmed, Suga gently chastised him, saying ARMY would be disappointed. "I want to become an adult," Jungkook went on, undeterred. "I want to do everything that I want to do, quickly."

In 2014, tattoos were still taboo in Korea, especially for idols.

Jungkook's role model G-Dragon had tattoos, but given the scandals that plagued him and BigBang, the general public may have found them distasteful but tolerable for the "bad boy" group. The first time I worked on a K-pop music video shoot, I stared blankly as a dancer requested a thick roll of skin-colored tape and began wrapping it around his arms, neck, and chest, covering up the ink. Much like in Japan, Koreans associate tattoos with *jopok*, or gangsters. Since 1992, tattooing can only legally be performed by licensed medical professionals; in 2021, celebrity tattoo artist Doy was fined five million won (approximately $3,800 at the time) for being unlicensed. When I was growing up in the 2000s, tattoos were still an uncommon sight and considered ugly.

The first public sighting of Jungkook's tattoo occurred in September 2019 when fans glimpsed the word "ARMY" on the knuckles of his right hand. Then came another, and another, and another, until his entire right arm was covered in a colorful sleeve. Given Jungkook's clean image, it was shocking that he, as a leading K-pop star, would defy the norms to such a visible degree, covering his body with tattoos, some he considered meaningful and others meaningless. There is a crown on top of the *A* in "ARMY," and a *J* from his nickname JK. His favorite woozy face emoji on his middle finger. A heart that used to be purple, the BTS fandom color, which faded with time. Clouds and lightning bolts. His debut date, 0613, on the side of his palm. A tiger lily, his birth flower. A snake on his forearm. A clock set to his birth time, linked to a microphone and music note that imply he was born to be a singer.

Next came the piercings: a barbell in the eyebrow; two in the lip; somewhere around nine in the ear, though he has taken them in and out. He grew his hair out, experimenting with unconventional styles like a ponytail, a mullet, a long curly bob with bangs. Some fans were unhappy, saying he looked better before. There was general backlash from those who found tattoos and piercings unbefitting for a member of the nation's representative idol group. Jungkook knew that very well. After he got his second lip piercing, he commented on a livestream, "There might be ARMY that hate it but . . . I'm sorry, I really wanted to do it," with an innocent laugh. To avoid scandal, most celebrities would have apologized, then removed or covered up their body modifications. Actress Han So-hee, for instance, removed the bulk of her tattoos before starting her acting career in the late 2010s. Jungkook persisted, and due in part to his influence, the country's attitudes toward tattoos and piercings have certainly improved. Koreans are generally more open-minded about them now.

Though not the first K-pop artist to receive ink, Jungkook made a powerful push forward for tattoo acceptance due to his good reputation, the contrast with his clean-cut looks placing tattoos in a new context. It went so far that representative Ryu Ho-jeong used photographs of Jungkook in 2021 to promote a bill that would legalize and regulate tattooing in South Korea. The same went for his many piercings, including the ring through his lip, another defiant stance against the country's conservative beauty and fashion. Not only through their music, but through quiet encouragement, Jungkook and BTS have pushed against the conservative strictures of Korean society, seeking to be positive role models that encourage youth to think more freely yet remain respectful. On another livestream, Jungkook was asked for advice from a fan who wanted a piercing despite their parents' disapproval. "Our mom and dad gave birth to us, so of course we have to listen to them," he said. "But there's only one life, and it's my life, isn't it? So . . . why can't I do it? I'm going to do what I want in my life." A good boy with a bad-boy image, or a bad boy with a heart of gold—character tropes, perhaps, but with Jungkook, it feels unposed and authentic.

On the other hand, Jungkook's tattoos and piercings appeal to a Western audience. They function as a signal that he is not a cookie-cutter idol; he is an individual and an artist, which makes him a K-pop visual for the globalized age, when catering to the Korean public alone is no longer enough. When Bang Si-hyuk selected the members of BTS, he had no way of knowing how to create a globally minded group. By happenstance, he assembled seven members that were more attuned to Western tastes than those who had come before. In the past, companies that adhered more closely to Korean beauty standards debuted idols that tended to lack very distinct features. Moles and freckles were zapped away by a laser, jawlines sharpened with a quarterly shot of slimming Botox; minor imperfections were swept away to create the ideal image, a human fantasy, adulated and adored.

There was a viral Bangtan Bomb, a casual YouTube short, from June 2014 called "Finding Jung Kook by Jimin PD," where Jimin went searching for Jungkook, then sixteen years old, and found him quietly eating pudding in the corner. Jimin then embarked on what he called "an ugly person special feature," where he walked around attempting to capture each BTS member except for Jungkook. He went off to find Suga, who was sitting cross-legged on the floor, and told him he wanted to film all the ugly people he could find.

"Then you have to film yourself, film yourself," Suga said, pointing at the camera.

"Of course, I appeared first," Jimin said proudly, making Suga and the staff laugh.

Though tongue-in-cheek, the video revealed the domestic perception of BTS at the time. Compared to other idol groups, they were thought to be full of "visual holes," a term referring to members with unconventional looks that appear to bring down the group's beauty and balance. I've heard countless Koreans call them "ugly" in an indifferent way—not meant as an insult or offense but a mere statement of fact. "Why didn't they fix themselves?" is another one I used to hear every so often.

BTS encompassed a wider range of facial structures, their distinct features making them easier to recognize for non-Korean fans, who might be less familiar with Korean characteristics. There have been several psychological studies of a so-called cross-race effect that explore the difficulty of recognizing faces from other racial groups due to lack of exposure. When someone cannot identify members, it becomes difficult to emotionally attach to them. BTS managed to sidestep this hurdle. Globally, each member has cultivated their own feral fan base, whose thoughts are too obscene to print. All the members of BTS are good-looking, but I personally noticed V first. He drew me into BTS, fulfilling his role as a visual. The first K-pop album I ever bought was *The Most Beautiful Moment in Life: Young Forever*, which I picked up at the Music Korea record shop in Myeongdong in the summer of 2016, after seeing V's pretty peach-colored hair and striking *manjjitnam* visage. When I met him on set for American *Vogue*, I was pleasantly surprised to see that he looked exactly like his photographs, down to his boxy smile, a man truly torn from a *manhwa* page.

Looking good demands maintenance, which demands dedication. In other cases, it requires a surgical knife. Plastic surgery is destigmatized in South Korea and among its K-pop stars in particular. Statistically, plastic surgery per capita is high; according to the International Society of Aesthetic Plastic Surgery (ISAPS), 13.5 cosmetic procedures were performed per every 1,000 individuals circa 2011. South Korea has the highest rate of plastic surgery in the world. Anecdotally, I can only attest to the nonchalant way my friends and family have treated the subject. Though my mother and sister were born with natural *sok ssangapul*, a half crease or hidden double lids, I inherited my father's monolids, and my grandmother used to insist that I get blepharoplasty, eyelid surgery, which would make me "look prettier." I have at least two cousins who received, around age eighteen or so, a version of the K-pop combo—a silicon implant in the nose and double eyelids, maybe with a bonus jaw shave—and were praised for becoming more beautiful. A colleague spent a year or so overseeing trainees at a K-pop label, and I once listened as she dispassionately discussed which girls should be sent off to get a small procedure before their debut. One time, a rookie was scheduled to be sent back to the surgeon for de-plasticization, after they deemed that she had in fact been prettier before.

Thanks in part to the influence of K-pop and K-dramas, as well as promotional efforts and aid from the government, Seoul has become a global destination for medical tourism and beautification. The Ministry of Health and Welfare (MOHW) announced that more than 600,000 international patients visited Korea in 2023, the largest number since the agency began keeping track in 2009, with the aggregate number of international patients reaching 3.88 million. Whenever my foreign friends or friends of friends visit, I'm asked for two recommendations: a Korean fried chicken joint and somewhere to get cheap Botox.

There's a lot to be said about this history. The double-eyelid surgery can be traced back to the work of an American military surgeon, stationed in South Korea in 1954, who reportedly noted in a 1955 essay the procedure's origins: "A slant-eyed Korean interpreter speaking excellent English, came in requesting to be made into a 'round-eye.' His future lies in his relation with the West and he felt that because of the squint in his slant eyes, Americans could not tell what he was thinking and consequently did not trust him. As this was partly true, I consented to do what I could." When Korea was war-torn and destitute, dependent on American protection, these Westernized beauty ideals began to take shape. Now they have morphed into their own byzantine set of standards. The trendy buccal fat pad removal, a surgery to create hollow cheeks, would never have been popular in Korea since Koreans value facial fat for its youthful appearance. But the influence remains; aestheticians and surgeons took that postwar influence and ramped it up to 2,000, as they did with so much else.

In the entertainment industry, plastic surgery has been viewed as a necessary sacrifice and an inevitable part of becoming an idol, yet stars must still walk a fine line. Idols who have had too much work done are called "plastic monsters." Fans love to argue over whether or not their favorites have gone under the knife, praising those that seem to be natural and attacking those who seem too plastic. Pre-debut photos are a source of rampant discussion, allowing fans to compare the bridge of the nose, the shape of the eye; they provide expert analysis of a drooping nose tip, which suggests the presence of a silicone implant. Even hairlines are scrutinized for the sign of implants. There are members of ARMY who are passionate that none of the members have had any work, viewing it as a point of pride. Whether they have or haven't matters less than the general impression that was left: once again, the idea that BTS is more real, their nonuniform features erasing the illusion of "sameness" that plagues other groups.

That word, "real," describes Jungkook's appeal rather well. Working in the industry, I've seen members of EXO, SHINee, Blackpink, BigBang, NCT 127, and so many more groups in person; I've even seen Cha Eun-woo, the face genius. So, people always find it surprising when I say that the best-looking man I've ever seen, the one who caught me completely off guard, was Jungkook. Jungkook hits that intangible spot between real and unreal. He is striking but approachable. Pretty yet still handsome. A strong jaw and nose, a sweet smile with those bunny teeth. Charming and charismatic. Perfectly imperfect, and imperfectly perfect.

CHAPTER 6

HIS AUTHENTICITY

In the 2015 music video for "Dope," RM walks up to the camera dressed in a hotel porter uniform and asks, with a knowing smile, if it is the viewer's first time with Bangtan. In hindsight, the iconic opening line would have been better suited for "Dynamite." A textbook pop song in the style of Katy Perry's "Firework," according to its co-songwriter Jessica Agombar, "Dynamite" premiered in August 2020, months into the global Covid-19 pandemic. Sung entirely in English, the uplifting summer song blends disco, funk, and bubblegum pop, the horns and synths bright like rays of sunshine. It was the first track by a Korean act to debut at number one on the Billboard Hot 100 and the first Grammy nomination for a K-pop group, reaching millions of Americans for the first time. In the music video, Jungkook takes a sip from a glass of milk, grinning like a model from the nineties "Got Milk?" campaign. There are burger shops and powdered-sugar doughnuts, palm trees and blue skies and white clouds, a distillation of Americana performed by a Korean act. This is the image of BTS most prevalent in the cultural consciousness.

Anyone working their way through the BTS discography would

have traced a path from "Dynamite" to "No More Dream." A far cry from "Dynamite," their 2013 debut single is a provocative howl of youthful rebellion. Rap verses comprise most of the song; even Jung-kook, the main vocalist, primarily raps. Given the pop image associated with BTS from 2020 onward, the casual listener may never guess that BTS was originally conceived as a crew of hip-hop idols, dressed in thick chains and snapback caps. To the Western public, this contrast can be jarring. But for the Korean public, BTS's debut was considered a return to K-pop's origins, which are closely intertwined with hip-hop due to the direct influence of Black American culture, which was first exposed to Koreans because of the long-standing US military presence. This influence is one prevailing theory as to why Korean artists have had more international success than Chinese and Japanese singers. It is a thorny relationship that has given rise to cherished musicians, as well as painful and tangled issues. But it is crucial to the understanding of K-pop and Jungkook.

K-pop contains heavy traces of hip-hop in music and dance, blended with a fusion of elements from electronic to pop to dance music and choreography. Efforts have been made by Korean media networks to preserve the history of K-pop, including *Archive-K*, a documentary miniseries that aired on SBS. When discussing the origins of Korean hip-hop, witnesses and historians traced it back to Seoul in the 1980s. President Park Chung-Hee had been assassinated in 1979, ending seventeen years of authoritarian rule, and the emergency measures that prohibited free and critical speech were repealed, allowing new modes of expression. Before sites like YouTube and Instagram accelerated the globalization of media, Koreans were in close contact with American culture since the US military entered the country at the end of World War II, committing forces to the Korean War in 1950 and establishing the United States Forces Korea in 1957. One of the most direct and influential pathways in the seventies and eighties was the American Forces Korean Network (AFKN), the US government television and radio broadcast service provided to troops stationed in South Korea, easily accessed by Korean citizens at VHF Channel 2. "The seventies and eighties, Korean TV at the time was not only boring, but there was a curfew," said Dr. Kyung Hyun Kim, a Korea-born UC Irvine professor known for his academic research of Korean pop culture. "AFKN was nonstop, twenty-four/seven. That was the fun station where you could watch *Sesame Street* and zombie movies, uncensored."

American programs provided the cultural building blocks for the generation who would lead Korean culture onto the global stage. Oscar-winning director Bong Joon-ho, for example, grew up watching Alfred Hitchcock and Brian De Palma and Sam Peckinpah films on AFKN, which shaped his cinematic style. In August 1981, MTV premiered on American cable and made its way to Korea via AFKN. Michael Jackson's iconic music videos like "Billie Jean," "Thriller," and "Smooth Criminal" were absorbed by artists in the 1980s like Park Jin-young, the founder of JYP Entertainment, who would pass that influence down to future generations like Jungkook, who referenced Michael Jackson with "Standing Next to You" in the 2020s. "From the moment I saw [Michael Jackson], my eyes were blinded," said Park of seeing the artist on AFKN for the first time. "From his movement to those clothes and those socks, all of it. Musically Quincy Jones, for stage performance Michael Jackson became my musical standard."

Solid Gold, an eighties American pop music program, was also influential, according to Park. But it was *Soul Train*, the iconic musical variety show that celebrated Black artists, that left the deepest impression. "Every Korean of my generation knows that was the coolest thing," said Dr. Kim. "We knew exactly when *Soul Train* was coming on." On Saturdays, Koreans crowded around their TV sets to watch dancers breakdance and groove down the Soul Train Line, a window into a distant culture that seemed joyous and free. Koreans, confined by their oppressive society and authoritarian government, yearning for these freedoms, recorded episodes of *Soul Train* and replayed them, practicing the dance moves over and over.

To witness hip-hop music off-screen, Korean youth went to the neighborhood of Itaewon, about a twenty-minute walk from the Yongsan Garrison, where the US military was stationed until 2018, and down the stairs to a basement club called Moon Night. Moon Night was run by a man named Seo Chi Hoon, who, having witnessed racial discrimination against Black soldiers at Itaewon clubs, first opened Soul Train, which welcomed only Black customers and banned white ones, as reported by the local news. With Moon Night, Seo opened the doors to all club-goers, including Koreans, who were allowed to absorb the hip-hop dance steps they witnessed on *Soul Train*, their eyes glued to the figures on the black-and-white checkerboard floor, spinning beneath a disco ball. Artists like Run DMC, Public Enemy, and 2 Live Crew could only be heard at Moon Night, their records brought in from the US army base to bypass censorship laws. Photographs captured Yang Hyun-suk, founder of YG Entertainment and member of Seo Taiji and Boys; Lee Hyundo and Kim Sungjae of influential hip-hop duo Deux; and Hyun Jin-young, the first artist signed by Lee Soo-man to SM, passing their evenings at Moon Night. "They would be the ones who would hang out there all of the time to try to get the firsthand experience of dancing and hip-hop culture," said Dr. Kim. "That's the exposure you need, so it's not filtered." Hyun Jin-young was particularly acclaimed for his skills. Having grown up near the military base with American friends, he mastered jazz, break, and street dance before they were mainstream. Before Lee signed him to SM Entertainment, Hyun was a member of a B-boy team called Spark and the only Korean allowed into the Soul Train club to learn to dance. He picked up "skill, groove, feel," from friends like Damon William, said to be the best of the US soldiers, who later rapped on Hyun's song "Sexy Lady." Hyun's success preceded that of Seo Taiji and Boys, but his career was derailed by two drug scandals, which shaped SM's close and restrictive approach to idol development to prevent future disgrace.

Thus, Moon Night became the birthplace of K-pop in the late eighties, according to Dr. Kim. It is allegedly where Seo Taiji encountered Yang Hyun-suk, making it the spiritual birthplace of Seo Taiji and Boys, the hip-hop trio who popularized rap in Korea in 1992. Their first three albums sold more than 1.6 million copies each to a population of just 40 million, according to a *Billboard* article from 1996, and they remain one of the bestselling Korean acts of all time. Seo got his start as a member of the heavy-metal band Sinawe, led by Shin Daechul, son of Shin Joong Hyun, the "godfather of Korean rock, the most important Korean musician of all time," according to Dr. Kim. Refusing to support President Park after he seized power in 1961, Shin Joong Hyun was imprisoned and tortured, banned from performing until Park's assassination. With Seo Taiji and Boys, Seo continued Shin's legacy, the antiestablishment spirit that gave birth to Korean popular music, using his songs as social critique and notably employing hip-hop, which he learned from Yang, who learned it at Moon Night, to mainstream success. It is a narrative that mirrors the origins of rap in 1970s New York as a genre of expression outside of the existing norms and providing social commentary to criticize repressive governments.

Seo Taiji and Boys arrived during the presidency of Roh Tae-woo, who served from 1988 to 1993. Although Roh was the first democratically elected president, his term was marked by corruption and human rights abuses, including police brutality that led to the death of a student protestor one year before the group's debut. Seo Taiji and Boys released songs that rallied against the country's education system. Their music was banned from public radio; compositions critical of the government and expressing revolutionary thought were censored, until fan outcry led to the repeal of the Public Performance Ethics Committee's pre-censorship practice. Through Seo Taiji and Boys' success, musicians were granted more freedom and continued to use music as an outlet. H.O.T. debuted with an album titled *We Hate All Kinds of Violence* and a single, "Warrior's Descendant," that decried the extreme bullying epidemic in Korean schools. Shinhwa's "The Solver" criticized the greed and hierarchy of their society, calling for complete reconstruction.

And so, academics like Dr. Kim have argued that Korean hip-hop, at its origins, had a realness and authenticity due to the direct influence of Black culture on Korean society, which resonated more strongly through commonalities in lived experience. "Although we're supposedly sovereign subjects of that peninsula, we've often been subjugated even in that land that we call ours," Dr. Kim said, pointing to the presence of the US military in Yongsan for seven decades, land formerly held by Japanese troops for thirty-five years. "For generations, the filet of Seoul real estate had been occupied. You had that experience of living in subjugation, the cultural right, the inferiority that has to be expressed in some way, transforming it in a way that rearticulates who you are," Dr. Kim added. "That's always been a part of the Korean brand."

By the time Bang Si-hyuk was forming BTS, however, decades had passed since the days when artists like Yang Hyun-suk and Hyun Jin-young learned to dance from soldiers at Moon Night. Each generation of K-pop has been further removed from that source. Hip-hop became more ornamental than fundamental, the rap parts added like neat embellishments. Yang Hyun-suk founded YG in 1996 after Seo Taiji and Boys disbanded, and spent the early years focused on hip-hop artists like the trio Keep Six and group 1TYM. After the success of SE7EN, an idol-style singer, Yang decided to attempt his first real idol group in the vein of SM's Lee Soo-man. One year before BigBang's debut, Yang gave an interview to Yonhap News, where he said that he planned to model the group after the American R&B boy band B2K. He said he chose his idols for their musical skills over their looks. Although he noted that GD and Taeyang were talented and passionate about hip-hop, he thought they were better suited for an idol group than an authentic hip-hop duo. "Hip-hop, as a genre, places great importance on the rapper's values and worldview, which makes their young age more of a handicap," he said, noting their lack of life experience, suggesting it would be difficult for them to be taken seriously as hip-hop artists.

On June 12, 2013, Big Hit released the music video for "No More Dream," off the first BTS single album *2 Cool 4 Skool*, which was advertised as a fresh take on nineties hip-hop from a boy band. In an interview with the online music magazine *Weiv*, Big Hit producer Pdogg discussed the challenge to find the right musical direction, an identity that was true to hip-hop but would still please the public. "In the Korean major music scene, no matter how you look at it, hip-hop is about untangling love stories through rap," he said. "Or YG-style, about swag. But if you're going to be like that, ultimately you have to have done really well, have a lot of money, have something to brag about, but of course we have nothing. Truthfully, it's not something people will acknowledge." Despite naming BigBang as role models, BTS veered away from Yang's new mold and took the direction of his original work with Seo Taiji.

G-Dragon, one of Jungkook's childhood heroes, may have sparked his interest in hip-hop, but RM shaped his understanding of hip-hop culture. The leader and artist around whom BTS was formed, RM grew up wanting to be a writer or a poet, not an idol. By his second year of elementary school, he was composing poems about despair and loneliness, comparing himself to a fallen leaf. By age thirteen, he was active in the underground rap community, making songs with amateur beats uploaded online. He spent hours in Hongdae, absorbing the work of hip-hop crews like Jiggy Fellaz and rappers like Verbal Jint. He gathered his influences: "In Korea, Epik High and Garion, in overseas, Nas and Eminem," he recalled in a 2015 interview with *Singles* magazine. "All their lyrics were just so real that I couldn't help but have the thought that I want to do music like these people too."

In 2009, he auditioned to join BigDeal Squads, an underground hip-hop crew that was an offshoot of the former BigDeal Records label. Though he flubbed it, forgetting most of the lyrics, RM's performance impressed Sleepy, one half of the hip-hop duo Untouchable, who had signed to the label TS Entertainment. One night over drinks, Sleepy shared RM's work with his friend Pdogg, and Pdogg brought it to Bang Si-hyuk, who was so enthralled that he decided to build a project around him. Given RM's rap background, the first Bangtan trainees were similarly rappers who passed the Hit It Auditions. There were around thirty in total, as Pdogg said in a 2013 interview with *Weiv*; Suga, who was part of an underground rap crew in the city of Daegu, joined the company after auditioning with an original version of RM's "Seventeen," both of their lyrics dealing with the struggles of youth.

By the time Jungkook entered Big Hit, the direction had shifted. In a 2011 video advertising Hit It the Second Audition, Bang called for trainees who could sing and dance. He hoped to explore a wider definition of hip-hop, aware that it was a cultural movement that emerged from the Bronx in the 1970s, encompassing more than rap. Despite this awareness, it seemed as though Bang was trying to fit two discordant halves together to make a new whole: a hip-hop crew and an idol group, the rap line combining with dancers and singers and visuals to make something new.

At the time, BTS received criticism in Korea for acting too similar to groups like H.O.T. In a 2015 interview with *Hiphopplaya*, a Korean web magazine, RM defended the group by stating that Korean teenagers were experiencing the same traumas in 1996, when H.O.T.'s "Warrior's Descendant" came out, and in 2013, when BTS debuted with "No More Dream." Listless and directionless, teens were not encouraged to find and pursue their dreams. Most studied with the aim to become a civil servant or make a comfortable living. "That's why we're just trying to plainly express the reality of now. 'A student that just studies hard even though they don't have a dream' is exactly who I was," RM said. "It's not something I was trying to pull out old stories for, but something that was purely my own story."

I have two cousins of a similar age to Jungkook who were raised in Daechi-dong, a neighborhood in Gangnam known for the thousands of *hagwons*, or private tutoring academies, that opened their doors there. *SKY Castle*, a popular K-drama set in the neighborhood, followed the zealous parents and beleaguered teenagers forced into ruthless academic competition, capturing Korean society in one extreme. In Daechi-dong, academics are the key to a successful life; my cousins slept maybe two or three hours a night, the remaining time devoted to school, then to *hagwon*, then to their bedroom, where they finished their homework from 10 p.m. until sunrise. They were forbidden from owning a smartphone, for fear of distraction. Though Jungkook would not have experienced this degree of academic rigor, having given up his normal high school years for idol life, this cutthroat mentality exists in all spaces. The stress and competitive mindset of the education system carries into working society. When you're given no free time, nurturing free thought and creativity is nearly impossible. Yet BTS, as led by RM, managed to do so, and to his credit, Bang did not hinder them. Suga once spoke about the great secret behind BTS's success, putting it in simple terms: "From before our debut, even after our debut, no matter what type of music we made or how we wanted to present it, 'just do it,' [from Bang and the company]. We know you'll get hate for it, but if you want to do it, just do it."

To pursue authenticity—not only in conveying the Korean youth experience but in the portrayal of American-style hip-hop—was an unusual directive that felt counter to the idol system. By the time BTS debuted, the industry was far removed from Moon Night and largely left with a shallow understanding of hip-hop's origins. Artists who were misinformed or ignorant about the complex relationship between K-pop and hip-hop, between Korean and Black culture, made the genre difficult to recommend to Americans. Often, K-pop artists cherry-picked the elements they found "cool," the surface-level trimmings like guns and grills that, when removed from their context, perpetuate harmful stereotypes. Even in the late 2010s to 2020s, singers have lip-synched racial slurs in rap songs, donned blackface "by accident," and put locs in their hair when singing a reggae-style track. When I worked at a K-pop record label, a coworker asked me why foreigners got so angry whenever artists wore cornrows or locs. I tried to explain, but she did not seem to understand. To her, hip-hop style was simply a visual aesthetic, disconnected from people's real lived experiences. She was a woman from the generation that helped build the industry from scratch. She thought it looked pretty, and to her, imitation was a form of flattery.

I found her opinion to be common in the industry. A small and largely homogenous country, Korea can feel like a bubble; the longer you stay, the more closed off you become. Over the years, I've found myself falling out of touch, the news from America feeling like stories from a distant land that have little to do with me. It's as though I'm slipping into a stupor, and I have to force myself to wake up and stay engaged with the world. That inherent lack of connection to global culture was a nonissue when K-pop was focused on markets like China and Japan with more similar perspectives, but for K-pop to be worldwide, companies and artists must be aware. Efforts should be made to understand. Instead, artists are asked to apologize for things they do not understand; others never apologize at all.

A look at the Circle Chart, run by the Korea Music Copyright Association (KOMCA), shows that the top track from a male idol group in 2013 was SHINee's "Dream Girl." I adored "Dream Girl," a funky pop song as easy to down as a fizzy drink. The music video was the pinnacle of K-pop production at the time, slick and stylized with multiple sets and conceptual outfits, the boys' voices blending beautifully, their dancing clean. It was the perfect package, SM's bread and butter. BTS's "No More Dream" lacked the high-cost gloss of SHINee's due to the dire financial straits of Big Hit, who had sunk its resources into debuting the girl group Glam to low returns. Yet that rawness worked in their favor. As a trainee, RM curated a playlist of fifty-some tracks, from Nas and Biggie and Tupac, and he and Suga and J-Hope taught the others everything they knew about hip-hop, driven by sheer passion and respect. Those songs became BTS's educational soundtrack. The lyrics to "No More Dream" were written by RM, Suga, and J-Hope, and RM composed twenty-nine versions, arguing with Bang Si-hyuk for hours. The primary directive was to speak about the lives of Korean youth, as only they could do; Jimin recalls that the rap trio had asked him to describe his classmates, their daily lives, and the dreams they wanted to pursue. The final version of "No More Dream" is meaningfully aimed at the Korean youth, trapped by the country's academic pressure, the need to study, to work, to succeed at all costs. In that way, BTS positioned themselves as radicals like Seo Taiji and Boys, rebelling against their hellish society, daring to dream of something different.

Big Hit's emphasis on authentic hip-hop from the beginning fascinated me. Was it even possible for a Korean group to be true to a culture so grounded in the Black American experience? In the early days, even BTS made missteps. In the music video for "We Are Bulletproof Pt.2," uploaded in July 2013, RM's hair is teased into an Afro, shaved at the back and sides; in some cuts, he holds a pimp cane with a dollar-sign handle. There are cuts to scenes of pistols firing, gunshots ringing in the background; though they allude to the name *bangtan*, which means bulletproof, the reference to the gang violence associated with rap music is obvious. That said, J-Hope, Jimin, and Jungkook perform a dedicated breakdancing segment, honoring one of the foundations of hip-hop. The lyrics are an earnest expression of their underdog status, referencing their sleepless nights and calling out those who might look down on them—rappers in other idol groups, underground rappers who found the concept of hip-hop idols ridiculous. Unlike most K-pop stars, BTS tried to engage with hip-hop and understand it. This effort was largely driven by RM, who craved a more honest interpretation of the music he loved.

Though it came from a place of admiration, RM made many mistakes in his youth. RM was only a teenager who, beyond family trips and four months studying in New Zealand at age twelve, had not left the South Korean bubble. He was tasked to guide the others on topics beyond his depth. He was guilty of appropriating Black hairstyles and had a habit of speaking African American Vernacular English

(AAVE) and an affected accent; on the *SimSimTaPa* radio program in June 2013, he said his individual talent was speaking as a *"heug hyung"* or "Black bro." The worst occurred when BTS was asked to perform a special stage on MBC's *Show Champion*, performing two covers of Shinhwa songs. In the introduction to the 1999 single "T.O.P.," RM said the N-word, as written in the original lyrics. The damage done to his reputation was massive; many have never forgiven him for it.

What he needed was education and experience, which Big Hit, in their own way, attempted to provide over time. "Bang Si Hyuk was absolutely more respectful of Black culture, and he understood that we have to learn directly from the experience," said Dr. Kim. A year after they debuted, BTS flew to Los Angeles to film a reality series called *BTS American Hustle Life*, where they trained with "hip-hop tutors" including Coolio, Tony Jones, and Warren G. The program is difficult to watch now. The series begins with a staged kidnapping. Two Black American men jump into the boys' transport van and drive them to Skid Row, where, fearing for their lives, they are shepherded into a room and stripped of their socks and shoes. "The show had serious problems with racial representation because there are some elements in there that are almost insulting," Dr. Kim added of those negative stereotypes (e.g., associating Black men with crime and violence) perpetuated by the show. On-screen, through its editing and framing, the series incidentally captured the ignorance most Koreans possess toward racial issues. But off-screen, the boys themselves learned a great deal.

So, we return to RM, the leader and first member of BTS. RM possessed a genuine love for hip-hop, nurtured by the older brothers he met as an underground rapper. Yet I believe that RM's time in L.A. gave him a wake-up call. It was a life-changing experience, and the members who returned from L.A. were not the same as those who had left. In that 2015 interview with *Singles* magazine, RM spoke of collaborating with Warren G, noting the most unforgettable teachings he took away: that hip-hop was open to anyone, regardless of race or country of origin. "Hip-hop is a type of music that is always ready to give you space for anyone who enjoys hip-hop. So, don't restrain yourself behind any type of prejudiced thought," RM said.

That same year, RM spoke to *Hiphopplaya*, exhibiting a growth and understanding unlike what I had ever seen from a Korean rapper—particularly celebrity rappers, who avoid speaking out on politically charged issues for fear of inviting scandal. He spoke of learning from Warren G that negative stereotypes like drug use and gun violence were not representative of the original hip-hop culture. The interviewer confronted him about the controversial moment in "If I Ruled The World" (2013) where he shouted "Westside till I die." "I was really wrong then," RM said, laughing at his past self. When pressed further, RM responded that at the time, he didn't understand the true meaning behind the phrase and his uninformed use was not respectful to West Coast hip-hop artists. "I believe there are many meanings inside the words 'Westside till I die.' Sweat, struggles, pride, etc. . . . As a result, I was thoughtless," he said. "Further than a mistake, it was a wrong. I have nothing to say."

BTS was not the first K-pop act to gain international fans, but left in charge of their own Twitter account, they interfaced with those fans in a more direct way than the groups before them. This also made them more globally connected, and the feedback from international ARMY, who were affected by issues of cultural appropriation and outright racism, was taken to heart. As the designated English speaker, RM must have seen the comments, the discourse on social media. And unlike many Koreans, trapped in the bubble, he listened. In a livestream, he reflected on the need to change his mindset after 2016, realizing that his actions, his music, and his words could hurt people, regardless of his intent. "I thought I need to hold responsibility for that and I need to think more about those things," he said. "I need to know how to change my thinking if it's wrong. I learned that I have to listen to the words of many people."

I believe what BTS took away from their time in L.A. was a simple truth: that they could not authentically express the type of hip-hop they had attempted in their debut. What followed next changed the course of their success, as the group spent several years searching for their direction—the style of hip-hop that fit them best.

BTS returned to their original ambition: to explore the beauty and pain, the triumph and anxieties of youth. Yet in place of the aggression that characterized songs like "No More Dream," rather than biting back against society like Seo Taiji and Boys or H.O.T., they changed tact and went for something more sentimental and softer. *The Most Beautiful Moment in Life Pt.1* was released after their trip to L.A. Suga later revealed that at the time, he had felt sure the album would be their last, but it is widely considered BTS's breakthrough. The lead single "I Need U" was a melancholic rhapsody that let Jungkook's breathtaking vocals truly shine and earned them their first win on a weekly music show. The music video's atmospheric visuals recall the films of directors like Wong Kar-wai, who explores human relationships with a poignant beauty.

BTS began to show softness and emotion, using hip-hop music to convey the sentimental uncertainties of life. Their music resonated with the N-po Generation, a term used to describe young Koreans in their twenties and thirties who had given up on a long list of things, from dating and marriage and childbirth to finding a job or owning a home. It also spoke to fans overseas, who were struggling with the same issues. *The Most Beautiful Moment in Life Pt.1* was my introduction to BTS, and I spoke to two fans who go by Aditi and Rinne, active ARMY who fell into the fandom at the same time. "I was captivated by the way the music video showed the breakdown of a friend group as they transitioned into adulthood," said Rinne. "It felt so real and vulnerable, and I found myself connecting deeply with their storytelling."

"Something in the videos and the music just seemed so beautiful, but in a very particular, sentimental way," said Aditi. "They're incredible storytellers. I think it's their biggest strength as a group and I think it's what drew me in as well."

Ultimately, BTS carried away two tenets of hip-hop: to be true to themselves and to possess open minds and empathetic hearts. Even as Jungkook changed to a more mainstream pop sound, he remained honest in his self-expression. In that 2015 *Singles* interview, RM was asked to define hip-hop. "Defining hip-hop is the same as trying to define love. If there are six billion people in the world, then there are six billion definitions of love, and each definition is different for each person," he said. "In one word, it's something that can't be explained."

Understanding that some things cannot be understood but can still be respected and appreciated. It's a painful yet beautiful lesson in life, one of many that Jungkook learned from his *hyung* RM and carried further than he ever dreamed he could.

CHAPTER 7

HIS HUMILITY

It seems every few months, a K-pop star is caught smoking—holding a vape in the greenroom, on the beach, in a public restaurant—and, due to the fandom outrage, forced to make an earnest apology for not living up to their expectations. So, when Jungkook was photographed by paparazzi outside Matsuhisa in Beverly Hills, a lit cigarette between his lips, the comparative calm of the fandom spoke volumes. No longer judged strictly by idol standards, Jungkook was on his way to straddling the worlds of Western and Eastern celebrity, which demanded a tricky balancing act between behaving like a rebel or a role model.

One might think that K-idols are not too dissimilar from the teen pop idols of past and present: Britney Spears, Miley Cyrus, Justin Bieber, and other Disney Channel stars with their squeaky-clean personas. (Think the Jonas Brothers' infamous purity rings of the 2000s.) There are subtle differences and distinctions—even between Japanese and Korean idols, who are often lumped together. J-idols are considered more general entertainers, who do not need to sing or dance at a high level, as long as they can charm their audience. Many of the most beloved J-idols are "incomplete," works in progress, who often begin their careers lacking skills and are expected to exhibit growth over time, like a protagonist undergoing their training arc. Their awkward overtures and willingness to do their best, despite their clumsiness, are endearing.

In Korea, idols undergo years of training and their debut is earned through sweat and sacrifice. K-idols meet their fans as complete, polished works. They are entertainers, but they are singers, dancers, or rappers first and foremost, placing them closer on the spectrum to Western pop stars. Idols are born from institutions and systems and structures, in the same way that major labels in the West create pop stars like Dua Lipa, who had the full weight of Warner Bros. behind her debut. "Dua was really smart—she signed to Warner Bros. partly because they didn't have a big female pop artist and they needed one," manager Ed Millett said in an interview with *Music Business Worldwide*. "They really wanted her, so she had the focus of the team from day one."

Yet the act of creation in the idol industry is more systemic, more rigid and controlled, each idol incubated and nurtured from egg to hen. It is a fact that executives like Bang Si-hyuk consider with pride. When asked by Bloomberg about HYBE's expansion into Latin music, Bang explained his desire to bring K-pop's "modularized" infrastructure into the region, referring to the formulaic method of creating a successful group. "So, we believe that by entering the market and providing our modularized formula and infrastructure, we can accelerate growth and foster innovation," he said. "In this process we can extract the strengths of K-pop, such as efficiency, vertical integration, and rapid industry growth, and use them as a driving force for innovation." SM Entertainment founder Lee Soo-man famously had a written "culture technology" manual that he kept somewhere in his office, as he told CNBC, explaining that it combines both culture and technology in a "logically formulized" way. The SM playbook allegedly encompassed all situations, such as the best chord progressions and shade of eyeshadow to be used in a particular country. "Because I'm an engineer, it is to be understood by logic," said Lee of applying his computer engineering background to producing cultural works. "It lays out formulas. So, I can say that I am an engineer rather than an artiste."

Thus, the K-pop industry resembles the Western pop industrial complex with everything souped-up on steroids to create a pop star in a more efficient manner with a more intimate connection to their fans. The fans are the currency; their love and devotion are the fuel that keeps the machine running. Compared to Japan, South Korea has absorbed more Western influence for popular music and aesthetics, even as far as the types of entertainers that the public prefers. Large J-pop-style rotational groups have not stuck in Korea; Lee Sooman tried several times, beginning with Super Junior to EXO, which he split into EXO-K and EXO-M to promote in Korea and China, respectively, before they folded back into EXO. His grandest ambition, the NCT project, was meant to have idols graduate through units with specific concepts, perpetually expanding. For example, Dream consisted of teenagers, who would depart once they came of age, being replaced by new teens. Yet after four years, the plan was dropped and Dream was cemented as a seven-member group; Mark Lee, the one who "graduated," returned. On a spectrum from orthodox Japanese fan tastes to Western pop tastes, Korean tastes seemed to fall somewhere in the middle. The eventual success of NCT and its many subunits played into that: with twenty-five members in six subunits, as of 2024, NCT had a large and diverse roster that was still fixed.

As time went on, the K-pop industry gained more global ambitions than J-pop, which remained focused on Japan. This can be attributed in part to the unexpected worldwide success of BTS, who introduced the genre to a more international audience than any executive could have anticipated. As the scope expanded, companies and idols learned to cater both to Westernized tastes—to generalize, smaller groups with defined artists and personalities—and those of East and Southeast Asia. The globalization of K-pop presented a challenge, as the opposing cultural standards made it impossible to please everyone.

Jungkook appears to be, as of this writing, one of the miracle cases—a K-pop star with a still-golden reputation. Given how far they've come, the Western public might not even know that the members of BTS are technically idols. Bang Si-hyuk put aside his initial goal of making a hip-hop crew when he realized the potential of K-pop's particular fandom culture. Yet he knew that fans could "get angry very easily— offended and angry. So, there were things that we were not to do as well," he told *The New Yorker* in 2024. Despite their incisive and critical music, BTS stayed clean, exhibiting the role-model behavior expected of them. No smoking. No drugs. No drinking until they were of legal age, and even then, no drinking to excess. No partying or clubbing (at least don't get caught). No dating (likewise). But for Western fans, this pristine image can be off-putting, registering as inauthentic and inhuman.

In the mid- to late-2010s, I-fans and K-fans began to pay more attention to idols that seemed "real," seeking a friend, not a fantasy. Idols who could provide a sense of comfort, not through escapism but through relatability. Authenticity became a powerful currency as misinformation and unrealistic imagery spread more readily over social media. This shift occurred, in a chicken-and-egg situation, around the time that K-pop became more popular overseas, and BTS certainly had a large part with the unfiltered content they shared online. A counterpoint to the traditional idol, the Western pop artist embodies traits like independence and individuality, possessing strong vision and ambition. There is no clear divide between Eastern and Western tastes, but there are certain alignments that occur. It comes down to a matter of preference—not all East Asian fans want perfect idols, not all Western fans want relatable ones. Should an idol be real or perfect? There are some who expect idols to be both.

No one aside from Jungkook can truly know him. But having spent hundreds of hours watching his livestreams and reading his interviews, I found myself convinced of his humility. He has a rare quality that makes you want to believe in him. Jungkook is humble and hardworking; in group interviews, he rarely seeks the spotlight and diligently does his best. But he is also refreshingly honest and straightforward. Jungkook speaks in a very simple and clear manner. He is not prone to the sophisticated, metaphorical language of someone like RM, who speaks more like a scholar. Though Jungkook's manner of speech may not be as poetic, it is no less beautiful, as though he speaks in haikus, not sonnets. Jungkook always gets to the point, in a way that seems to convey an honesty and authenticity with each syllable.

I've always struggled with translating quotes from Korean to English, especially for K-pop artists. Done one-to-one, the responses become dry and lacking flavor, as though they were written up by an intern providing the bare minimum. Korean is, on the whole, a more blunt, more brusque language than English, where context and delivery are integral to understanding. For instance, the phrase *ma-shi-tta*, "it's delicious," translates literally to "there is flavor," "there is taste."

It makes it even more difficult to come across as "real" when your translated speech feels stilted. Jungkook's way of speaking is uncommon, even among Koreans. When he first joined Big Hit as a trainee, he spoke atypically as a child, not knowing how to properly use *jondaenmal* (formal speech) with upperclassmen and finding *banmal* (informal speech) to be more natural.

This in itself is unusual. Formal speech, respect levels, and hierarchical structure are ingrained in Korean culture. When I, a Westerner, first moved to Seoul, I did not mind at all when people younger than me addressed me casually by first name or spoke to me in *banmal*; I did not fuss over titles or honorifics. Yet as time passed, after working at a company for several months, I grew to understand the underlying shade of informal speech, what it meant when someone didn't even attach the basic honorific suffix *-shi*. There is a character quirk of some Koreans who use informal speech freely to indicate an open mindset—the more Western idea that all people are equal, regardless of age. Jungkook may have been open-minded as a child, or he may have picked it up from a favorite character or role model. I'm inclined to believe in the former, given the way he quickly understood and adapted his behavior, even as a teenager. Once he entered the Big Hit trainee dorm, he quickly noticed how others reacted to his informal style of speech and began speaking in formal Korean. To him, speaking in formal Korean became a matter of understanding, deference, and empathy toward those around him—*nunchi*, a Korean concept of situational awareness that equates to the ability to read the room, picking up on social cues and looking out for others' comfort.

These traits of understanding and empathy were taught to him by his older brothers—all of whom, by Bang Si-hyuk's intuition or unparalleled luck, seem to be genuinely good people, according to industry accounts. "I knew they would succeed when I met them," choreographer Choi Youngjoon said in a YouTube interview, marveling at the boys' kind and considerate behavior, even toward the dancers and staff. These qualities remained with Jungkook as the years passed. On a Weverse livestream in February 2023, Jungkook was scanning the comments rolling across the screen, when he saw a fan ask him how he would feel if they liked other male idols, tossed out like bait for a slice of fan service. On some nights, Jungkook might have played along, feigning jealousy. Instead, he spoke simply. "Jungkook, if I like other male idols . . . What about it? If you like them, you like them. What can I do?" he said in an easy manner. "It's not my life. I have to respect yours . . . Respect, understanding, consideration. A person should always have those three."

As BTS began promoting actively overseas, it became more important to satisfy fans who wanted an artist *and* those who wanted an idol, causing them to perform a mind-boggling balancing act, like Philippe Petit walking a steel wire between the Twin Towers. The pressure of representing their country overseas added another layer of complexity. Korean pop culture and entertainment received substantial investment from the government in the late 1990s, following the 1997 financial crisis. The Ministry of Culture, Sports and Tourism was given funding to promote K-pop, building the country's soft power, and in 2012, an advisory committee was established to sustain the growing wave of popularity and allocated hundreds of millions of dollars to do so. Like all effective forms of soft power, K-pop stars became national representatives, building positive perceptions of the nation wherever they went. And with this investment, what was once a lower form of entertainment, a fleeting escape, became a powerful export. BTS became—like Olympic figure skater Yuna Kim, footballer

Son Heung-min, and other South Koreans who earned international plaudits—the nation's pride.

Consequently, BTS spent more and more time overseas, becoming exposed to new cultures, new ways of thinking, expanding their views outside the domestic echo chamber. Though asked to represent their nation and its values overseas, Jungkook may have absorbed new ideas. "I think he's become the most open-minded of all of us," V said in their 2019 Festa video. BTS has always been consistent, effectively using their role-model reputations to speak out for just causes, where other celebrities are reluctant to do so for fear of public backlash. Instead of merely releasing a statement in support of Black Lives Matter in 2020, BTS donated $1 million to the movement, affecting many of their fans overseas, which inspired ARMY to match the amount in twenty-five hours. "It's about us being against racism and violence," Suga explained in an interview with *Variety*. "Most people would be against these things. We have experienced prejudice as well ourselves. We just want to voice the fact that we feel it's the right of everyone to not be subject to racism or violence."

In 2018, BTS was invited to the United Nations to help UNICEF promote a campaign for global education and training, after launching the "Love Myself" campaign with UNICEF the previous year and partnering with the organization's program to end violence against children. Four years later, during the global pandemic, President Moon Jae-in brought BTS to the UN General Assembly, giving each of them a burgundy diplomatic passport and a certificate appointing them special presidential envoys for future generations and culture. Dressed in suits, they performed "Permission to Dance" at the Assembly Hall, encouraging people to get vaccinated and to uplift the youth, struggling through the pandemic. In a prerecorded video speech for the seventy-fifth UN General Assembly, each member had taken their turn. Jungkook, seated on a chair in head-to-toe black, his silver hoops glinting in his ears, spoke calmly and steadily.

"We live in uncertainty, but really, nothing's changed. If there's something I can do, if our voices can give strength to people, then that's what we want and that's what we'll keep on doing." Simple, honest, straightforward, and humble.

CHAPTER 8

ARMY

In episode 18 of season 34 of *The Simpsons*, which aired in April 2023, Homer insults a female pop idol and earns the wrath of her fandom, who launch glitter bombs and send a murder of crows to his workplace. "You don't know these fan armies, they're all ruthless psychos," Lenny says to Homer, before turning to address the camera directly. "Except for the BTS Army, who are just and pure of heart," he adds, breaking the fourth wall in a moment that the official *Simpsons* Twitter account shared with the caption "Not like the other fans. #BTSArmy."

Such is the reputation of the BTS fandom, who were christened ARMY (an acronym for Adorable Representative M.C. for Youth) in July 2013 and have become as famous as the artists they adore. If I were to point a finger at the largest source of Jungkook's success, the key ingredient to making him a global pop star, it may very well be the love and devotion of ARMY, who launched not only Jungkook but all of BTS and their individual solo careers to record-breaking numbers.

Devoted fandoms are not exclusive to K-pop, nor are they a new phenomenon. In middle school, I had a classmate so dedicated to the Backstreet Boys, she wrote "KTBSPA" (Keep the Backstreet Pride

Alive) on notebooks and palms. She wrote the acronym everywhere, to the point where I remember that phrase all these years later. Beliebers, Directioners, Swifties, Beyhive, Little Monsters; Cheeseheads, Potterheads, all kinds of heads. Fame and fandom go hand in hand.

K-pop fandoms precede BTS. What makes ARMY unique for their time is their highly international composition. ARMY pioneered the cross-cultural work of supporting a group that was originally geared toward an East Asian audience and promoted them on a global scale. International ARMY, or I-ARMY for short, are super savvy online, linking up via Twitter and Discord, Reddit and Tumblr, YouTube and TikTok, populating each platform as it arises and using it to share the gospel of Bangtan. Their pièce de résistance: uniting with other K-pop fandoms in 2020 to fight white supremacy and anti-Black racism by drowning out the harmful propaganda on the #WhiteLivesMatter hashtag with K-pop fancams and reaction GIFs. BTS is more socially aware than most K-pop artists, one of the few to donate a substantial sum to the nonprofit Black Lives Matter Global Network Foundation. Thus, it made sense that ARMY comprised a large part of the group effort, and Jungkook became the face of a meme that remixed three stills from *Lord of the Rings: Return of the King*, an edited exchange between the characters Gimli and Legolas.

GIMLI: Never thought I'd die fighting side by side with a Kpop stan
JUNGKOOK'S head on Legolas's body: sksksks anyway stan jungkook
GIMLI: Aye. I could do that.

What I-ARMY accomplished broke ground for all K-pop artists. Their contributions are legendary and numerous. An example is the work of subtitling and fan translations, or TL. It may be common sense but is often not given due credit: translations have been integral to the spread of K-pop, and much of the initial work, before the companies themselves realized the value of addressing their international audience, was done by fans. Much has been said about how YouTube, Twitter, and other online platforms allowed K-pop artists to communicate more directly with international fans. Now English subs are applied to most videos and company notices are duly translated, but before BTS became a global group, English subtitles were sparse and rarely attached to K-pop content by the companies and creators, who would not have found it worth the time or effort. Big Hit Entertainment did not apply official subtitles to BTS videos until sometime in 2019, years after the group had won international acclaim.

Living in South Korea, thousands of miles from the States, I find it incredible how far away it all seems. Major milestones like *Parasite*'s success at the Oscars or BTS's at the Grammys register as no more than a brief flicker on the news. As recently as 2022, I had a conversation with two members of the Blackpink team who, even after their breakout performance at Coachella in 2019, asked me whether the group really was popular in the US and seemed amazed by the thought of it. That is how insulated Korea can be, which is why international outreach has not been prioritized by corporations.

One of the most influential fan translator groups from the early days was Bangtansubs, who has been crucial to putting BTS's content before a wider audience since their debut. Bangtansubs is the video subtitling arm of BTS-Trans, a nonprofit, fan-run organization that provides unofficial English translations for "media and content produced by, or related to, BTS—consisting of social media posts (tweets, Instagram, Weverse, and Naver posts), blog posts, and song lyrics," according to the group. I remember the first time I found Bangtansubs on YouTube circa 2014, I was surprised to see such an organized and concentrated effort at promoting content for a smaller Korean group, not one from a Big Three label. In hindsight, it should have been a sign of things to come—smoke signaling fire.

I had the pleasure of chatting over email with several members of the team, which, since its founding in 2013, has grown to around thirty members: four different language translators (Korean, Japanese, Mandarin, and Indonesian to English), video timers and typesetters, video encoders, secretaries, team coordinators, and administrative staff. Their ages range from sixteen to thirty-seven; they live in Germany and the Philippines, India and the US, and are PhD candidates and working professionals, architects, graphic designers, high school students. The founding members began following BTS when they were no more than Big Hit trainees and started BTS-Trans about one month before their official debut. Translated videos were originally uploaded to Tumblr, Dailymotion, and YouTube, where the group gained a following. In late 2024, they had 1.46 million subscribers on YouTube and more than one thousand videos subbed. Their most popular video dates back to October 12, 2016: a Bangtan Bomb group reaction to the "Blood Sweat & Tears" MV with 9.8 million views.

K-pop fandoms are extraordinarily well organized, and the members of BTS-Trans are no exception. With a large team working together across time zones, they communicate via Discord, and translations and files are passed along the digital pipeline between designated roles through Trello and a shared Google Drive. Each video has at least one translator, a timer who creates the subtitle files, and an uploader, according to a translator who goes by Rinne, as well as the secretaries and administrators who help keep things moving. Rinne translates videos from Korean to English. The shortest videos can be done in a few hours, while more difficult projects (an episode of

Run BTS, for example) require a team of spot-checkers and can take months or even years to complete. The one-hour-eleven-minute stream for BTS's first-anniversary event required four translators, one timer, two typesetters, and one encoder/uploader. Additional notes and references are added to provide context, ensuring that the original meaning is conveyed as closely as possible.

"Most of our members join this team because they want to bridge the language gap so that ARMY with no Korean language knowledge can enjoy BTS's content just as much as those who do. Our YouTube channel (Bangtansubs) started out of a desire to add English subtitles to BANGTANTV content, in the hopes that more non-Korean speakers around the world would be able to enjoy these videos, and understand BTS's message in the process," the group said.

In the West, subbing and TL culture has long existed for inaccessible foreign media; when I was a child, I puzzled over how to join an IRC (Internet Relay Chat) that would let me download subtitle files for my favorite anime series. Thanks to sites like YouTube and Twitter, K-pop content became more accessible than before, making it less of a niche interest. With increased exposure via the YouTube algorithm, K-pop groups no longer felt so foreign and strange, but translations were integral to the process and experience. Fans do it for free. Like all fandoms, ARMY's work is a labor of love. They are not directly compensated by the idols or their companies. Why, you ask? It comes down to the desire to share that which you love with more people.

"I like to think of Bangtansubs/BTS-Trans (and translators in general) as the 'glue' of the fandom [and] beautifully, our fandom has grown to encompass the whole globe," said Dhara, a typesetter for the group. "Translators work hard to streamline messages so everyone can understand them. So, everyone can find a reason to stay and love BTS in their own way. Over the years, the fandom has grown through this ability to communicate our love for a common thing, and I truly don't think this would have been possible to this extent without the help of the translators."

"It sounds a bit cheesy to say this, but our work is motivated purely by love," explained Aditi, a translator. "We do it because we have this deep love for BTS. While there are other reasons, the main reason I translate is because I think BTS say, sing, write, and create beautiful words that deserve to be heard and understood by lots of people. If I can play even a small role in helping people understand and appreciate the members, that means a lot to me."

A fan's love for their favorite artist is expressed in many forms, and each form helps to expand that artist's foothold. In addition to translators, there are content creators, who make fanart, memes, and clever video compilations (e.g., "an unhelpful guide") that—in entertaining and well-edited chunks, painstakingly edited from hours of footage—advertise each member in a shareable format. Videos like "jungkooks duality being a threat to humanity for 8 minutes," by the YouTuber KOOKIESTAETAS, which had more than 2 million views at the time of writing, showcase Jungkook's natural *aegyo* (charms or cuteness), contrasting with his powerful stage presence. "Jungkook hates losing at anything | 'you always have to let jk win' - Hobi" by SugArmyy, which has more than 5.8 million views, highlights Jungkook's competitive and stubborn nature and is edited with meme sound effects and graphics that make him appear all the more endearing. Compilations serve as grassroots marketing efforts. Fans showcase the most engaging sides of their favorite idols in a way that feels more authentic than anything the company can put out.

Elsewhere, the fancam is a significant vehicle for exposure. After watching dance practice videos, I enjoy going to fancams, which are different close-up videos of the idol dancing and singing at performances. You can see the moment they wink at the camera, the exact swoop of their perfectly styled bangs, their footwork and arm movements. Fancams possess great power: the girl group EXID was reportedly saved from disbandment after footage of member Hani dancing to "Up & Down" went viral in 2014, sending the song from the bottom of the charts toward the top. Hani's legendary fancam now has more than thirty-eight million views and is credited with sparking the fancam craze. "That was actually almost our last performance, because we were thinking of disbanding at that time. If it wasn't for that fancam, I wouldn't be here right now," she said on the TV show *Running Girls*. "I felt like I had been saved by that fancam then. It felt as if I had finally been found by someone after being lost in the woods for ages."

Fancams are generally captured by fans of each idol, who dedicate significant amounts of time and money to follow them around the city and around the world. Fancams are shot, edited, and uploaded with a frenzied speed that rivals professional news corps, often in stunning 4K quality that's higher definition than the official concert footage. Once, I went to KCON with my sister and we sat next to two fans of The Boyz, who had traveled from Japan to New York to see their biases, holding HD cameras with hefty zoom lenses. One of them gifted a handmade picket, or fan, to my sister with a photograph she had taken of Sunwoo, sharing her love.

In Korea, a *homma*, or home page master, will run a fansite for their favorite idol, a hobby that feels more like a full-time job: taking photos of their idol leaving shows like *M Countdown* at odd hours, flying to capture their showcase in Osaka, sneaking the camera equipment into the venue by smuggling it under their skirt, taped to their thigh. Though *homma* can make money from these photographs, selling fan-made merchandise, most of them spend more than they make. A former *homma* once disclosed that their idols even recognized them, seeking them out during performances to make sure they got the best photos—knowing that a good photo has the potential to help their career.

Jungkook's fancams are spectacular and show off his range. Take his April 2019 official fancam of "Boy With Luv" on *M Countdown* (more than sixty-two million views). Wearing a beige suit and blue floral tie, he moves lightly on his feet, the camera zooming in to capture his sweet smile, even when he's not center stage. Four months later, an unofficial fancam of BTS's performance of "Idol" at the Lotte Family Concert (more than eighteen million views) captured Jungkook in a black suit, dancing with raw power, tossing his sweat-drenched hair back and forth, completely lost in the stage, leaving ARMY speechless.

Streaming and charting are another large component to the fandom experience. Jungkook tops the Billboard charts. How? The efforts of his fans, who follow comprehensive guides on how to stream and buy during comebacks with different guides for each chart. There is a prominent Twitter fan account called @btschartdata (BCD) with 2.4 million followers that popularized Stationhead, a site where fans can connect and stream songs together, when they began organizing streaming parties for BTS comebacks in 2020. A May 25 streaming party for "Butter" attracted more than 400,000 listeners and drove 5.4 million streams in one session, turning Stationhead into an indispensable tool for K-pop fandoms (the official page for BTS ARMY has 4.63 million members). Jungkook himself hosted listening parties for "Seven," "3D," and *Golden* on Stationhead, signing on to chat with ARMY as they racked up millions of streams. Platforms like Stationhead turn the solitary act of streaming into a social call, playing into one of the core driving forces behind K-pop.

The psychology of fandom is complex, based on a search for community and social identity. All fandoms, across sports and music and fictional series, share the same positives and negatives. The act of choosing a favorite artist, a bias, is also choosing a social group and your identity within that group, and fostering close relationships with people who share your obsessions. These friendships keeps fans engaged, and ARMY are among the most committed and close-knit. "To me, ARMY feels more like family than any other fandom," said Adele, a timer with BTS-Trans, during our email exchange. "I have a plethora of interests within and outside of music and K-pop, which I may enjoy with others online or in person, but there's a deeper, shared feeling of acceptance and love that ARMY creates, which I have yet to find within other communities of the things that I love.

"I think that part of this stems from the diversity of ARMY and their willingness to share unconditionally," Adele continued. "As ARMY, we understand our differences and that each one of us battles our own struggles, but we also have our own strengths, and because of this, ARMY strives to make the world a little bit easier for others who may be experiencing the same things. We reach out, we donate, we work together, all as one family, and it's a beautiful thing."

Since the fandom is the foundation of the K-pop industry, the companies encourage close relationships with the artists. These relationships are more personal than those in Western pop fandom. In the digital age, they have grown even closer. Idols spend hours on livestreams. Jungkook is particularly well-known for them. Livestreams used to be supervised by a staff member, according to BTS, who made sure everything went smoothly. Once the boys moved out on their own, Jungkook began going off book, streaming whenever he wished. On February 1, 2023, he turned on an impromptu live and mused aloud that surely, he was big enough to do this, giving the camera a cheeky smile. During the pandemic, his Weverse lives were a bright spot in many ARMYs' quarantined days. He streamed from his home at odd hours. In June 2023, Jungkook fell asleep on Weverse in front of more than six million viewers, who watched him doze peacefully for about forty-five minutes before a staffer switched off the live remotely. He talked about this in an interview:

"You go on this livestream sometimes," Jimmy Fallon said to him on *The Tonight Show*, "and sometimes you do karaoke, sometimes you're cooking, this thing that made me laugh, this is my favorite thing that you did, you fell asleep, and you fell asleep and just slept for forty-five minutes and everyone—six million people—tuned in to watch you sleep."

"I think my fans, ARMY, liked it because it was something very unexpected, but actually it's a little embarrassing," Jungkook responded, looking sheepish.

The pandemic played a key role in pushing BTS, who had been gaining ground overseas since 2016, to a new level of mainstream success, putting them in front of people who couldn't care less about Billboard charts and music award show wins. The song "Permission to Dance" is often cited as a benchmark, the group's third full-English single that, along with "Dynamite" and "Butter," comprised a pandemic-era trilogy of songs designed to bring happiness during the outbreak. "Permission to Dance" stands out in particular. Cowritten by Ed Sheeran for BTS, the upbeat song and music video celebrated essential workers and ended with a montage of people removing their face masks to reveal their smiles. BTS's joyfulness struck a chord with people during this time: seven good-looking boys, dancing and singing to lighten people's spirits. Again, they were at the right place at the right time, as people stuck alone and indoors sought comfort and connection. This brought them new fans and made their existing relationships stronger. "BTS's ability to capture hearts through their honest experiences and thoughts transforms their music into a source of inspiration and comfort, allowing them to stand out among other K-pop groups and truly connect with a diverse global audience," Rinne from BTS-Trans said.

The connection between ARMY and Jungkook is the backbone of his success, the result of a loving relationship carefully fostered over the years. His love for ARMY is genuine, and BTS themselves care about the fans, who, through their many efforts, lifted them out of obscurity and allowed them to achieve their dreams. Yet I also understand that this benefits companies, which encourage unhealthy attachments. After all, it would take several thousand "normal" fans like me—who add a few BTS songs to their shuffle playlist, pick up one album on a whim to place on the shelf—to measure up to one fan deep in the grips of the parasocial relationship, who buys twenty-plus albums to collect enough photocards and, even more important, to earn the chance to meet their idol in person at a fan meeting.

The parasocial relationship can veer down darker paths. *Sasaeng* fans are notorious in K-pop fandom, stalkers who violate celebrities' *sasaenghwal*, or private life. *Sasaengs* will track down an idol's address and wait outside their homes; on the penultimate Weverse live before his enlistment, Jungkook remarked, with light frustration, that *sasaengs* were still outside his house, as a passing comment. Some *sasaengs* go even further, breaking into their idols' homes or hotel rooms and stealing their belongings. Jaejoong of TVXQ once woke up to a *sasaeng* fan in his bed. *Sasaengs* obtain their idols' phone numbers with regularity and text and call them, so idols often change their digits; they also acquire idols' schedules in advance, down to their flight and seat number, so they can purchase seats near them. There are accounts online dedicated to selling idols' personal information (numbers, flight schedules, hotels), allegedly received from employees at either their music labels or third-party companies (travel companies, for instance) that sell it for profit. In September 2023, HYBE organized a task force to combat this. *Sasaengs* are not limited to Korea but exist across all countries, even the US. Last year I flew to Japan on the same flight as Mirae, a seven-member boy group that disbanded a few months later. Even they were surrounded by six to eight fans, who stood by taking photographs and flew on the same plane in nearby rows.

The fansign is another aspect of the idol industry that differs greatly from pop. Fan club members who buy x number of albums receive entries into a lottery to attend a fansign, which is a private event held by the idol or idol group. They perform plenty of fan service (e.g., song covers and skits) and spend time signing albums and chatting individually with the fans, who file down the line one by one. Idols will answer requests, from putting on a pair of cat ears to holding hands and making eye contact. Fans who've followed a group from debut or who simply purchase enough albums to score repeat visits may even be recognized and remembered by their idols. K-fans share close-up videos, as I-fans watch longingly: Jungkook reaching out to briefly hold hands with a fan, interlocking fingers; Jungkook putting on a fuzzy hood shaped like Cinnamoroll, the Sanrio mascot, shaking his head back and forth so the ears flop.

During the pandemic, when in-person fan meetings could no longer be held, companies switched over to fan calls, which marked a seismic shift for the industry. With a video call, which no longer required you to be in Korea, I-fans had access to the same level of intimacy that was once reserved for K-fans. International album sales spiked as fans bought dozens of albums in an attempt to get fan calls; some of them are repeat winners, who become obsessed with the opportunity to chat regularly with their bias. There is a compilation of fan calls Jung-kook conducted for *Golden*. One fan mixed cider and soju and beer together for a virtual toast, asking Jungkook to have a drink sometime, to which Jungkook said he would drink one during a live. Another fan showed Jungkook his own baby photos and asked him to mimic those expressions, which he did cheerfully.

It all serves what Weverse president and HYBE executive Joon Choi once described in 2023 as the company's ethos: "The thing we're really digging into is the psychological mechanism of falling in love." I am fascinated by this corporate analysis of idol fandom, which appears to be more invested than pop fandom (there are exceptions, of course; e.g., Swifties, Directioners). There are many reasons why the typical idol fan is more prone to attachment.

Where Western teen idols are more generally marketed toward fellow teens, maintaining a demure public image to maintain parental approval, J-idols and K-idols, while certainly appealing to younger fans, home in more closely on an element of escapism to target older fans with wallets of their own. In their purest incarnation, idols are a fleeting escape, a dose of pure dopamine delivered onstage, a "shining and special existence," as Sunoo of Enhypen said on the first episode of the audition program *I-Land*. They provide endless amounts of content, producing music and videos thrice as fast as Western artists, a wormhole you can fall into at any moment, losing hours to a K-pop binge. Bright and smiling, they help you forget your troubles for a little while. With escapism in mind, the most important aspect of the idol industry—the reason for the profound attachment that forms between idols and fans—is the story being told.

More than pop stars, idols become characters in a story unfolding before your eyes. Their personas, at times carefully constructed, mimic character tropes, beloved by fans of the subculture. There's the "cold city man," the cool and unexpressive and stylish *tsundere* (slang borrowed from Japan to describe someone that seems prickly on the outside but is soft and sweet once you get to know them); the "happy virus," a cheerful ray of sunshine that lifts the entire group, like J-Hope; the responsible leader, who keeps the others in line, like RM; the resident genius or all-rounder, who seems effortlessly good at everything, like Jungkook. Then there's the group dynamic, which is carefully curated and cultivated: the moments of bickering, of affection, each snapshot coming together, episodically, to portray a lovable found family.

It's well known that Bang Si-hyuk is a self-proclaimed *otaku*, a Japanese term that refers to a form of superfan, sharing series like *Nichijou* and idols like Akina Nakamori on his Twitter account. In popular culture, *otaku* are most associated with fans of anime and manga and video games, but it is not enough to simply enjoy those hobbies. To be an *otaku* is to possess a consumptive passion for the subject. One can be an *otaku* of any hobby or genre—an idol *otaku*, for instance—as long as you demonstrate the single-minded fixation. With the overlap between idol fans and *otaku*—two subcultures with roots in Japan—similar tropes tend to emerge across mediums. If I had to guess, Bang's *otaku* inclinations may have helped him understand the mechanisms of superfandom on a deeper level than other CEOs.

Joining a fandom and finding your favorite member is called *ipdeok*, an obscure portmanteau of the prefix for "enter" and a twist on "obsession." The same term exists in idol, anime, and game fandoms, as the same structures and principles apply. Fans become a part of the journey and, in the case of idols, your actions directly affect the outcome. You cheer for them, cry with them, fight for them, buy CDs and stream their songs to boost their numbers. Watching them struggle, you want to help them succeed. Their everyday trials hit like story beats in a regular series, in which you are highly invested. There can be, as Joon Choi said, the sensation of falling in love, whether that love feels romantic or friendly or maternal or paternal. The sensation is difficult to explain to outsiders. Do fans ascribe to these artists the same traits that one would to a favorite fictional character? Idols, especially those that follow the orthodox rules, can seem too good to be true. To create the perfect escape and preserve the dreamlike fantasy, an idol must cast away or conceal the uglier parts of themselves.

The act of quitting a fandom is called *taldeok*, loosely translated, to escape the obsession. Some of the decline of the idol industry can be attributed to the frequent scandals that arise. Due to their regularity, most are minor bumps in the road, quickly brushed under the rug with a handwritten apology, uploaded by the artist on social media, leaving the barest blemish behind. Dating scandals, for instance. A Korean tabloid called *Dispatch* reveals a secret celebrity couple almost every year during the Korean New Year; in 2024, they revealed that Aespa's Karina and actor Lee Jae-wook were dating. Karina issued a handwritten apology. She'd broken her fans' trust and shattered their romanticized image of her by being in a relationship, making herself unavailable for the imagination of her fans. For that, she had to beg for forgiveness. The couple broke up five weeks later. The matter was quickly forgotten. There have been idols with secret wives, those that rushed into marriage after a surprise pregnancy, DUIs and dog attacks, abuse and harassment. I know more than one fan who, disenchanted by the unhappy realities of their once-favorite idols, fled to the comfort of fictional versions, who can generally never disappoint you. Many K-pop fans experience burnout and leave, too jaded by the industry to fall under its illusory spell for good.

When Jungkook returned to Seoul on June 22, 2023, there were hundreds of fans waiting at Incheon Airport's international arrivals;

he stepped through the door and gave several 90-degree bows, after which fans began to break through the barricades, wailing and running with their phones in the air. It gave me secondhand anxiety. Some fans become so attached that the prospect of their idol dating can send them into a frenzy. When Jungkook became embroiled in dating rumors, which the company soundly denied, some fans posted graphic photos of their self-harming behavior in response to the news. The inability to distinguish fantasy and reality can lead to troubling outcomes. It's love at its darkest.

The public would be surprised to know that many of Jungkook's biggest haters come from within his own fandom. There are OT7 (one true seven, in that the one true form of BTS is seven members) fans who believe that all members should receive equal love and care, a bit like parents who insist they love all their children the same. Then there are the *akgae*, or solo stans. *Akgae* support only one member of their group and resent the other members for either holding their bias back or taking too much of the spotlight. It saddens me to say that Jungkook has always had an astonishing number of anti-fans, *akgaes* of other BTS members who resent his visibility in the group. Back in 2015, I remember seeing Jungkook receive a lot of hate online: for being in the center too often, despite that being his official position; for being pushed too much by the company, even though he himself worked diligently in the background, not putting himself forward. A cover of "Rainism," performed at the 2016 MBC Gayo Daejejeon show, was criticized for appearing like a Jungkook solo showcase with the other members relegated to backup dancer roles.

ARMY often told me Jungkook was the most popular member, but I saw more haters than fans online, their negativity overshadowing all else. It was painful to see people ripping on him for periods of bad acne, which he experienced as a teenager going through significant stress. I once had a recurring incident with a Jimin *akgae* who, after I complimented Jungkook's looks in a feature for American *Vogue*, left hateful comments and messages, for how dare I compliment Jungkook and not Jimin? The greatest irony, of course, is that Jimin and Jungkook are incredibly close, supporting each other's solo careers and accomplishments, as are the other members of BTS, who are always good to each other. Many K-pop fans lament *akgae* dynamics—the toxicity that drives many away and defines the public perception of the "unhinged K-pop fan," even though most fans are sweet. For that one Jimin *akgae*, I encountered hundreds more wonderful ARMY who wanted to help spread BTS's message of love and acceptance.

"I believe a lot of hate and discrimination in this world is born out of ignorance and fear of the unfamiliar," said Adele from BTS-Trans. "If just one more person can understand the messages that BTS creates for the world, then maybe the world can brighten a little more wherever that person roams. The more we can understand each other, the more we can feel more similar as humans, and you can't put a price on that connection."

"My main motivation is for the fandom," said Annie, a BTS-Trans translator. "It might sound weird but I feel like we're this one big family, even though I haven't met them. BTS are my role models and they always go above and beyond for us ARMYs, and so I feel like I have to pay that forward and somehow contribute as much as I can."

The media often focuses on the negative sides of K-pop fandom, the unhealthy relationships and echo chambers that develop around real people. Jungkook would prefer to focus on the positive: the love that ARMY gave to him that allowed him to stand on the stage and find out who he is, what he hopes to share with the world through his voice. As he so often says, it's a precious gift that he'd like to spend his whole life trying to return. At the prerecording for Jungkook's performance of "Standing Next to You" at *M Countdown* in November 2023, Jungkook prepared a special gift for the 180 fans who won the lottery to attend. A bottle of Golden perfume, its custom blend chosen by Jungkook: tiger lily, his birth flower; suede; and amber, with flecks of gold floating inside the glass. "Blooming splendidly in a resplendent display, just like the flower language that means 'Love Me,'" read the accompanying note. "It resembles autumn, melancholic yet filled with brilliant GOLDEN moments, all captured within. Centered around the fragrance of the tiger lily that elegantly blooms in this enchanting season, Deep amber forms a harmonious and sensual blend with the flowers. Only for ARMY." Jungkook signed each note with gold pen and enclosed a second handwritten note, simple and straight to the point as always: "I'm happy that you all can listen to my song. Thank you. -JK-"

Even once he enlisted, ARMY was on his mind and he was on theirs. I had seen people predict that Jungkook's time in the military would dampen his popularity. But those predictions underestimated the strength of the bond he and ARMY had forged over the years. Close to midnight on December 18, 2024, after one year of his service had passed, Jungkook returned home for the winter holidays and, without any notice, began an impromptu Weverse livestream titled "Oh I missed you, a lot." He gave a brief tour of his new apartment, then sat down and began singing karaoke for ARMY beneath a deep purple light. It was like nothing had changed. Comments flooded in from around the world: Brazil, Pakistan, India, America, Japan, an endless stream of purple heart emojis.

In two hours and fourteen minutes, he had gained 17.5 million viewers. In eight more minutes, the number jumped to 19 million, and by the time he went to bed at 2:04 a.m., he had amassed 20,190,330 viewers and 291,799,096 likes, breaking his own 2023 record for most viewers on an individual Weverse live. "I want to come back soon, really," he said, with a heartfelt smile. When he does, ARMY will be ready and waiting to make history yet again.

CHAPTER 9

HIS SOLO CAREER

In the months following the June 14, 2022, announcement that BTS would be taking a hiatus, each member did, for the first time in nine years—longer, if you count their training period—what they liked, freed from the need to place the group first and foremost. J-Hope released his solo studio album *Jack in the Box* in July, Jin released the solo single album "The Astronaut" in October, and RM dropped his solo studio album *Indigo* in December. In March, Jimin released his solo mini album *Face*; Suga released *D-Day* under his alias Agust D in April. V released two singles, "Love Me Again" and "Rainy Days" in August, ahead of the September drop of his solo mini album *Layover*.

Jungkook took a long break. Having worked nonstop since he was thirteen, sacrificing his chance at a normal adolescence, he came to a full stop. No longer forced to keep moving, he found himself at a rest that went on for five months, after he returned from the Qatar World Cup in November. As one of the last members to move out of the group dormitory, he lived alone for the first time. He nested in the luxury apartment he'd purchased. He stayed up as late as he wanted, getting up at 4 a.m. to make chicken stir-fry with a slice of cheese if he felt like it. He played music on the speakers, sitting in a darkened room, green lights sparkling on the walls like a constellation of stars. He boiled buckwheat noodles, adding three spoonfuls of Perilla oil, two spoonfuls of *cham* sauce, one spoon of Buldak sauce, and one spoon of Buldak mayo to a bowl, slipping an egg yolk into the mixture and stirring it well. The *deulgireum makguksu* recipe went viral. He honed his cooking skills for other dishes, watching YouTubers like YOOXICMAN score the gleaming white fat on a strip of pork belly and sear it to a golden crisp; he went to the gym, drilling his right hook with his personal trainer; and he sang karaoke to ARMY on Weverse livestreams whenever the mood struck. Some nights he grew introspective, even somber, musing on the importance of health and happiness. "While I'm still young, I have to enjoy it," he said in March. "There's only one life. Everyone, we only have one life."

As time passed, and each member released their solo projects, the anticipation for Jungkook's individual debut began to build, simmering like a pot on a long and low boil. A feature on Charlie Puth's song "Left and Right," released shortly after the group hiatus, and his historic performance at the opening ceremony of the 2022 FIFA World Cup suggested a strong future in global pop. Publishing his first solo album with the weight of so much expectation must have felt like an impossible task. After all, Jungkook was an accomplished songwriter who began writing with guidance from the other members, particularly Suga, who watched over Jungkook with pride. When reviewing Jungkook's work on "Outro: Love Is Not Over" on *The Most Beautiful Moment in Life Pt.1* from 2015, Suga remarked, "Ah, our Jungkook has a talent for this and is good at it."

In the early days of his career, Jungkook possessed the ambition to compose his own music. The night before the interview for the *Wings* concept book in 2017, he stayed up until seven in the morning to compose songs with his MIDI keyboard. Though he kept asking Big Hit for piano lessons, he hadn't yet learned any chords, and had to press every key to find the sound he was seeking. The interviewer asked whether it was necessary for every member of the team to write songs, and Jungkook protested that he didn't want to leave all the songwriting to two or three members. "Besides, the kind of music and emotions I like are different from what the other members like," he said. "I want to make my emotions into a story and hear it in sound."

In 2024, Jungkook was promoted to a full member of the Korea Music Copyright Association (KOMCA), after earning substantial royalties for twenty-two song credits. His first solo song, "Still With You," cowritten with Pdogg, was a gorgeous jazz ballad and fan favorite. Despite never receiving an official release or promotion, it gained more than 250 million streams on Spotify. A known perfectionist, Jungkook had a habit of writing songs and deleting them the next day. There was an original song called "Decalcomania" that Jungkook intended for his first mixtape; soft and moody, the unfinished ballad read like a journal entry, almost too intimate to share: "When I see you smile in the screen, you're good at everything, you're just perfect / Feels like I've never been you." The demo was uploaded on Twitter on September 1, 2019, but when fans inquired about its release two years later, he said he had deleted the files.

In an interview published in *Weverse Magazine* in June 2022, Jungkook spoke about his reluctance to release his own compositions. Writer Kang Myeongseok asked whether Jungkook might hesitate to release a song he had written, if he wasn't personally satisfied with the work. Jungkook seemed to latch onto this train of thought, sharing that he had written many songs and sat on them. Upon listening to them later, he found them lacking and, instead of making the effort to edit them, chose to simply erase them, despite his older brothers encouraging him to keep at it. "The other members tell me, 'You have to keep making releases. That's how you figure it all out,'" he said. "So, I'm writing songs lately." In February 2023, however, during a Weverse stream, a fan asked if he was preparing his solo album and he confessed that although he was anticipating his future album, he had come to "an all-stop," comparing his lifestyle to that of a rock that had ceased its forward motion.

For HYBE, this was a nightmare scenario. Even back in 2017, when I visited the Cheonggu Building following their first win at the Billboard Music Awards, a Big Hit staff member fretted about the need to maximize the boys' time and earning potential before the dreaded military enlistment period, which cut male celebrities' careers short by taking them out of the industry for about eighteen months in their prime. Jungkook possessed such massive promise, particularly in the Western market. HYBE could coax him gently, trying to encourage him to work on his solo projects, but he was no longer a trainee, nor was he beholden to the group members he cherished. The group was on an official break. No one could make Jungkook do anything against his will, and Bang Si-hyuk had always taken a more laissez-faire approach to BTS because he wanted their music to be an authentic expression of their youth.

While Jungkook settled into his time of rest, Andrew Watt, the Grammys' 2021 Producer of the Year (Justin Bieber, Lady Gaga, Post Malone), and Cirkut (Katy Perry, Miley Cyrus, The Weeknd) were wrapping production on "Seven." The track, which was originally written for Bieber, was finalized over a year before its debut, according to an interview with *Forbes*, and inspired by the UK garage sound in vogue at the time. Watt played the song for his manager Scooter Braun, who had sold his company Ithaca Holdings to HYBE in 2021, becoming the CEO of HYBE America, to the chagrin of many fans but the delight of Bang Si-hyuk, who had ambitions for K-pop in the US. He saw that the Southeast Asian K-pop market was stagnating and there was potential for growth in America. HYBE America is a fascinating project. Bang is not the first Korean CEO to set his eyes on North America, but HYBE America was a large step for the company into foreign territory. To spearhead the effort, Bang leaned on Braun. Braun's greatest success was stumbling across a thirteen-year-old Justin Bieber on YouTube and signing him. Former clients include Ariana Grande, Kanye West, and Demi Lovato.

Braun was credited with A&R, artists and repertoire, for Jungkook's solo output. The A&R typically scouts and signs new artists then maintains a close relationship in developing their early career, liaising between the artist and the label. This type of A&R does not exist in the K-pop industry, where artists are more directly managed by the company and the company head takes a hands-on role in their artists' development. What is known is that Braun heard "Seven" and thought of Jungkook, then made the connection. "Scooter was the one that actually said this could be the biggest song in the world if Jung Kook sings it," Watt told *Forbes*. As CEO, Braun was responsible for the success of HYBE's American venture, and in Jungkook, he likely saw the potential for a crossover pop act that could catapult the subsidiary to success. Braun took the song straight to Bang, sharing it with him over a meal, and pitched it specifically for Jungkook. Bang then personally took it to Jungkook, who, at the time, was still unsure if he would release an album anytime soon, as Bang revealed in an interview with Bloomberg.

That all changed after Bang sent him "Seven." In an email interview with *Variety*, Jungkook commented, "Upon hearing 'Seven,' I thought, 'This is it.' As this is my first step forward in the spotlight as a solo artist, I want to show a more mature and grown version of myself." The moment he heard the song, he felt that switch flip. It was not a planned project or an artistic concept he had envisioned for himself. It came down to his instincts. The same instinct that led him to choose Big Hit over larger music labels, including JYP of the Big Three, told him to go for it. Ultimately, "Seven" was the song that sparked his next move, as he told Kang Myeongseok in another issue of *Weverse Magazine*: "I only have one, big goal, and it's to be a giant pop star."

On April 8, 2023, fans had lined up by 7 p.m. at Incheon Airport Terminal 2 for international departures, standing on step stools and makeshift risers, armed with phones and DSLR cameras. Barricades were set up beside the entrance and security guards in black safety vests patrolled the area. Jungkook entered to cheers, flanked by bodyguards and a videographer, dressed in a Calvin Klein denim jacket and T-shirt, his hair pulled back into a small ponytail at the nape of his neck. He waved to the fans who had come to see him off, bowing every few feet, then boarded a flight to Los Angeles and checked into the Beverly Hills Hotel. On April 10 at 1 p.m., he headed to the studio, seeming slightly anxious to record overseas with a non-Korean producer, his first official schedule for his solo work. He sighed and spent the fifteen-minute car ride performing vocal exercises with a black drinking straw in his mouth, a technique he had researched online to strengthen and balance his vocal cords.

Accompanied by Bang Si-hyuk, a testament to the importance of this project to HYBE, Jungkook arrived at Andrew Watt's Beverly Hills home, where he maintained a recording studio in the basement, decorated with paisley tapestries and string lights. This was an environment completely different from the functional recording booths that HYBE used. Watt sat on a sofa a few feet away from Jungkook as he recorded his lines, listening through headphones and providing guidance and cheering him on, getting up to give him thumbs-ups and high fives, hooting and clapping.

His positivity put Jungkook at ease. Jungkook had arrived feeling, as the opening lyrics of "Seven" described, the weight of the world on his shoulders. There was the need to represent BTS as the group's main vocalist, which he continued to feel a decade on. Even after impressing Chris Martin, who directed his session for "My Universe" in 2021, Jungkook felt pressure more keenly when recording outside his comfort zone, particularly with non-Korean producers. It was not only BTS's reputation on the line but that of all K-idols, as he and Suga discussed on *Suchwita*: the pride he carried as a Korean artist and the desire to represent his nation on the stage of Western pop.

He spent hours going over the lines with Watt, at times requesting an attempt at different phrasing, a lyrical run, adding a breathier quality to the high notes. He stayed in good spirits the whole way through. "This kid is perfect, baby," Watt shouted, enthused, impressed by his positive attitude and willingness to sing a line, over and over, until it sounded right. Once they finished recording, Jungkook came out of the booth looking a bit weary and jet-lagged. But after listening to the recording, he felt uplifted, finding confidence in his ability to perform in these unfamiliar styles and conditions, which pushed him toward the next goal. Jungkook was humble as usual but his dreams were spectacular and unmatched. When asked whether his dreams had changed following the session, Jungkook replied, "I'm Korean, but I'd like to be the one and only singer who can cross back and forth between K-pop and pop songs. I'm going to conquer all genres, if I could. I'll just stick with these two for now and perhaps I could do Latin music later. And opera. I could also do musicals. And classical singing." Without question, Jungkook's ambitions and potential to achieve them had no limit.

"Seven (feat. Latto)" debuted at number one on the Billboard Hot 100 and Global 200 with nearly sixteen million Spotify streams, the first K-pop act to reach number one on the US Spotify chart and the first Korean solo artist to debut on the top of the global chart. It debuted at number three on the UK Singles Chart, then the highest debut for a Korean soloist in that chart's history, tying with BTS for the highest Singles Chart debut for a Korean act. "Seven" became the fastest song to reach one billion streams in Spotify history and was the fourth most streamed song in 2023, after Harry Styles's "As It Was." To ensure the success of Jungkook's release, HYBE pulled on every connection in their Rolodex. Choreographer Brian Puspos came on as a backup dancer. Bradley & Pablo (Harry Styles, Rosalía, Lil Nas X, Charli XCX) directed the music video, costarring Korean actress and then–it girl Han So-hee. The rest of the album received the same level of support and push from HYBE HQ and America, from Bang and Braun.

"Hearing him on his own on this song, it's pretty clear how massive of a run this guy is about to go on," Watt said. "It's pretty dangerous what's about to happen."

Mere moments after finishing "Seven," Watt played two demos for Jungkook, one of which was "Standing Next to You." His fingers woven and resting on his chest, Jungkook closed his eyes tightly, as if he could see himself performing it onstage. He began to snap his fingers, his face lighting up. Jungkook left and spent the evening with the demo track and lyrics, learning the song overnight in order to record it the next day, humming the notes into his straw. The next morning, leaving the hotel, he seemed in shock over the skills required to sing the song. He clutched his iced coffee, the practice straw still in his mouth. This was classic Jungkook: relentless and hardworking.

An article in *The New York Times* said, "This is what all the hard work of being in BTS was for, ostensibly—a shot at extending his career beyond the very wide boundaries of the group's accomplishments. Or put more plainly: more hard work . . . If he celebrated his ample successes—including a No. 1 single and No. 2 album on US charts—the cameras were not there. If he acted out or pushed back, we'll never know." From a Western point of view, it may appear that K-pop stars like Jungkook are overworked. While there is certainly truth to that, it is not a black-or-white issue. No one at HYBE, not even Bang Si-hyuk, could force Jungkook to work as a solo artist against his will—his long-delayed album, *Golden*, and his refusal to pick up numerous lucrative luxury brand endorsements, despite the number of companies begging for him, are proof of that. When he stays up till dawn poring over the melodies, practicing each note with care, it is not due to a company directive. To be frank, Jungkook could have recorded "Standing Next to You" with minimal effort, and his fans would have loved it. He works hard because he wants to do his best, and he wants to give his absolute best to his fans. That is who he is.

Hopping on Weverse live in November, after his *Golden* promotions were over, Jungkook said his solo schedules, though jam-packed and stressful, had been far more fun than he expected. The whirlwind experience had also provided moments of meaningful introspection, as Jungkook realized that he was the type of person who preferred to be active, working toward something, even if it made life more difficult. In other words, his eight months of hectic solo work were ultimately more satisfying than his five months of near-sedentary rest. In a 2022 interview for *Weverse Magazine*, Kang asked Jungkook why he always did so much. "Because, in the end, I want it," he said. "I want to see myself being able to do all those things." He has always found joy in doing so.

Back in the same spot as the day before, with Watt on the sofa,

Jungkook crooned as though he'd been practicing the song for weeks, not mere hours. Watt said he sounded like Michael Jackson, Jungkook's eyes growing wide in disbelief. He sang over the course of about four hours, after which he left the recording room in a daze. Would he receive recognition from others, he fretted to himself often, riding in cars between rehearsals and recording sessions, in L.A., in New York, in Seoul, looking pensive, at times unsure. Crossing over from K-pop to US pop required crossing countless cultural barriers, not only the language, but the ways of doing things, the systems at work. But, as Bang later told a reporter for a *New Yorker* feature, Jungkook had always dreamed of being a "U.S. pop star"—what should have been an impossible dream for a boy from Busan, but now seemed frighteningly possible.

"Standing Next to You" became the title track of his solo album, *Golden*, which came out in November 2023. Originally, he had planned for a small EP, filled with only the songs he loved, but as Braun and Bang presented him with more and more options, the little EP became a full album with eleven songs, selected and recorded at a breakneck pace once he returned to Seoul. As he told Suga and V over barbecued meat on *Suchwita*, Jungkook recorded five songs in a week, nearly one song a day, singing three hours a day for five days straight. In the booth, he fussed over the rhythms and the pronunciation. Once, he stumbled over a tongue twister of a phrase in "Yes or No" but was determined to push through. It was after recording "3D" that Jungkook decided to proceed with an album fully in English. The decision was no doubt supported by HYBE America to help him fulfill his ambitions of being a global pop star, and also expose him to a greater audience as they did when BTS released their song "Dynamite," which was completely in English. It also would have presented an enticing challenge for Jungkook, who had been studying English for years. In

2019, he shared on a VLIVE livestream that he wanted to help RM, who shouldered most of the overseas interviews. He ran through his vocabulary list—confidence, interpret, admire, anxious, thoughtful, shocked, jealous—and detailed his struggles with the verb tenses, adverbs, and prepositions he had been learning through Siwon School, a language academy with online courses. By 2020, when BTS filmed an interview with Jimmy Fallon for *The Tonight Show*, Jungkook capably fielded a few questions in English, as RM watched him, beaming with pride. Still, by Jungkook's own admission, he had a long way to go to reach RM's level of fluency and continued to practice at every opportunity.

"This album was prepared for the overseas music market, so we chose all English songs," he explained in an interview with the *Hankyoreh* newspaper, assuring his fans that he would release Korean songs in the future. "I wasn't working on an album, but after listening to 'Seven,' I came out of a break," Jungkook said in an interview with Spotify. "We rushed to record the music, shoot the music videos, and album photos. Since ARMY have been waiting for so long, we worked very fast."

By July, Jungkook had flown back to New York to prepare for his first solo performance at the GMA Summer Concert Series. One day ahead of the show, in between dance rehearsals at New 42 Studios in Times Square, he went to a doctor's office to have his throat examined as it had felt dry and irritated for weeks, and received a temporary treatment to relieve the soreness. The morning of the show, still struggling with his poor condition, Jungkook was slightly taken aback when, due to the threat of rain, *Good Morning America* pushed up his performance. Yet by the time he climbed the stairs, he had settled into the usual groove, intending to take it as easily as he could.

Much like he had years before at the Chile show, where he collapsed backstage, Jungkook sang each song perfectly, no evidence of his throat trouble. Seconds after he left the stage, the rain began to fall, causing him to nearly slip on the stairs, his left foot sliding out of his Balenciaga sneaker. His throat hurt, and his body was racked with coughs as he entered the trailer. Looking up at the rain clouds that had put a halt to what should have been a triumphant live stage, Jungkook couldn't help but lament. "Isn't this too much?" he said. "I'm so sad." Rolling down the window as they drove away, Jungkook waved at the fans, pointing sadly at the sky. "This was my first performance," he said. "I've never had things go well at the beginning."

One week later, Jungkook was backstage at *The One Show* in London, warming up his body with a bout of shadowboxing and his vocal cords by singing strains of "Seven," downing cough syrup to keep his symptoms at bay. The weather was clear, and he performed the song for the ARMY that had come to see him in front of the Thames, the sun low in the sky. Skipping down the hallway, he seemed overjoyed. Two days later, he was back in New York to perform at the Global Citizen Festival, which ended with a teaser of his next single, "3D," which he had recorded in Seoul in July, taking notes and a video call with the producer David Stewart. In the car after the show, driving through the city at night in the falling rain, Jungkook pulled up the lyrics to "Hate You," rehearsing them in the quiet darkness.

Over the course of eight months, Jungkook traveled to five countries, recorded twelve songs, performed in more than ten shows, and released three music videos and four performance films. Though he didn't address it often, ever present, looming in the background, was the impending enlistment that would cut short his nascent solo career. In April, after recording "Seven" and "Standing Next to You," Jungkook walked through the Beverly Hills Hotel, pondering the best way to drop his singles. "Before I go to the military . . . I'll release the singles . . ." he thought aloud. "Singles before I go to the military . . . it's already April now. How many singles should I release?" he said, slipping into his Busan *satoori*. There was a drive to prove himself in the short time he had left, to establish a foothold for him to return to after one and a half years away. "I received approval as Jung Kook of BTS. I received lots of it. I have proven myself," Jungkook said. "But I've never done anything as a solo artist. The general public doesn't know me. So, what I was ambitious for was satisfying the public solely by myself without the power of BTS."

A change seemed to come over him again, witnessed by collaborators like Pdogg, who had been with Jungkook since before his debut and noticed that as a solo artist, no longer needing to balance with the team, Jungkook was free to delve into different sounds, manipulating his voice in new ways. Stewart, who had also produced "Dynamite," noted that Jungkook's accent and Western pop vocals had grown more natural since then, describing him as a professional with an innate "feel."

Each of the three singles, chosen by Jungkook, served a different purpose and test for the artist. "Seven" was selected to show his maturity, dispelling his image as the *maknae* of BTS, evidenced by the explicit version. According to an article in *The New Yorker*, Braun advised Jungkook to follow the lead of Justin Timberlake, who went for "edge" without NSYNC (think: "Rock Your Body," which was rather provocative for 2002). The single "3D" felt like a direct nod to Timberlake, a 2000s-style R&B pop song with a "retro vibe" that could have been on Timberlake's first solo album, *Justified*; a remix featuring Timberlake himself dropped a few months later, showing that Jungkook's pop vocals stood up to the onetime "prince of pop." Not only this, but the collaboration with Timberlake showed that Jungkook was being modeled in his image. Just as Timberlake broke out of NSYNC into a successful solo career, so too would Jungkook, with a similar pop-forward, edgy sound that showcased his versatility and star power.

Then there was "Standing Next to You," the title track, a bombastic homage to Michael Jackson, who nearly every K-pop star, including Jungkook, considered an inspiration. Michael Jackson remains the paragon of song and dance to many K-pop stars. His legacy lives on. To properly pay tribute to Jackson required not only vocal prowess but dance skills, which Jungkook had been carefully honing over the last decade. In order to live up to the performance he had envisioned in his head, Jungkook elevated his dance. Son Sungdeuk, who had taught the teenage Jungkook to dance, said he himself became a fanboy, seeing Jungkook reach a new level of skill. In October, Jungkook flew to Budapest to film the music video, which featured several exacting dance breaks, Jackson-style footwork, and pelvic thrusts. Resting on a bed during the shoot, Jungkook mulled over what the public might think. "I think the fans will really love it. In the eyes of the public . . . maybe . . ." he said, his eyes closed and his voice trailing off. "'This kid who sang 'Seven' and '3D' can even dance like this?' I hope they react like that. 'Wow, as expected, BTS still has it. They are still at the top of their game.' I hope I can hear that. I hope there are a variety of reactions. That's why I work hard, to hear those things."

With his own name on the line, Jungkook received the acknowledgment he craved from more people than he might have ever thought possible. On her website, Diana Ross said of Jungkook, "I really like his songs and his videos. MJ is coming through all of the moves. I just think he's great!" "Standing Next to You" was remixed by Usher, who Jungkook had been a fan of growing up. In an interview with iHeartRadio, Usher shared that he was eager to collaborate with Jungkook. "'Standing Next to You' was obviously a smash when Jungkook put it out. I just wanted to participate in the magic," he said. "I love this song because it made me feel like early Michael. Something about it made me think about those days, made me think about 'Rock With You.'"

When they met on set to film the performance video, Jungkook's eyes glowed. This was a childhood fantasy being fulfilled; he smiled as he signed a copy of *Golden* to give to Usher, writing his name with a gold marker and being careful to make sure the message didn't smudge. Backstage, he mulled over how he had studied Usher's dance moves when he was a trainee, and it was an honor to work with the legendary artist now. Usher was so impressed by Jungkook that he later invited him to perform at the 2024 Super Bowl halftime show, though Jungkook was regrettably in the military by that time.

By the metrics, *Golden* was a groundbreaking success. It sold more than two million copies on the day of its release and stayed on the Billboard 200 for twenty-four consecutive weeks. Jungkook was the first K-pop solo artist to have all three of his singles reach the top ten of the Billboard Hot 100 and land three top-ten singles on the official UK Singles Chart, and the first Asian solo artist to simultaneously debut at number one on three major global charts. Still, some fans and critics were left disappointed. Compared to "Decalcomania," a raw and intimate composition, and the solo albums of RM and Suga and J-Hope, the songs on *Golden* were mainstream pop songs that had been preproduced by Western names, gathered by Braun and Bang and presented to Jungkook on a sampling platter. Unlike the solo output of RM and Suga and J-Hope, whom Jungkook himself had always admired, it was not the personal work of an artist. Harsher critics derided it as "derivative pop," a collection of songs that could have been sung by anyone. Yet most pop stars, even those in the West, do not take a heavy hand in writing their own music; thus this criticism felt unwarranted.

All creatives can relate to the pressure behind releasing your first work. Being unnecessarily precious about that debut can lead to a permanent stall, a state of paralysis. As a perfectionist, I imagine this was part of what kept Jungkook in stasis, while the other members were steadily putting out their solo music. In early November, having returned to Seoul, Jungkook went live on Weverse to discuss *Golden*'s successful release, noting that his primary goal was to be acknowledged as a pop singer. Aware of ARMY that were disappointed he had not written any songs himself, he confessed he was not in the headspace to do so. He didn't have anything to say, nothing to resolve or explore. "Even if I try to convey something, my knowledge and my vocabulary and expressions, I am really simple and direct," he said. "Lyrics are hard, but I do want to write lyrics." He seemed to be working through his own worries out loud.

Ultimately, Jungkook chose to adjust his mindset. His first solo album took the form of a new goal, a new project, a new phase in his life, where he considered his voice an instrument, a tool offered up to better songwriters to tinker with. Though he respected artists like RM and Suga and J-Hope, who wrote their own lyrics and composed their own songs, he wanted to rely on better songwriters and composers who might be able to express his feelings in a more eloquent way. By his own admission, he still lacks self-confidence; releasing his own music may take a lot of time. He was moved by the music he was presented with and wanted to make it his own—and he did to the joy of millions of fans around the world.

In the future, he may return to his own songwriting, once he has something new to express, and no doubt he plans to tackle different genres once he's returned from his military service, including songs in Korean. But with *Golden*, Jungkook achieved something remarkable. Those who criticize *Golden* for its formulaic pop sound may forget the radical transgression of the fact that these mainstream pop songs—written for artists with names like Justin Bieber—were given to a boy named Jeon Jungkook from Busan. The mere act of recording them made them groundbreaking. In a perfect world, this would not be so, but only by infiltrating and working within the existing systems can an outsider begin to enact meaningful change. To see Jungkook perform a flawless tribute to Michael Jackson on *The Tonight Show*, receiving the acknowledgment of the Western public, is moving, and an act of representation I did not think I'd ever see in my lifetime. Whether or not *Golden* was Jungkook's perfect album, whether it encompassed his entire ethos as an artist, is frankly unimportant. As a first step into the unknown, it accomplished everything it needed to do and more.

"I think it was a year where I showed who I am," Jungkook said, looking back over the start of his solo career. "It was fun. It was extremely tough. I was super happy. The goal I'm set on is not that clear, but if I just keep growing, growing and improving, and experience failure now and then, then I'll be stronger and more solid. And I'll get there without me knowing it. I'll keep moving forward."

CHAPTER 10

HIS LOYALTY

In the winter of 2023, Jungkook sat down in a chair in a pristine white marble bathroom with his hairdresser Park Naejoo. Draping a white cape over Jungkook's shoulders, secured neatly at the back of the neck, Park took a hair comb and clippers and began the arduous task of shaving Jungkook's head before the artist's military enlistment. Jungkook faced forward, with an air of acceptance, as the electric razor clicked on. At the end of November, Jungkook had held his first solo showcase, Jung Kook *Golden* Live On Stage, for twenty-eight hundred fans at Jangchung Arena, a triumphant final live performance to close out promotions for *Golden*. He performed twelve songs for the crowd, international chart-topping hits like "Seven (feat. Latto)" and "Standing Next to You," styled like a global pop star who had come home again. Yet before the last song, when Jungkook appeared, dressed comfortably in gray sweats, the mood shifted as he took on a more contemplative tone. As he gave thanks to ARMY, sitting cross-legged onstage, Jungkook seemed quietly emotional. As he prepared to give his farewell song, he said, as if in parting, "Please never forget that whenever or wherever I am, I am always with all of you."

"It was fun, right," Jungkook said quietly, his eyes closed as Park moved a comb across his hair, reflecting on the eight-month journey they had just finished. Performances for *Good Morning America* and *The Tonight Show*, collaborations with Usher, live shows on the Thames in London, in Times Square, New York, and that final showcase, his first solo show in his homeland. It was a promising start to a global pop solo career that saw him push himself further into uncharted territory. And yet it was already time to press pause.

Park made pleasant small talk, as he began removing the artist's hair in small tufts. Jungkook kept his eyes closed or looked at his phone, singing softly to himself, seeming calm and steady. He noted that washing his hair would become easy, said with a lightness that undercut the situation. As Park swept the clippings away with a sponge brush, Jungkook asked if they'd finished, brushing the stray hairs off his face. Running his hands over his newly shorn head, he smiled with enthusiasm.

Park began to weep, overcome with emotion, as Jungkook stood up and gave him a hug. "I almost cried too, but I won't," Jungkook said. "I'm holding it in."

From the background, a staff member told him that he had worked hard, the words ringing like a solace, a consolation, a quiet lament.

The scene will be familiar to any K-pop fan but is unique to the experience of K-pop boy group fandom, as every male Korean citizen is required to enlist in the military. It is a profound and emotional experience, different for every fan and every idol who goes through it, summoning Kübler-Ross's five stages of grief: denial, anger, bargaining, depression, and acceptance, as military enlistment often spells the end of an idol's peak career.

Once BTS became the biggest K-pop act in the world, fans would often discuss how long they could possibly last. Many pop groups that rose in a like manner succumbed to in-fighting or egos, contractual disputes or creative differences (the Beatles, NSYNC, One Direction, and so on). For a Korean pop group like BTS, there was the added factor of military service. With the frantic pace of the industry, now debuting more than fifty new groups per year, it's easy to understand why most expected BTS's popularity to wane by the time enlistment began. Their global popularity was a complicating factor, given how difficult the details behind Korea's military service policy can be for foreigners to grasp. But I'd argue that the unusual way in which Jungkook tackled his duty set him up for the best possible outcome: a future in which he can regroup with his bandmates and chart a course forward for his solo career.

In Korea, conscription has existed as far back as the Three Kingdoms period, according to historical records, due to frequent invasions from foreign countries by land and sea. Military service became compulsory in South Korea in 1949, when the Military Service Act was established, a few years following the liberation of Korea in 1945 from Japanese occupation. One year later, with the outbreak of the Korean War, it became indispensable. Living in Seoul, one can never forget that the Korean War never ended, having only achieved a ceasefire with an armistice agreement signed in 1953. Though tensions ebb and flow, changing month by month or year by year, the conflict lives on in the background like white noise. Seoul is some thirty-five miles away from the DMZ, the stretch of land that separates North from South. My friends and neighbors make morbid jokes that if a conflict were to arise, we would be the first to die when the bombs fell since we lived so close to the new presidential residence in Yongsan. One day, when I went to meet a friend, they asked if I'd heard the sirens that morning, calling for us to evacuate underground. "I really thought that was the end," he said with a laugh. We tried to integrate the danger in the background into our lives. Still, when I hear the roaring sound of jet engines, planes flying too closely overhead, I feel a spike of fear, knowing that it could be my last moment.

That is all to say that military conscription is an unfortunate necessity, even now, when decades of relative peace lie between us. Though the threat may be minimal, laughed off with a jest, it remains present and engraved in our shared subconscious. Military service is a duty and rite of passage among Korean men. It is an act of patriotism and men are expected to publicly embrace it with pride and perform with a smile. Yet in private, they look grim. The rules have changed over the years, but as of 2023, the year Jungkook enlisted, they are as follows: men between the ages of eighteen and thirty-five are eligible to serve and must perform their mandatory service before age twenty-eight; women are not compelled but may volunteer. There is a physical examination and a psychological test to determine if they are fit to serve; those found unfit may qualify for social service positions—working a nine-to-five-style job monitoring a subway station, for example—away from combat duty, but requiring a longer length of service. The term, which used to be two years, was shortened to an average of eighteen months in 2022. I can go on about the physical and mental burdens of enlistment, the culture of toxic masculinity, the hazing, all the many reasons why men might dread going. But as it applies to Jungkook, I'd like to focus on what is widely regarded as the most painful aspect of conscription: the loss of nearly two years of the prime of your life.

It's a loss for any man, but especially for K-pop idols, who are in the business of conveying youth and beauty onstage. Shaving their head is not a mere practicality, demanded by the military, but a symbolic act: a ceremony marking a brief exit from idol life and return to a civilian one. It also marks the end of an era. Things are never quite the same once an idol returns from service. "You became a man" is the de facto return greeting. When RM, V, and Jungkook recalled meeting J-Hope during his service, they remarked that their sunshiny Hobi had also "become a man," carrying himself with more gravitas. That's not a bad thing: idols grow, mature, they come back and find new paths. But there is always sadness in seeing one phase of life close. It is the ending of something. And unlike a natural phaseout, it is more abruptly closed, like a plant being ripped from its roots.

For fans, the start of the enlistment era marks a period of mourning. You can feel the shadow cast over the fandom, the idols themselves, as the group's eldest member inches toward thirty. Once the first one goes, the rest begin to follow like falling dominoes. A friend who worked at HYBE once told me that by their internal metrics, boy groups generally require more time than girl groups to hit their stride, the benchmark being about three years to break through with the public. Once they've had a few good years, the momentum built up behind them, it's time for the oldest members to enlist. Another friend of mine confided that one male idol friend, in the months prior to his enlistment, grew haggard and withdrawn, drinking more often than before, as he grappled with his impending loss. Even Jungkook, who tackled his enlistment with positivity, must have struggled to some degree. His final official schedule—recording the performance video with Usher for the remix of "Standing Next to You"—was a career highlight, the chance to collaborate with a childhood hero. Once the shooting had wrapped, he faced the camera that was filming behind-the-scenes footage to provide a final comment.

Jungkook announced that it was officially his last schedule and that he had learned a lot over the last eight months. Rocking back and forth on his feet, he promised to keep practicing and growing as an artist, who would deliver an even better run on his return from the military. "ARMY . . . you would probably feel melancholy by the time you watch this video . . ." he said, his eyes drifting away from the camera, as though trying to hold back some emotion. "You guys go and live your lives, and I will be back as if I had never left."

In the air, one could sense a tinge of sadness that, after all he had done, it was already over. Then there was his choice of farewell song at the showcase: "Still With You," a moody jazz song he cowrote and coproduced in 2020. The lyrics ache with yearning, the sensation of missing someone and being missed. Even if Jungkook himself held no regrets, his fans felt at least a shred of it. If Jungkook had stayed out of the military, he could have made further strides in the Western pop world, carrying the momentum of *Golden* forward. While Jungkook and the members were serving, other K-pop groups made their moves, breaking records that BTS had set. Female idols continued their careers undeterred, while younger male groups filled the empty space.

This melancholic sentiment is shared among all Korean men who serve. When I look at my two cousins, I see two different tales. Some men, like my youngest cousin, might make the decision to enlist early, ripping the Band-Aid off in their early twenties. A year into college, he has planned to go as soon as possible, taking that time to, more or less, "get it over with," setting course for the rest of his life once he's out. Yet that means he's currently adrift as he waits to serve, and he's unable to take any concrete steps for himself. He hasn't established himself before enlistment, and the repercussions of that decision will alter the course of his life. Others, like his older brother, knee-deep in postgraduate coursework, delay for as long as they can, trying to lay their foundations before their lives are interrupted. When one is drowning in anxiety, careers cannot blossom and relationships are put to the wayside.

There is grief over losing two years in the most consequential period of your life, and it takes a toll on men when faced with the difficult decision of which two years to sacrifice. Idols rarely have a choice, and it stings either way. With the rapid pace at which the industry moves, casual fans and the public will have moved on to the next new group in a matter of months; companies encourage this regardless, releasing new idols from the wings to begin their careers, waxing as those before them begin to wane. As a former fan of SM groups, I watched Super Junior phase into the military as EXO rose up, then NCT 127 stepped in after EXO, followed by NCT Dream and on to Riize.

It is a painful process for loyal fans to witness. Hence why someone like Jungkook, who is always mindful of ARMY, would handle it with the greatest care. In late May, almost seven months before his enlistment, Jungkook shared on a Weverse livestream that he would do what he could to make it easier for fans, to soften the shock of seeing him go overnight from their shining idol to a civilian soldier. Rather than shaving his head suddenly, he resolved to cut his hair slowly, bit by bit, like "*mobal*-lighting," a play on the words for hair (*mobal*) and gaslighting. As he rested his hand on his then-shoulder-length wavy hair, he tried to help ARMY imagine the process as a natural one. He kept his promise, as the months went on, trimming his hair a little at a time. The mop of curly hair became a neat mullet, then a wolf cut, until the back was trimmed for a more classic short style.

On December 5, 2023, Jungkook, V, Jimin, and RM gathered for their first group Weverse livestream since Jin's enlistment. The four of them sat down before a spread of pepperoni and Hawaiian pizzas, liter bottles of soda, and chicken wings, as though setting up for a party. Solemnly, Jungkook announced that it was their last group live broadcast before they enlisted in the military. V nonchalantly gnawed on a chicken thigh, as RM pronounced it a gloomy occasion.

For the next thirty-eight minutes, the four tried to lighten the mood, despite the heavy atmosphere, reassuring their fans that they'd be safe and well, that they'd come back stronger, that time would pass quickly, that they'd prepared content as gifts to be unwrapped in their absence. Jungkook expressed his relief that he had managed to complete his album before he left, giving him a clean finish. RM swore that one and a half years would go by in no time, and that ARMY had weathered ten and a half years by their side already. Jimin and V joked about their soon-to-be shorn heads, Jimin swearing he would go in and out quietly, without showing his shaved head to fans, like a true idol (though he revealed his shaved head on a farewell livestream of his own) and V commenting that with a shaved head he would look like the Pokémon Chimchar or Aipom. Jungkook revealed that he had already shaved his head, though he kept the buzz cut hidden beneath a black cap and hood.

It's often said that mandatory enlistment is one of the core reasons for Korea's growing gender division. According to some men, women will find it difficult to make pleas for equal treatment in society when they won't be conscripted alongside them. The matter of gendered conscription was brought to the constitutional court once in 2014 and once in 2023, the latter case by a group of five men who filed a petition on the grounds of gender equality. In both, the court unanimously upheld that the Military Service Act was constitutional and fair, for the time being.

Beyond the grief and anger men might feel, however, there is always acceptance. Enlistment is an unavoidable facet of life. In that last livestream, the final foursome expressed it:

"It's unfortunate, but it's time to go," Jimin said.

"We have to go now," they all agreed.

"Of course, we have to go," RM, a true leader, said, as if it were a matter of course.

"Everyone goes," Jungkook said.

Certainly draft dodging is not uncommon, as some search for discreet ways to be found unfit to serve. I've personally seen it all, from purposefully gaining a great deal of weight to failing the psychological exam. I've heard of families that pay money to get information on the best times to enlist, to get placed in the best base or civil station. These practices are kept hush-hush. The problem begins when one expresses an overt desire to sidestep service. The singer MC Mong was sentenced in 2011 for allegedly having two teeth unnecessarily removed to deliberately delay his enlistment. In 2023, Ravi of VIXX left the group after his suspected involvement in a corruption scandal with a military broker, who allegedly helped more than forty individuals falsify health conditions to evade enlistment. The most famous case occurred in 2002 when singer Yoo Seung-jun, who had postponed his enlistment date to travel overseas, went on a trip to Los Angeles and obtained American citizenship, renouncing his Korean citizenship and his duty to serve. The public was so outraged, the government declared it an act of desertion and banned him from entering the country. Yoo has spent the last two decades trying to fight the decision; his most recent and third attempt to receive a visa was denied in September 2024. Yoo has never been able to return to his homeland.

I don't think you'd find any Korean with much sympathy for him. The double-edged sword of a collectivist society is that the suffering is meant to be shared. Fairness, or the appearance of it, is integral, where things are not really fair—the widest gender wage gap among OECD countries in 2022, the second-fastest-rising income inequality rate as of 2023. President Yoon Suk Yeol, who won the election in 2022, campaigned on a promise to restore "fairness and common sense"; his wife has since been compared to Marie Antoinette, embroiled in a scandal after accepting a Dior handbag as a gift, and he himself was impeached after declaring martial law in 2024. So when Jin, the eldest member of BTS, approached enlistment age, and the government began to consider whether the group had earned an exemption from military service, I saw many international fans excited over the prospect. Yet I never imagined for one second that BTS would take an exemption, even if it were offered.

The public perception of BTS, the pride of the nation, would have been irreparably hurt. Even celebrities who properly serve but receive "cushy" civil service jobs that allow them to commute rather than live in barracks receive side-eye and a heap of judgment, as the public wonders whether they benefited from preferential treatment. Even documented injuries are examined with suspicion. Yes, there is precedent for receiving exemptions for notable achievements that elevate the country's "prestige" overseas, an incentive introduced in 1973 for athletes and artists. Soccer player Son Heung-min for winning gold at the 2018 Asian Games; Lee Sanghyeok, aka "Faker," and the members of South Korea's League of Legends team, who won gold at the Asian Games in 2023; pianist Seong-Jin Cho, who won the 2015 International Chopin Piano Competition with a stunning forty-minute performance of Piano Concerto No. 1 in E Minor, Op. 11. I'd argue that BTS easily made even greater contributions to the country's global presence and esteem than an Olympian has, but the incentive program itself is wildly controversial. Its recipients are not immune to public backlash. Exemptions given are few and far between, and lawmakers have not found a clear benchmark for idols, whose contributions are less tangible than a shiny medal awarded on a podium. Why should my favorite idols have to serve when others do not? What makes one better than the other? The fighting over who deserves this privilege would have been acrimonious.

In 2020, after wrestling with the matter, the National Defense

Committee of the National Assembly did pass a bill that was dubbed "the BTS law," a special law that allowed "a pop culture artist who was recommended by the Minister of Culture, Sports and Tourism to have greatly enhanced the image of Korea both within the nation and throughout the world" to defer service for an additional two years, enlisting by age thirty instead of twenty-eight. The bill passed two months before Jin's twenty-eighth birthday. The introduction to the amendment read, "Whilst these young pop stars are contributing to the image of Korea as much as people in traditional arts and sports, they are not receiving the equal protection of rights [to pursue their careers] as the others have been . . . these young pop artists tend to make the most achievements in their 20s, and to force them into military service during their prime not only hurts their careers, but also does a disservice to the nation." The matter of a full exemption remains contentious. In 2022, not long before the group visited the White House to meet President Joe Biden, Military Manpower Administration (MMA) Commissioner Lee Ki-sik connected military exemptions to matters of fairness. "[We've] been on track to reduce cases of military exemptions until now; however, the issue has been brought up again with BTS," Lee said. "It's important that we reconsider whether this kind of program is appropriate bearing in mind fairness and equality . . . which are key topics of conversation among young people in Korea."

BTS themselves never asked for an exemption and seemed reluctant to accept one, no doubt concerned over the growing furor. Without fuss, Jin announced his enlistment in December 2022 at age thirty, followed by J-Hope in April 2023 at age twenty-nine and Suga at age thirty in September. RM enlisted that December at age twenty-nine. What was surprising: Jimin, V, and Jungkook, who had two to three years left to go, chose to enlist alongside him, an aberration from other K-pop groups, who commonly enlist in waves, to keep some form of public presence and musical output. Staggering enlistment is a clear and easy attempt to minimize loss.

On December 8, a few days after their last group live, Jungkook turned his camera on to see ARMY, on his way home from a run, his shorn head still concealed by a black ball cap. Back at his apartment, Jungkook settled in for the night, taking a seat beneath the glow of a warm orange light, a setting he had saved under the name izakaya. As fans commented that they were sad, he remarked thoughtfully that he was sad too. "The army is the place that all men go. I don't have any particular thoughts on it but . . . I think that I definitely have to go." It was a glimpse at his inner self, the feelings of Jeon Jungkook, in direct contrast to his public self, the idol BTS Jung Kook, who had a duty to enlist with a patriotic smile. The clash between his two selves must have made the process more difficult.

One of the greatest mysteries behind the BTS enlistment era: as the youngest, Jungkook did not have to go for several years. So why did he choose to serve, so soon after releasing his first solo album? It was loyalty not merely to his country but to his group. The cultural nuances behind enlistment may be difficult to grasp if you are not a part of Korean society. But this factor is clear and obvious and has been throughout Jungkook's career. He is, above all, and always has been, a loyal member of BTS. In his November 2023 Weverse stream, after returning from his overseas promotions, Jungkook could not have said it more clearly: "To me, BTS is more important than my solo work." On their final group stream, he looked sentimental as he spoke of how much he missed the noise of the BTS greenrooms and dress rehearsals.

Of course, we cannot know the personal reasons behind Jungkook's decision. I can only expand on the way that decision was received and perceived. The way in which Jungkook chose to enlist—as the youngest, alongside his older brothers—is a testament to his character, his values, and the beauty of what he holds dear. By putting the group above his own individual needs, he let his actions speak louder than any words and empty platitudes and well wishes could have. "To be honest . . . we also want to see BTS as a full group sooner than later. That's why we came to that decision," Jungkook said. "I have no regrets. I feel relieved . . . I think it's a great decision."

It was a stunning act of loyalty and devotion, consistent with the loyal and devoted character that had endeared him to a global audience over the years. The fact that Jungkook, Jimin, and V did not make a fuss about enlisting so early or a show about what was a clear sacrifice made them more admirable. Following *Golden*, the time was ripe for Jungkook to blossom as a global pop star. It would have been within his rights to take advantage of the opening and put himself and his solo career first, as so many of his Western peers have: Michael Jackson, Justin Timberlake, Harry Styles, Beyoncé. Yet Jungkook quietly chose to stay with his group, an act of selflessness that was a refreshing counter to the pop status quo.

In the early hours of December 12, the day that Jungkook was due to enlist, he turned on his phone one last time for a Weverse live. At under eight minutes, the live was brief, the mood sober. He had just sent RM and V off and was doing laundry, the sound of clothes tumbling in the background. His fans teased him for running the dryer before his enlistment, treating the significant day like any other.

"I came to say my final goodbyes," he said. "Everyone be healthy and well. I'll come back safely.

"By tomorrow, all of our members will be serving in the military. Up until the moment we left, thank you so much for supporting us.

"Goodbye," he said in formal Korean. "Bye-bye," he added in English. He seemed reluctant to go.

"Bye-bye," he said with a wave. "Love you. Love you guys."

One might reason that Jungkook left for the sake of ARMY, who would hope to see BTS together as seven members sooner than later. The enlistment era may have felt bittersweet, but BTS made their name by taking the bittersweet moments in their lives, the lows and highs, and transforming them into meaningful music. While I think that's true, I consider his loyalty to be the greatest factor—to the six older brothers who are more than bandmates, more than friends, more than family, to whom he has said, over and over, that he owes everything.

"I always think that I stopped growing up mentally at age fifteen," Jungkook said in the documentary series *Burn the Stage*. He spent his middle school years training and living in a dorm, then his high school years as a full-time working idol, unable to attend school and socialize like a normal teenager. His waking hours were devoted to his six older brothers, who were always around him, exerting influence without even meaning to. Like a sponge, he absorbed their knowledge, their personality tics, their shared dreams. "The guys filled me in one by one, and I think maybe that's how I became what I am now," he said. "You might say, I could be a manifestation of all their personalities coming together."

BTS has always been strongest together, and together they changed the enlistment era, making it far less forlorn than in previous years. Each member prepared an individual cornucopia of content, prerecording songs and videos to drip-feed to their fans while they were away. RM released the album *Right Place, Wrong Person*; Jimin, his second studio album, *Muse*; Jimin and Jungkook released *Are You Sure?!*, a reality series on Disney+; Jungkook dropped his documentary *I Am*

Still, as well as the single "Never Let Go," which he recorded as a fan song for BTS's eleventh anniversary. With so many songs and videos, the fact that soldiers are now allowed to use their phones when off duty—allowing for short Weverse updates—and the shortened length of service, it feels like they've hardly been away. When you're young, two years feels like a lifetime. Post-pandemic, two years is nothing.

One day in June 2024, I looked through my news feed and was surprised to see that Jin had finished his service and was due to be discharged. Already, I thought. Despite the requests to stay away, a few fans and reporters turned up to catch his exit from the military base in Yeoncheon, setting up their tripods and cameras across from the gate. Dressed in his fatigues and beret, he exited the compound and gave a proper salute, before RM strolled up with a grin and a saxophone slung around his neck, playing a riff from "Dynamite" to welcome him. The full group reunited to celebrate his discharge, taking a selfie together for the first time in years. Four months later, J-Hope completed his service and was greeted by Jin, who was dressed in a burgundy setup and sunglasses, the two of them prepared to hold things together until the full group came out in June. The day after his discharge, Jin declared that he wanted to give "light hugs" to a thousand fans—originally three thousand fans, but HYBE talked him down to a thousand—in a fan meeting unlike any other. J-Hope flew to L.A., getting straight back to work on undisclosed projects—part of the alleged "six-month post-discharge plan," as teased by Suga.

As for Jungkook, one can only wonder what he'll do once he gets out in June 2025. He once said that he might come out with more drive. That might suggest a jump start on his second solo release, a slew of collaborations. He might return to the studio and, with clarity of mind, revisit his own songwriting. HYBE's CFO Lee Kyung-Jun shared in a November 2024 earnings call that the company was in talks with BTS to resume their group activities in 2026. There's nothing ARMY would love more than a tour to make up for the Map of the Soul Tour that was canceled due to Covid-19. Whatever direction he chooses, there's no doubt that Jungkook will do whatever he can for BTS and ARMY, whom he wants to see smile.

In that final livestream with RM, Jimin, and V, Jungkook closed out the last moments by instructing V to hold the camera steady, promising a surprise for ARMY. As V gave a thoughtful speech, motioning toward their youngest, Jungkook sprinted past the camera, his hood down, yelling out, "We were BTS!" with a broad smile, making everyone else laugh, ending their farewell stream on a joyous note. In the same flash, he would be back, in the blink of an eye, as if he'd never left.

WHO IS JUNGKOOK?

What kind of artist was BTS's Jung Kook, who is the solo artist Jung Kook, and who is Jeon Jungkook? What makes him special, the K-pop male idol that the Western public gravitated toward the most? Jungkook's solo journey has been brief, yet it's already been commemorated and exalted by the industry.

On August 30, 2024, eight and a half months after Jungkook's enlistment, HYBE, in the artist's absence, opened an exhibition dedicated to his solo career. *Golden: The Moments* was installed on the first and second floors of Le Méridien and Moxy, a dual-brand hotel in Myeongdong, a tourist district known for street food carts peddling cups of fried chicken and broiled cheese scallops in the shell, where shops in the underground subway station are stocked with Jungkook photocards and key chains and baubles.

A portrait of Jungkook on the cover of *Golden* was draped over three stories of the building. Fans reserved a time slot and went to the second floor to enter in small clusters, paying 35,000 won to receive a golden entry ticket and an emerald-green folded card, containing an image of him. Portraits from his entire promotional run were blown up and framed in roughly a dozen separate spaces, wrapping around two floors. There were areas celebrating his record-breaking accomplishments, from hitting 1.8 million Melon streams in twenty-four hours for the clean version of "Seven (feat. Latto)" to the silver Billions Club plaque he received from Spotify for hitting a billion streams with "Seven." His microphones and in-ear monitors, which he used as a member of BTS and as a solo artist, were encased in glass displays. Fans passed beneath a replica of the *Golden* marquee and posed in front of the many photo spots with their friends, giddily inching close to the mannequins that wore Jungkook's apparel, the black pin-striped suits and baggy jeans arranged along a red carpet.

In the gift shop, HYBE offered a selection of merchandise that flew off the shelves. According to fans fighting in the trenches, the most coveted items sold out each day in the first few hours, generally before noon, despite the one-item-per-person limit and a daily restock. There were fourteen printed photographs, a photocard set with fifteen cards, two posters, one photo holder key ring, one image picket or handheld fan, a "golden bar," a simple chain necklace with a gold ring, a bottle of perfume, a green velvet jewelry box, and a purple microphone charm on a key chain that resembled the custom microphone (purple, studded with Swarovski crystals) on display beside Jungkook's purple in-ears.

There was a room with white walls left like a blank canvas for fans to scrawl messages with black and blue and gold markers, and scribble hearts and crowns and bunnies. Messages were written in Korean and Chinese, English and Japanese, penned by visitors from all over the world, Taiwan and Hong Kong and Ukraine and Russia. Some fans, who had come on September 1, wished him a happy birthday. Messages of love and thanks, wishing him well and good health. "jeon jungkook the whole world loves you, i love you, jeon jungkook kpop legend," one fan wrote in simplified Chinese. "The whole world will love u," they ended simply in English. By the end of the run, the walls were completely covered. Tens of thousands of guests reportedly visited the Seoul exhibition, and *Golden: The Moments* went on the road to L.A. and Tokyo.

The exhibition included all the highlights of Jungkook's solo run and curated them in a perfect arrangement. It was a presentation of Jung Kook, the artist, all the best moments from the amazing superstar. Infallible, untouchable, a shining golden boy. On the surface that is who the public sees most often, as promoted by HYBE and presented in the media, and that is an essential component to Jungkook. His image as the perfect, can-do-everything golden *maknae*.

Yet as Jungkook explores who he is as a solo artist, the image of perfection does not seem to align with his own personal view of himself. He's said many times on his promotional tour, over and over in interviews, that he does not consider himself a genius. In a July 2023 interview for *Weverse Magazine*, as he began his solo promotions, Jungkook expressed his lingering uncertainties. "Why am I so popular? Is it just because they like my voice? Or maybe the way I dance? I still can't figure it out—about why I'm loved by all these people." Any fan who peers beneath the surface will see the contradictions within Jungkook. Modest and kind, never ostentatious and arrogant. I certainly have no way of knowing who Jungkook truly is, but when I consider how Jungkook appears to me, my thoughts wander to "Decalcomania," his unfinished song from 2019. He sings about the perfect person he sees smiling on-screen, the one who's good at everything, and not recognizing this person as himself—not recognizing Jung Kook as Jungkook. "Decalcomania," as defined by the Tate Britain, is a blotting process where paint or ink is applied to paper that's folded to create a mirror image. Jungkook sings about longing to become decalcomania, the desire to become the mirror image to the idol that everyone sees.

There is a sense of loss—and a sense of being lost. When I hear his soulful voice, I can't help but picture the boy who moved from Busan alone at age thirteen, practicing his dancing and singing without rest, as though his life depended on it. I think about "My Time," a solo song released on the 2020 BTS album *Map of the Soul: 7*. There Jungkook sings about how quickly he was forced to become an adult, the idea that his life has been a movie, a performance he has acted out on-screen for the enjoyment of others. Despite all he's accomplished, achieving his dreams of superstardom, becoming the "cool" artist he had fantasized of being as a child, he meditates on what he has lost in exchange: his childhood, relationships, precious time that has slipped through his fingers. Unlike "normal" children, Jungkook was never given the time to find himself outside of the confines of BTS. He has spoken about feeling empty without them, clinging to them as a form of identity. In *Bangtan Attic*, the introspective talk video filmed for the group's 2019 anniversary stream, he confessed, "BTS Jung Kook shines brightly, but Jungkook is shabby . . . I didn't study from when I was young and am slower than the others."

These songs are revealing of Jungkook's true inner self. They speak to the sensation of being unmoored, wanting connection and stability. A quiet anguish that speaks to a common human experience: a search for identity, to find himself. The desire to face the emptiness inside yourself and confront the question of who you are as a person. What makes me unique, what do I have to share and give to the world that only I can do? Until now Jungkook spent much of his career embodying whoever he needed to be. He could be the flawless idol, the talented superstar, the friend and confidant. Once BTS announced its group hiatus, he could finally pause and reflect; he was given a bit of time, at last, to question who he was beyond BTS. In December 2023, he and Jimin both entered the army's 5th Infantry Division in Yeoncheon County in Gyeonggi Province, about thirty-seven miles north of Seoul, where Jin was stationed as an assistant drill instructor. After completing his five weeks of basic training, he began his duties as a cook, chopping vegetables and preparing mass portions of meat with shovels to feed the ranks. Other than a single word posted to Weverse on January 17, 2024 ("Unity," the slogan of his military division), he stayed off social media until March 2024, when he shared an update:

ARMY are you doing well?
I'm doing well
I'm working out a lot
I'm doing a great job at cleaning, up to the ceiling
I'm doing well at cooking too
It's already mid-March, isn't it
I'll come see you again
I miss you a lot
Unity!

While he took time to fulfill his service, missing his dog Bam and ARMY and resting his image, HYBE continued to release and promote the content that was prepared in advance: "Never Let Go," the English fan song cowritten by Jungkook and released for 2024 BTS Festa; *Are You Sure?!*, the travel reality show with Jimin that streamed on Disney+; the documentary *I Am Still* about his solo career. Jeon Jungkook may have been away quietly living a civilian life, but for the figure Jung Kook, HYBE's global superstar, there was no such thing as rest.

•   •   •

In many ways, Jungkook's journey as an artist is one of self-discovery that is universal. All artists work to receive love and give love to the fans, but when I see Jungkook, at times I can glimpse an element of emptiness and loneliness, a vulnerability that I find very human and compelling. In preparing *Golden*, he said one reason he did not participate in the songwriting was because of his personality. He considered himself a simple person, incapable of holding on to the past, for better or worse—a trait he must have admired and acquired from Jin, who is known for the same sort of easygoing disposition. He shared the challenge of writing lyrics, perhaps subconsciously comparing himself to someone like RM—who is known for his skill with a pen— and his frustration with trying to find the right words or expressions. He called himself too simple and direct, but at other times, he has confessed that he is full of contradictions. In those contradictions, he is more relatable than any other celebrity I have ever encountered. That relatability, hand in hand with his incredible talent, is a powerful combination.

If I were to simplify it, Jungkook's global appeal can be drawn to the qualities he shares with his predecessors and peers, who walked a similar path. Michael Jackson, the consummate performer, tireless hard worker, possessing the skills to sing and dance at the highest level, while sacrificing his childhood for stardom. Justin Bieber, the experience of debuting at a young age, growing up in the spotlight with the fans witnessing his journey, fostering an unprecedented amount of closeness through social media. Harry Styles, the ineffable charisma and raw star quality that he projects without overt effort or meaning, never trying too hard. Jungkook, too, possesses a rare combination of talent and humanity, care and authenticity that have allowed him to foster a special relationship with his fans, who are the most important part of the Jungkook equation. Because ultimately, at the end of the day, as Jungkook himself would tell you, he stands where he is today because of them.

Toward the end of his final solo showcase for *Golden*, Jungkook grew sentimental, taking the time to give ARMY a heartfelt thank-you. Without them, Jung Kook the idol and Jung Kook the pop star would never have existed. As he wondered aloud what he would have been doing if he had never become an idol, a fan yelled out that no matter what he did, he would've done great at it, and he demurred. "I'm not that amazing of a person," he said. "But after meeting all of you, I could become an amazing person. It's all thanks to you."

In the globalized age, where people are more open to diverse artists and content than ever before, Jungkook was blessed to step onto the stage at the right time, to have turned the right heads, and he had the skill to take advantage of that timing when the moment arrived, backed by a dedicated legion of fans. Of course, the fans alone aren't enough: it has been almost two decades since Rain topped the *Time* 100 reader poll for most influential person yet could not make headway in the Western music industry due to the fundamental prejudices in American society that relegated people of color to side roles. Thanks to a cultural shift, brought on by a more open-minded generation willing to embrace diverse perspectives, we now live in an age when the dream of an East Asian pop superstar isn't as impossible as it once was.

The day before his surprise live show in Times Square on November 9, 2023, Jungkook went to visit a Barnes & Noble in the city, clutching an iced coffee as he took in the display for *Golden* with genuine awe. Even with all he had accomplished, he still seemed the same as he had all those years ago. As he perused the shelves, looking over the different album covers, he wondered, if he wasn't a singer, if he would come to buy someone's album to support them. Whose fan would he be, he mused to himself. On the afternoon of the show, he woke up after sleeping for twelve hours or so and ate a burrito bowl in his hotel room to recharge. The TSX Stage was located behind the billboard at the center of Times Square, and Jungkook was keenly aware that its prime position meant non-ARMY would be in attendance, putting pressure on him to perform at his absolute best.

"I'm in good condition, and it's a good day to wrap up," he said in a car on the way. "And then it's done," he added, biting his knuckle.

The Instagram account for TSX Entertainment sounded the alarm with a post: "You've got 30min New York. Jung Kook is performing LIVE on the TSX Stage. 5:30 p.m. See you soon." Yet ARMY was far ahead of the curve, having analyzed the small handful of clues (a cryptic post from Big Hit, teasing a special surprise; the TSX digital billboard switching over to Jungkook's Calvin Klein advertisement) to guess that Jungkook would be performing a surprise show. Fans accordingly scouted out the location the day before and lined up in the early hours of the morning. By the time Jungkook was ready to hit the stage, the crowd had filled the area, crammed together on the pedestrian square and neighboring blocks. He could hear their cheers from the hotel room above the square, where he warmed up his vocals. Local news helicopters flew overhead and radio hosts dubbed it his coronation as a solo artist, a grand performance in Times Square, where he ran out onto the stage, high above the crowd, to the triumphant opening chords of "Standing Next to You." "Hey, New York City! I'm Jungkook of BTS, let's have fun," he said, before giving an incredible performance of five of his songs. His microphone was on, his unprocessed vocals projecting over the city landmark, as he danced without missing a beat, each step carved into his memory from hours of practice.

The Times Square performance felt like a zenith for his solo career, a sign that Jungkook had arrived and come into his own. The hard-working boy, who kept his high school uniform hanging on a ward-robe rack backstage at *Show Champion*, had become an international pop star. One couldn't help but think back to a scene from the *BTS American Hustle Life* reality show BTS released in 2014 where Jung-kook walked along the sidewalk in Los Angeles, clutching a simple white paper flyer, asking skeptical strangers to come to see their free concert. Now, with thirty minutes advance notice, he could gather an adoring crowd—reportedly thousands in Times Square and more than 280,000 who streamed from home—and keep them enthralled.

At the end of it all, the core of Jungkook's success, the key mecha-nism behind his coronation as a pop star, comes down to the nature of Jungkook, of the honest and openhearted boy who put his group and his fans before himself. No matter where he went, his two pillars—BTS and ARMY—stayed ever present in his mind. In an interview with 103.5 KISS FM, he spoke about how much he missed each of his older brothers. "Most of all, when I engage in solo activities, I deeply miss the moments we shared together," he said. "I missed the casual mo-ments when we were doing different things in the waiting room, and even going to Suga-*hyung*'s concert, I missed that, and even when per-forming alone, I missed it . . . I want to stand onstage with the mem-bers as soon as possible."

I remember the first time I heard "Begin," a solo song by Jung-kook on *Wings*, released in 2016. He was nineteen years old then, three years into performing as Jung Kook of BTS. As RM recounted on a livestream, Jungkook wanted to write his own lyrics, but could not convey his feelings. So it was up to RM to capture Jungkook's story, and together they drew a poignant self-portrait. Around January 2016, the seven members of BTS had gathered together to cry, airing their grievances and comforting one another. According to RM, Jungkook was not prone to tears or complaints. Jungkook never spoke up when he was having a hard time, always diligently performing his work, telling the other members he was just fine. But on that day, Jungkook cried openly for the first time, surprising all his older brothers, who had never seen their *maknae* weep so much. When asked to share his hardships, "Jungkook said, 'I don't have any hardships . . . at such a young age, when I knew nothing, I signed a contract, came up here, and, because it's what I wanted to do, I sang and danced as hard as I could,'" RM recounted. What Jungkook tearfully confessed was that it only hurt to see them suffer—the six older brothers he lived with, who had helped him grow and to whom he pledged his love and loyalty.

The first time I heard "Begin," I was surprised. Even back then, in 2016, Jungkook was often talked about as the member with the most solo potential, as the golden *maknae*, the all-rounder center of the group. I expected a light and easy song that would highlight his blossoming skills as a pop act, not a nearly four-minute ballad about how much he loved his *hyungs*. Jungkook sang about how much he owed to them, the ones who took the small and empty boy, lacking his own "scent" and identity, and taught him how to feel. I have had conversations with members of the K-pop industry from rival companies, who have remarked, with great cynicism, that the only reason why BTS hasn't broken up is due to HYBE's iron fist, as it spent years demanding that all the members remain on equal footing with one another. Only BTS knows the truth, but given every small gesture of support, of pride and affection that the members share with each other after ten years have passed, I doubt that's the case.

The making of Jung Kook and the triumph of BTS comes down to a single word: devotion. It is the devotion between Jungkook and the members of BTS, who raised him and made him who he is. It's

Jungkook's single-minded devotion to his craft, the countless hours he's spent in rehearsal rooms and practice spaces, singing and dancing, building up his world-class skills from nothing. It's his devotion to his journey as an artist, as he takes the slow and steady steps to find his mode of self-expression. His devotion to his country, as he fulfills his military service without complaint. And his devotion to ARMY, the fans he cherishes above all, who return his devotion with their own in spades. As an admirer of his, I can say that, no matter what happens next, whatever path he chooses to take, it has been a privilege to watch his rise, to hear the name Jungkook on the English-speaking lips of TV and radio hosts, editors, directors, producers, at the top of the world. To see an honest and hardworking boy from Busan become an international pop superstar.

ACKNOWLEDGMENTS

To my parents, whose love and support are limitless, without whom I could not follow my own dreams. To my sister, who pulled me into K-pop in the first place, turning it into a shared activity that always brought me joy. I love you and I thank you three, above all, always.

To my agent Clare and my editor Hana, without whose patience and wisdom this book would not be possible. To Jonathan Karp, whose vision and passion for this book truly inspired me. Thank you for your trust. To the team at S&S, thank you for your hard work and care.

To my friends in real life and online, who kept me going through many sleepless nights, my sounding board on a million different topics. Thank you for showing me the beauty of fandom and friendship that transcends time zones.

To my past and present colleagues, who encouraged me, suffered with me, celebrated with me, without whom I would never have found the courage to break free.

To BTS and ARMY, whose passion and persistence changed the course of many lives, including mine. *Borahae.*

NOTES

INTRODUCTION: WHAT IS IT ABOUT JUNGKOOK?

1   *It took forty seconds*: "Jungkook's GMA Concert Tickets Sell Out in Seconds," Jungkook Global, July 14, 2023, https://jungkookglobal.com/news/f/jungkook %E2%80%99s-gma-concert-tickets-sell-out-in-seconds.

1   *. . . a crowd of 5,000 across three days at AX-Korea in 2014*: Seunghun Ji, "The Group BTS Will Have Time to Look Back on the Last Performance Together through '2024 Bangbang Concert,'" *Maeil Business Newspaper*, June 4, 2024, https://www .mk.co.kr/en/musics/11033050.

1   *two sold out nights at London's Wembley Stadium in 2019 for 120,000*: Mark Savage, "BTS Are the First Korean Band to Headline Wembley Stadium," BBC.com, June 2, 2019, https://www.bbc.com/news/entertainment-arts-48487862.

2   *number in the tens of millions by unofficial counts*: Kat Moon, "Inside the BTS ARMY, the Devoted Fandom With an Unrivaled Level of Organization," *Time*, November 18, 2020, https://time.com/5912998/bts-army/.

3   *1iota opened the raffle for tickets at 12:00 p.m. EST and closed it down before one minute had passed*: Mun Wansik, "방탄소년단 정국, 美GMA 서머 콘서트 K팝 솔로 최초 출격→티켓 매진 대란..역시 '월드 슈스,'" *Star News*, July 10, 2023, https://m.entertain.naver.com /article/108/0003165840.

3   *the line of ticket holders began to form on Monday at Seventy-Second Street, stretching down Fifth Avenue*: Kirsten Fleming, "We're Waiting Five Days—in 90-Degree NYC Heat—to See BTS' Jungkook," *New York Post*, July 13, 2023, https://nypost.com /2023/07/13/were-waiting-in-line-five-days-to-see-bts-jungkook-in-nyc/.

3   *co-opting the Apple Store bathroom on Madison Avenue as an outpost*: r/bangtan, "Jungkook @ Good Morning America (GMA) Summer Concert Series 2023 Questions and Meet up Megathread," Reddit, July 2023, https://www.reddit .com/r/bangtan/comments/14wavn2/jungkook_good_morning_america_gma _summer_concert/.

3   *By Thursday afternoon, more than seven hundred people stood in line . . .* : Ibid.

3   *By sunrise, Jungkook, who had flown in from Seoul two days prior, made his way to Rumsey Playfield*: *Jung Kook: I Am Still*, directed by Park Jun-soo (HYBE, 2024).

3   *Still nursing a stubborn sore throat that had stuck around for several weeks . . .* : Ibid.

4   . . . *gained eighteen million views on YouTube by the time of the recording*: Good Morning America Summer Concert Series, *Good Morning America*, July 14, 2023.

5   *"he was born to perform & Rock on Stage Superstar Jungkook"* . . . : Ibid.

5   *the hundreds of fans who attended BTS's first public showcase*: "BTS on First Impressions, Secret Career Dreams and Map of the Soul: 7 Meanings," The Tonight Show Starring Jimmy Fallon, YouTube, February 25, 2020, https://www.youtube.com/watch?v=v_9vgidPJ8g.

8   *("everyone in BTS, except for Jungkook, he's too pretty for my taste.")*: "Yokel Hero," *The Simpsons*, season 32, episode 14, aired March 7, 2021, on Fox.

8   *topped the inaugural Billboard K-Pop Artist 100 list*: Jeff Benjamin, "The 2024 Billboard K-Pop Artist 100," *Billboard* (online), February 27, 2024, https://www.billboard.com/lists/k-pop-artist-100-list-2024-ranked/.

8   *being dedicated to the group*: JK, "Golden," BTS, Weverse (livestream), November 3, 2023, https://weverse.io/bts/live/0-128993548.

8   *potential "breakout" star*: Jeff Benjamin, "BTS, Blackpink, Taemin & Jungkook Lead Tumblr's Most Popular K-Pop Stars of 2017 Summer: Exclusive," *Billboard* (online), October 5, 2017, https://www.billboard.com/pro/tumblr-most-popular-kpop-stars-summer-2017-bts-blackpink/.

9   *stocks down by nearly 28 percent*: Thania Garcia, "BTS 'Hiatus' Spurs 28% Drop in HYBE Stock; Company Insists Word Was Mistranslated," *Variety* (online), June 15, 2022, https://variety.com/2022/music/news/bts-hiatus-hybe-stock-drop-1235295190/.

9   *They could even take a break if they so wished, which Jungkook did for almost five months*: "[슈취타] EP.15 SUGA with Jung Kook," BANGTANTV, YouTube, July 29, 2023, https://www.youtube.com/watch?v=ocDDLPLKe70.

9   *flew seventy-two hours round-trip to Argentina*: "[슈취타] EP.12 SUGA with Jin #2023BTSFESTA," BANGTANTV, YouTube, June 10, 2023, https://www.youtube.com/watch?v=tZscK8j5a5w.

10 *nicknamed the golden* maknae (maknae *meaning youngest) by RM*: "130514 랩몬 & 정국," BANGTANTV, YouTube, May 16, 2013, https://www.youtube.com/watch?v=9DD4xUC83tM.

10 *"The moment I saw the cover [of Golden], I thought, ah, a true pop star . . ."*: "[슈취타] EP.21 SUGA with 정국 II," BANGTANTV, YouTube, November 4, 2023, https://www.youtube.com/watch?v=0RKnjVL2kWA.

11 *my experience covering a HYBE group for the March 2023 issue of* Vogue: Monica Kim, "Tomorrowland: How Seoul Became Pop Culture's New Frontier," *Vogue*, February 15, 2023, https://www.vogue.com/article/seoul-portfolio-march-2023.

12 *"DNA," which they performed thrice across the city*: Monica Kim, "BTS Takes on L.A. With *Vogue*—And It's 'Hella Lit,'" Vogue.com, January 25, 2018, https://www.vogue.com/article/bts-kpop-band-in-los-angeles-vogue-video-shoot.

12 *his shaky grasp of English*: JK, "졸리다," BTS, Weverse (livestream), August 3, 2023, https://weverse.io/bts/live/4-126872661.

12 *ate the same red-hot Buldak noodles*: JK, "모두 아프지말고 편안한 하루 되세요," BTS, Weverse (livestream), April 25, 2023, https://weverse.io/bts/live/3-117661738.

13 *practically raised him, per his own admission*: BTS: Burn the Stage, episode 3, "Just

Give Me a Smile," directed by Park Jun-soo, aired April 5, 2018, on YouTube, https://www.youtube.com/watch?v=RmZ3DPJQo2k.

13   *ARMY is an international force of fans who are among the most internet-savvy in the world*: Moon, "Inside the BTS ARMY."

13   *his dancing style, which can be traced back to Michael Jackson*: *Thriller 40*, directed by Nelson George (Showtime, 2023).

CHAPTER 1: HIS UNDERDOG STORY

16   *In 2024, the city was home to about 9.6 million residents*: Seoul Metropolitan Government, City Overview, Population, accessed January 2025, https://english.seoul .go.kr/seoul-views/meaning-of-seoul/4-population/.

16   *New York City was estimated to have about 29,303 residents per square mile in 2020*: United States Census Bureau, QuickFacts, New York City, New York, accessed January 2025, https://www.census.gov/quickfacts/fact/table/newyorkcitynewyork /PST045224.

16   *the percentage of the population living in the greater capital area (50.6 percent) was the largest . . .* : Park Soon-bin, "Korea Has Highest Capital Population Concentration of OECD—BOK Says It's Hurting Birth Rates," *Hankyoreh*, November 3, 2023, https://english.hani.co.kr/arti/english_edition/e_national/1114875.html.

17   *the Big Three had amassed financial resources, stacked talent rosters, and cultivated relationships*: Jang Yunjung, "The Big 3 of Korean Pop Music and Entertainment," *The Dong-A Ilbo*, July 26, 2011, https://www.donga.com/en/article/all/20110726 /401789/1.

17   *idol music was generally regarded as a low form of entertainment by the Korean public*: Kang Hyun-kyung, "Rise of K-Pop Singers: From Low Culture 'Ttanttara' to Artists," *The Korea Times*, March 29, 2018, https://www.koreatimes.co.kr/www/art /2025/01/398_246443.html.

18   *Winter of the SM Entertainment girl group Aespa once spoke about this training . . .* : *Knowing Bros*, episode 303, aired October 23, 2021, on JTBC, https://www .youtube.com/watch?v=m2RK7E6Dw1o.

18   *"What did we say we'd do if you use satoori"*: "SEVENTEEN TV 시즌4," Want Woo Thailand, YouTube, November 1, 2013, https://www.youtube.com /watch?v=QVcpXKJ5oDU.

19   *made the SBS Eight O'Clock News*: *SBS 8뉴스*, September 11, 2011, https://www .youtube.com/watch?v=4dOWmskPPP4.

19   *It even went on to inspire a variety show called Are We Strangers*: Lee Woo-in, "'우리 가 남이가' PD 'BTS "팔도강산" 듣고 프로 기획,'" TV Report, Naver, February 20, 2018, https://m.entertain.naver.com/now/article/213/0001019270.

19   *. . . it was because of that song that he went to his Big Hit audition*: *New Yang Nam Show*, season 2, episode 1, aired February 23, 2017, on Mnet.

20   *"Sa-too-ri?" he said . . .* : BTS, "BTS Live : JK," BTS, Weverse (livestream), originally posted on VLIVE, November 30, 2016, https://weverse.io/bts/live/2-105470541.

20   *The company was financially strapped due to the public's poor reception of Glam*: Myeongseok Kang, *Beyond the Story: 10-Year Record of BTS* (New York: Flatiron Books, 2023), 53.

21 *the official book, positions Big Hit as a David going against the Goliaths*: Ibid., 41.

21 *there was little competition among new boy groups at the time*: Ibid., 94.

21 *In* Beyond the Story, *writer Kang Myeongseok makes a point to call out EXO*: Ibid., 73–74.

22 *in the one hundred days leading up to EXO's debut, SM dropped twenty-three teaser videos*: Ibid., 74.

22 *. . . didn't receive its first comment, according to Kang, until three days after it was posted*: Ibid.

22 *Kang talks about the blog, a Twitter account, a fancafe, and, importantly, the YouTube channel BANGTANTV*: Ibid.,75–76.

22 *On December 22, 2012, Jin introduced himself*: 방탄소년단 (@BTS_twt), "안녕하세요 저는 오늘부터 방탄 트위터를 같이 쓸 "진" 입니다! 잘 부탁 드려요~~ 자주 만나용ㅋㅋ," X, December 22, 2012, https://x.com/BTS_twt/status/282409074832850944.

22 *a second grainy selfie captioned "my lower lip is charming.jpg"*: 방탄소년단 (@BTS_twt), "아랫입술이 매력.jpg," X, December 24, 2012, https://x.com/BTS_twt/status/282872331342792704.

22 *"We heard that there are companies that wouldn't allow their artists to use SNS, but we can use it freely"*: "01/14 The Bridges Magazine," translated by KIMMYYANG, *BTS Interview Archive* (blog), July 24, 2021, https://btsinterviews.wordpress.com/2021/07/24/01-14-the-bridges-magazine/.

23 *"What we want is one company dinner"*: "흔한 연습생의 크리스마스 Video Edit by 방탄소년단," BANGTANTV, YouTube, December 23, 2012, https://www.youtube.com/watch?v=fnZsn-So-AU.

23 *"Our company, our boss, I don't like any of you . . ."*: BTS, "흔한 연습생의 크리스마스 (Full Version)," Soundcloud (streaming), January 11, 2013, https://soundcloud.com/bangtan/full-version.

23 *. . . RM revealed a piece of Bang's criticism . . .*: "130107 RAP MONSTER," BANGTANTV, YouTube, January 7, 2013, https://www.youtube.com/watch?v=srk5_rQVmmA.

23 *Jin said that the boss had commented on his weight gain*: "130122 진," BANGTANTV, YouTube, January 26, 2013, https://www.youtube.com/watch?v=L48qIsKFeCg.

23 *RM turned on "Kiss the Rain" . . .*: "130225 RAP MONSTER (Feat. SUGA)," BANGTANTV, YouTube, February 25, 2014, https://www.youtube.com/watch?v=YY-Fal6_WGfg.

23 *J-Hope showed off his new pants*: "130227 J HOPE & 정국," BANGTANTV, YouTube, March 5, 2013, https://www.youtube.com/watch?v=aaPnq3aaBvs.

23 *The first Bangtan Bomb, "130617 VJ Jungkook"*: "[BANGTAN BOMB] VJ 정국 - BTS (방탄소년단)," BANGTANTV, YouTube, June 19, 2013, https://www.youtube.com/watch?v=ELIOdaJ77lY.

23 *Jungkook sang a comedic trot (a Korean music genre) rendition of "N.O . . ."*: "[BANGTAN BOMB] N.O (Trot ver.) by Jungkook and (Opera ver.) by BTS," BANGTANTV, YouTube, October 23, 2013, https://www.youtube.com/watch?v=Qs2unC6IwBc.

24 *V began practicing a dance set to Run DMC's "It's Tricky . . ."*: "[BANGTAN BOMB] it's tricky is title! BTS, here we go! (by Run–D.M.C.)," BANGTANTV, YouTube, February 7, 2015, https://www.youtube.com/watch?v=PSdgzdDMIeE.

24 *Jungkook and V lip-synching to Linkin Park . . .* : "[BANGTAN BOMB] Just watching Jung Kook lip sync show," BANGTANTV, YouTube, February 2, 2014, https://www.youtube.com/watch?v=0-XR2iLEUQY.

24 *. . . the boys tossing their heads and crab-walking to "Show Me Your Bba Sae" . . .* : "[BANG-TAN BOMB] Show Me Your BBA SAE!?!? - BTS (방탄소년단)," BANGTANTV, You-Tube, March 19, 2016, https://www.youtube.com/watch?v=ttSLLgU8F_I.

24 *born in Busan by the sea, where he grew up with his father, mother, and older brother in Mandeok-dong*: Busan Metropolitan City, "BTS Pilgrimage to Jungkook's Home-town, Mandeok-dong, Busan," https://www.visitbusan.net/index.do?menuCd=DOM_000000302002001000&uc_seq=476&lang_cd=en.

24 *his father dressed up as Santa Claus for Christmas*: "[2019 FESTA] BTS (방탄소년단) '방탄다락,'" BANGTANTV, YouTube, June 13, 2019, https://www.youtube.com/watch?v=CPW2PCPYzEE.

24 *his mother took him to the playground in the evenings to exercise*: jungkook vids slow (@jjklve), "jungkook playing basketball and reminding of his childhood," X, August 21, 2021, https://x.com/jjklve/status/1429104757474578435.

25 *his grandmother lovingly raised the two baby chicks . . .* : *BTS Memories of 2019* (Big Hit Three Sixty Co., Ltd. & Play Company Corp., 2020), DVD.

25 *"I'm really grateful for that. To my parents" . . .* : BTS, "BTS Live: 전 눈물이 없는 사람입니다," BTS, Weverse (livestream), originally posted on VLIVE, June 3, 2019, https://weverse.io/bts/live/0-105457296.

25 *his dream to be a global pop star, which according to Bang Si-hyuk, had always been his ambition*: Alex Barasch, "The K-Pop King," *The New Yorker*, October 14, 2024.

26 *"Factory Girls"*: John Seabrook, "Factory Girls," *The New Yorker*, October 8, 2012.

27 *"The boys were fun to watch—heavily made-up moussed male androgynes doing strenuous rhythmic dances . . ."*: Ibid.

28 *"I found myself wondering why overproduced, derivative pop music . . ."*: Ibid.

28 *"perpetual foreigner . . ."*: Frank H. Wu, "Where Are You Really From? Asian Amer-icans and the Perpetual Foreigner Syndrome," *Civil Rights Journal* 6, no. 1 (Winter 2002).

29 *to talk with those their own age*: "[아카이브K 오리지널] #035. 방탄소년단 1편, 지금 다시 하라고 한다면 절대 못하죠," Archive-K, YouTube, December 18, 2023, originally aired on SBS in 2021, https://www.youtube.com/watch?v=wtgAUap1K2s; .

29 *"Actually, talking with your peers about what you're feeling at the moment . . ."*: Ibid.

30 *thrilled to receive even a little interest*: 방탄소년단 (@BTS_twt), X, February 12, 2013, https://x.com/BTS_twt/status/301255151317032961.

30 *"It became really natural . . ."*: "[아카이브K 오리지널] #035. 방탄소년단 1편, 지금 다시 하라고 한다면 절대 못하죠," Archive-K.

30 *Some studies suggest it has to do with human empathy*: Sunkyu Jun et al., "Effects of Un-derdog (vs. Top Dog) Positioning Advertising," *International Journal of Advertising* 34, no. 3 (May 27, 2015): 495–514, https://doi.org/10.1080/02650487.2014.996199.

30 *companies to engender attachment*: Ibid.

30 *"from normal working-class families"*: One Direction: This Is Us, directed by Morgan Spurlock (Tristar Pictures, 2013).

30 *"We tried to stay away from the typical boy band thing . . ."*: Ibid.

31 . . . *400-meter relay, expecting B1A4 or Teen Top to win* . . . : "BTS, B1A4 - M 400m Relay Final, BTS, B1A4 - 400m 릴레이 결승 @ 2015 Idol Star Championships," TV-People, YouTube, October 6, 2015, originally aired on MBC, https://www.youtube.com/watch?v=quLibKURtkc.

31 *"This is like real life . . ."*: Araceli Seráfico (@araceliserafico1008), comment on "[BANGTAN BOMB] a 400-meter relay race @ 아육대," BANGTANTV, YouTube, 2020, https://www.youtube.com/watch?v=9ZQ5koAQCtw&lc=Ugya0iJ5Wnoal OCzR6N4AaABAg.

31 *fifteen-year-old Jungkook, removed from his family* . . . : "130208 정국," BANGTANTV, YouTube, February 12, 2013, https://www.youtube.com/watch?v=NURcgb N4DGA.

32 *2015 to 2017 is named a particularly difficult period in the official biography*: Kang, *Beyond the Story*, 154.

32 *accusations of sajaegi, or chart manipulation*: Ibid., 155–56.

32 *Jungkook made a solo appearance on* Flower Crew . . . : *Flower Crew (꽃놀이패)*, "Pilot Episode 1," aired July 15, 2016, on VLIVE.

32 *Jo issued an apology*: Eunhwe Jo, "'꽃놀이패' 서장훈 "불편한 부분 있었다면 죄송하게 생각한다," Xportsnews, Naver, June 7, 2016, https://m.entertain.naver.com/article/311/0000616222.

32 *an estimated $32.6 billion contribution to the South Korean economy over one decade*: Lee Min-hyung, "BTS 10th Anniversary Celebration to Supercharge Domestic Economy," *The Korea Times*, June 15, 2023, https://www.koreatimes.co.kr/www/biz/2025/01/602_353041.html.

32 *Approximately eight hundred thousand foreign tourists visit the country each year* . . . : Ibid.

33 *In 2023, the Korea Post made special commemorative stamps* . . . : Ibid.

33 *Jungkook, who appeared to be on good terms with Jo, gave the man a warm embrace*: You Quiz on the Block, episode 99, aired March 24, 2021, on tvN.

CHAPTER 2: HIS WORK ETHIC

36 *"Not to the point of being an all-rounder . . ."*: "130514 랩몬 & 정국," BANGTANTV, YouTube, May 16, 2013, https://www.youtube.com/watch?v=9DD4xUC83tM.

36 *"BTS Jungkook Is Good at Everything - Golden Maknae Moments" has earned more than nineteen million views* . . . : "BTS Jungkook Is Good at Everything - Golden Maknae Moments," edited by Kookies And Cream, YouTube, April 17, 2018, https://www.youtube.com/watch?v=5y3fRM6kvfU.

36 *"Jungkook, you are known for being great at everything . . ."*: "BTS Responds to Rumors about Their Fan Base and Potential Stage Names (Extended) | The Tonight Show," The Tonight Show Starring Jimmy Fallon, YouTube, July 13, 2021, https://www.youtube.com/watch?v=qKuwYOIS_VQ.

36 *"He's like top-tier out of just like the whole industry . . ."*: "Chan's 'Room,'" episode 148, Stray Kids, VLIVE (livestream), March 13, 2022, https://vlivearchive.com/post/1-28341329.

36 *"I think because of you, our group was able to go this far"*: "2021 Winter Package in Gangwon," *BTS Winter Package* (Big Hit Entertainment, 2021).

37 *Kitagawa scouted fresh talent*: Bunna Takizawa et al., "No. 1 Hits, Sexual Abuse Scandal Mark Kitagawa's Lasting Legacy," *The Asahi Shimbun*, September 12, 2023, https://www.asahi.com/ajw/articles/15003474.

37 *Kitagawa's legacy was marred by accusations of sexual abuse that spanned decades*: Yuri Kageyama, "Johnny & Associates Founder Kitagawa Sexually Assaulted Hundreds of Teens, Investigation Finds," AP News, August 29, 2023, https://apnews.com/article/japan-johnnys-sexual-abuse-executive-resign-investigation-cd1b8c226ae52ef4ff3c8e7d5d78bcc4.

37 *Guinness World Records removed his distinctions in 2023*: Guinness World Records, statement published September 6, 2023, https://www.guinnessworldrecords.jp/news/press-release/2023/9/a-statement-from-guinness-world-records-757941.

37 *one inspiration for the idol trainee system was Detroit's Motown Records*: John Seabrook, "Factory Girls," *The New Yorker*, October 8, 2012.

37 *"This department would groom and polish them . . ."*: "Interview with Maxine Powell," WGBH radio station, September 1995.

38 *Seventeen, the Pledis Entertainment boy group with thirteen members, received gag comedy lessons . . .*: "Hoshi of Seventeen teaches the "3 keys of comedy" | EP.12 Seventeen Hoshi | Salon Drip2," TEO, YouTube, October 24, 2023, https://www.youtube.com/watch?v=qRN7TUC_CF0.

39 *took selfie and TikTok lessons*: "(ENG)Suffocating Timing Talk of Wonyoung Who Is Busy Winking and Precious Child Leeseo, Born In," MMTG, YouTube, April 14, 2022, https://www.youtube.com/watch?v=OOO6IyRPJq0.

39 *more than 1.26 million people aged fifteen to twenty-nine were unemployed in 2023 . . .*: Yonhap, "Over 1.2 Mil. Young People without Jobs after Graduation: Data," *The Korea Times*, August 27, 2023, https://www.koreatimes.co.kr/www/nation/2025/01/113_357866.html.

39 *a viral photograph taken during the summer monsoon in 2022*: CNA, August 19, 2022, https://www.channelnewsasia.com/commentary/seoul-flood-monsoon-rain-climate-change-south-korea-2887286.

40 *"2013 February eighth. Jungkook's daily log"*: "130208 정국," BANGTANTV, YouTube, February 12, 2013, https://www.youtube.com/watch?v=NURcgbN4DGA.

40 *The dormitory was tucked on a side street in Nonhyeon-dong, Gangnam*: "Run BTS! 2022 Special Episode - Telepathy Part 2," BANGTANTV, YouTube, August 23, 2022, https://www.youtube.com/watch?v=nbRKyymm4Eg.

40 *Sometimes, he would go there to buy a cup of instant ramen noodles . . .*: *You Quiz on the Block*, episode 99, aired March 24, 2021, on tvN, https://www.youtube.com/watch?v=CqA1Rq2Ty6Q.

40 *buy a single banana milk after practice*: "Spotify | Billions Club: The Series featuring Jung Kook," Spotify, YouTube, December 19, 2023, https://www.youtube.com/watch?v=fiUY03iIvGY.

40 *these spots offered the future BTS members a reprieve*: "Run BTS! 2022 Special Episode - Telepathy Part 2," BANGTANTV.

41 *all seven boys slept in a single bedroom with three sets of bunk beds . . .*: *BTS Rookie King: Channel Bangtan*, episode 1, SBS MTV, September 3, 2013.

41 *he was five foot seven*: "BTS," KBS World, February 21, 2014, http://world.kbs.co.kr/service/contents_view.htm?lang=j&menu_cate=artist&id=&board_seq=347978&page=40.

41 *waited to shower until everyone else had fallen asleep*: BTS: Burn the Stage, episode 3, "Just Give Me a Smile," directed by Park Jun-soo, aired April 4, 2018, on YouTube, https://www.youtube.com/watch?v=RmZ3DPJQo2k.

41 *Jin, the oldest, drove the boys in his Mini Cooper*: 방탄소년단 (@BTS_twt), X, October 8, 2013, https://x.com/BTS_twt/status/390981052241420289.

41 *The ceremony was attended by a smattering of photographers from BTS's first fansites*: The Qoo message board, February 5, 2021, https://theqoo.net/index.php?mid=hot&filter_mode=normal&document_srl=1835019099.

41 *Jungkook was seen smiling for the cameras . . .* : Ibid.

41 *Bang Si-hyuk rented a practice space*: Myeongseok Kang, *Beyond the Story: 10-Year Record of BTS* (New York: Flatiron Books, 2023), 41.

41 *In one of four basement studios*: "[공포]연습실에서 봤던 기이한 현상과 귀신 이야기!(심장주의)," Bitoon, YouTube, December 9, 2018, https://www.youtube.com/watch?v=-UrSWq-S7zI.

41 *On an average day, the boys woke up around 10 a.m. . . .* : Kang, *Beyond the Story*, 52, 55–56.

42 *Kim Sung-eun, who trained Jin, V, and Jungkook for more than one year*: Sunhwa Dong, "K-Pop's Hidden Hero: BTS, TWICE's Vocal Trainer Kim Sung-Eun," *The Korea Times*, April 26, 2020, https://www.koreatimes.co.kr/www/art/2025/01/398_288428.html.

42 *J-Hope and Jimin, trained and naturally gifted dancers, provided additional assistance . . .* : Kang, *Beyond the Story*, 57–58.

42 *"Hardship was an expectation at the time . . ."*: BTS Monuments: Beyond the Star, directed by Park Jun-soo (Disney+, 2023).

42 *Jungkook had recorded his first dance video*: "Dance practice by 정국 of 방탄소년단," BANGTANTV, YouTube, February 4, 2013, https://www.youtube.com/watch?v=Q3lL7zQ7kkA.

42 *a routine choreographed by Kyle Hanagami*: "Kyle Hanagami | SAVE YOUR GOODBYE," Kyle Hanagami, YouTube, May 28, 2011, https://www.youtube.com/watch?v=Nujl183jTWk.

42 *"Today I finally graduated . . ."*: "130208 정국," BANGTANTV, YouTube, February 12, 2013, https://www.youtube.com/watch?v=NURcgbN4DGA.

43 *one of 36 boy groups to debut that year*: "[Video] 2013 K-Pop Group Debuts," Soompi, January 3, 2014, https://www.soompi.com/article/566721wpp/video-2013-k-pop-group-debuts.

43 *. . . after boarding the twelve-hour economy-class trip from Seoul to Los Angeles . . .* : "흔한 연습생 막내의 미국 춤 연수기 (1)," *Bangtan Blog*, February 6, 2013, https://btsblog.ibighit.com/m/54.

43 *Son Sungdeuk, who chose Jungkook as the most promising trainee*: "[어딜맨 EP.11] 안무가 손성득이 직접 말하는 방탄소년단부터 투모로우바이투게더까지!," OK Pop!!, YouTube, September 27, 2022, https://www.youtube.com/watch?v=avcfbe1g_Eg.

43 *he emerged from Tom Bradley International Terminal at LAX* . . . : "흔한 연습생 막내의 미 국 춤 연수기 (1)," *Bangtan Blog.*

44 *Jungkook posed in the middle of a street*: Ibid.

44 *On the first day, Jungkook took two or three classes at Movement Lifestyle*: Ibid.

44 *BigBang, whom the members of BTS idolized*: "[슈취타] EP.3 SUGA with 태양," BANG-TANTV, YouTube, January 18, 2023, https://www.youtube.com/watch?v=N43HXJCShx8.

44 *Jungkook experienced a "mental breakdown"*: "흔한 연습생 막내의 미국 춤 연수기 (1)," *Bangtan Blog.*

44 *Son and Jungkook reviewed a difficult snippet*: "정국이의 춤 연습," BANGTANTV, You-Tube, February 5, 2013, https://www.youtube.com/watch?v=Bpcczy88UWg.

44 *Jungkook woke up and went to the Korean restaurant* . . . : "흔한 연습생 막내의 미국 춤 연수 기 (1)," *Bangtan Blog.*

44 *he went to a coin laundromat*: Ibid.

44 *On weekends, Jungkook went to the beach*: "흔한 연습생 막내의 미국 춤 연수기 (2)," *Bangtan Blog*, February 7, 2013, https://btsblog.ibighit.com/m/53.

44 *He ate corn dogs and lo mein*: "흔한 연습생 막내의 미국 춤 연수기 (1)," *Bangtan Blog.*

44 *Instructed by Bang Si-hyuk to let Jungkook enjoy himself and experience new things*: "[어 딜맨 EP.11] 안무가 손성득이 직접 말하는 방탄소년단부터 투모로우바이투게더까지!," OK Pop!!

44 *Jungkook struck a one-handed handstand that he called "the Nike"*: "흔한 연습생 막내의 미 국 춤 연수기 (1)," *Bangtan Blog.*

44 *and again on the manicured lawn*: "흔한 연습생 막내의 미국 춤 연수기 (2)," *Bangtan Blog.*

44 *skateboard for the first time and started to ride it* . . . : Ibid.

45 *He watched the sun set on the beach*: Ibid.

45 *Jungkook went to the Lobster on Santa Monica Pier* . . . : Ibid.

45 *"He gained the eyes of a tiger"*: "[어딜맨 EP.11] 안무가 손성득이 직접 말하는 방탄소년단부터 투모로우바이투게더까지!" OK Pop!!

45 *"I'm not someone with very high self-esteem . . ."*: Myeongseok Kang, "Jung Kook: 'I've Been Changing a Bit,'" *Weverse Magazine*, July 20, 2023, https://magazine.weverse.io/article/view/825?ref=&lang=en.

46 *the members worried about having enough songs to fill the set list* . . . : *BTS: Burn the Stage*, episode 1, "I'd Do It All," directed by Park Jun-soo, aired March 29, 2018, on YouTube, https://www.youtube.com/watch?v=j6zWwAoEi_w.

46 *There were more than five hundred thousand preorders for* Wings *in the first week* . . . : Nahee Kim, "방탄소년단, 정규 2집 선주문 50만장 돌파 . . . 가파른 성장세," *News1*, October 7, 2016, https://www.news1.kr/entertain/music/2795111.

46 *More than a hundred fans waited at the airport* . . . : *BTS: Burn the Stage*, episode 2, "You Already Have the Answer," directed by Park Jun-soo, aired March 29, 2018, on YouTube, https://www.youtube.com/watch?v=L38H9yVb3d8.

46 *. . . performed dance covers outside the venue and waved their pickets* . . . : Ibid.

47 *Jungkook walked backstage and slumped onto a sofa* . . . : Ibid.

47 *Medics held a can of oxygen to his mouth* . . . : *BTS: Burn the Stage*, "Just Give Me a Smile."

47 *he stumbled for a moment, his hand touching the floor to keep himself from falling*: "BTS

Fire 170312 Wings World Tour In Chile," Kpop&Drama Fan Fansub K&DF, You-Tube, March 14, 2017, https://www.youtube.com/watch?v=ex29snt1OaA.

48 *Jungkook staggered backstage into a room . . .* : BTS: Burn the Stage, "You Already Have the Answer."

48 *Suga went to the bathroom and cried in secret*: BTS: Burn the Stage, "Just Give Me a Smile."

48 *A gel ice pack was held to Jungkook's forehead . . .* : BTS: Burn the Stage, "You Already Have the Answer."

48 *"I was in bad condition . . ."*: Ibid.

49 *. . . the foursome was stunned and elated . . .* : "[BANGTAN BOMB] Grammy Nomination Night," BANGTANTV, YouTube, December 15, 2020, https://www.youtube.com/watch?v=m1aAyKMVUUU.

49 *The idea was suggested by J-Hope, the dance leader, who texted Jimin and Jungkook*: "[BANGTAN BOMB] The 3J Butter Choreography Behind the Scenes," BANG-TANTV, YouTube, October 3, 2021, https://www.youtube.com/watch?v=O84fLDIU-T0.

49 *It was the first gathering of 3J for practice in four years . . .* : Ibid.

49 *The thirty-second dance break was choreographed by Nick Joseph*: Nick Joseph (@nickjxseph), Instagram, December 2, 2021, https://www.instagram.com/tv/CTm3K_gh1Xv/.

49 *The trio danced through the sequence once, as J-Hope monitored the rehearsal with Son Sungdeuk . . .* : "[BANGTAN BOMB] The 3J Butter Choreography Behind the Scenes," BANGTANTV.

51 *It has received more than seventy-eight million views to date:* "[CHOREOGRAPHY] BTS (방탄소년단) 'Butter (Feat. Megan Thee Stallion)' Special Performance Video," BANGTANTV, YouTube, September 9, 2021, https://www.youtube.com/watch?v=IkeZX2hnoOk.

CHAPTER 3: THE WAY HE SINGS

53 *he was unable to perform at company evaluations, and instead fidgeted in place for fifteen minutes:* Park So-young, "[Oh!커피 한잔③] 방시혁 '성격 변한 정국, 변함없는 진..방탄 모두 순수해,'" Osen, Naver, April 24, 2017, https://m.entertain.naver.com/article/109/0003524214.

53 *Jungkook could not sing on command . . .* : New Yang Nam Show, season 2, episode 1, aired February 23, 2017, on Mnet.

53 *Jungkook is said to possess perfect pitch*: Brian Hiatt, "Charlie Puth on Getting (Allegedly) Ghosted by Ellen's Label, Recording With BTS' Jungkook—and His New Album's Songwriting Secrets," Rolling Stone, October 8, 2022, https://www.rollingstone.com/music/music-features/charlie-puth-new-album-bts-jungkook-adam-levine-1234606344/.

54 *Jungkook matched a sequence of seven notes*: "Run BTS! 2021 EP.150 - 전의 전쟁 호캉스 1," BANGTANTV, YouTube, December 24, 2022, https://www.youtube.com/watch?v=f8lY0NIHrdQ.

54 *"He's a low-key prodigy . . ."*: Hiatt, "Charlie Puth on Getting (Allegedly) Ghosted by Ellen's Label."

54   *"The only artists that have ever sent me perfect vocals or recorded perfect vocals in front of me are Jungkook, Boyz II Men, and James Taylor"*: "Charlie Puth: The Puppy Interview," BuzzFeed Celeb, YouTube, October 26, 2022, https://www.youtube.com/watch?v=2CRqxoYnaKk.

54   *Jungkook's recorded vocal range spans somewhere from a G2 to a B♭5 . . .* : "방탄소년단 정국의 음역대 BTS Jungkook Vocal Range (G2 ~ Bb5) [0옥타브 솔 ~ 3옥타브 시♭]," Riki Kudo, YouTube, August 18, 2016, https://www.youtube.com/watch?v=gaTlDM9MdZw.

54   *there are entire Twitter accounts dedicated solely to his voice*: JK Vocals & Praises (@jjkvocal), X, accessed April 4, 2024, https://x.com/jjkvocal_.

54   *Coldplay's Chris Martin was openly awed after watching Jungkook . . .* : "Coldplay X BTS Inside 'My Universe' Documentary," BANGTANTV, YouTube, September 26, 2021, https://www.youtube.com/watch?v=viM_c-Fc7sc.

55   *Cirkut, who coproduced "Seven" with Andrew Watt, commented on Jungkook's versatility . . .* : *Jung Kook: I Am Still*, directed by Park Jun-soo (HYBE, 2024).

55   *Watt . . . was also impressed by Jungkook's range*: Ibid.

55   *"I honestly just love his voice"*: "Charlie Puth Reveals Details on Jung Kook Collab and How Attractive the BTS Star Is," SiriusXM, YouTube, June 29, 2022, https://www.youtube.com/watch?v=MabRZws3hz0.

55   *the Guinness World Record for the largest official fan club in 2008 . . .* : "TVXQ in Guinness World Record," KBS World, March 24, 2009, http://world.kbs.co.kr/service/contents_view.htm?lang=e&menu_cate=enternews&id=&board_seq=168389&page=244&board_code=music_news.

56   *Pdogg has described him as the epitome of pop*: *Jung Kook: I Am Still*.

56   *Jungkook has curated playlists for ARMY*: "Jungkook's Playlist," Spotify, accessed December 19, 2024, https://open.spotify.com/playlist/68BVOzAqp8N8VvPfBn2dUy.

56   *"I think he's the only one in Korea who can pull off pop like this . . ."* : "[슈취타] EP.21 SUGA with 정국 II," BANGTANTV, YouTube, November 4, 2023, https://www.youtube.com/watch?v=0RKnjVL2kWA.

57   *Suga revealed that HYBE had asked him to stop using Jungkook to record his demo tracks*: "[슈취타] EP.19 SUGA with 김종완," BANGTANTV, YouTube, October 17, 2023, https://www.youtube.com/watch?v=0FH-NPFe2So.

57   *"Ay-yo, finally! Is this what you've been waiting for?"*: G-Dragon, "Heartbreaker," YG Entertainment, music video, August 18, 2009, https://www.youtube.com/watch?v=LOXEVd-Z7NE.

57   *draws the ire of Sony Music, due to its resemblance to "Right Round" by Flo Rida*: Sanghee Han, "Big Bang Leader Accused of Plagiarism," *The Korea Times*, August 24, 2009, https://www.koreatimes.co.kr/www/nation/2025/02/719_50616.html.

58   *filed a lawsuit against SM, citing the exploitative thirteen-year "slave contracts . . ."*: Kang Young-soo, "박찬종 '동방신기는 '노예계약' . . . SM, "준사기죄" 해당,'" 조선일보, August 4, 2009, https://www.chosun.com/site/data/html_dir/2009/08/04/2009080401107.html.

58   *They claimed the company held an unreasonable amount of power over their careers . . .* : Court of the Republic of Korea, "우리법원 주요판결 - 상세보기 | 서울중앙지방법원,"

accessed November 12, 2024, https://seoul.scourt.go.kr/dcboard/new/DcNews ViewAction.work?seqnum=6353&gubun=44&scode_kname=&pageIndex=1& searchWord=&cbub_code=000210.

58 *the Korea Fair Trade Commission to standardize entertainment contracts to not exceed seven years*: Kim Hyo-jin, "K-Pop Stars Punished by Unfair Contracts," *The Korea Times*, December 3, 2014, https://www.koreatimes.co.kr/www/culture/2025 /02/135_169279.html.

59 *he ran through a list of his childhood aspirations: 2015 BTS 花樣年華 on Stage* (Stone Music Entertainment, 2016), DVD.

60 *"It wouldn't be an exaggeration to say that [BigBang] made BTS"*: "[슈취타] EP.3 SUGA with 태양," BANGTANTV, YouTube, January 18, 2023, https://www.youtube .com/watch?v=N43HXJCShx8.

60 *BigBang, even calling them role models at their debut showcase*: Kim Sooki, "방탄소년단 '빅뱅이 롤모델, 많이 배우고 있다,'" *News2Day*, June 12, 2013, https://www.news2day .co.kr/28559.

61 *"They are incredibly inspiring and influential people . . ."*: *Kiss the Radio*, interview, June 29, 2013.

61 *"nation's little sister"*: Eo Hwanhee, "'국민여동생'부터 '음원퀸'까지 . . . 데뷔 15주년 아이 유가 팬들에 전한 말," 중앙일보, *The JoongAng*, September 25, 2023, https://www.joon gang.co.kr/article/25195278.

61 *IU was the first artist whose CD Jungkook bought with his own money*: "K-Pop Sensations BTS Talk Eminem, Fandoms, and Learning English from 'Friends,'" Yahoo, YouTube, June 1, 2017, https://www.youtube.com/watch?v=naaFZYEQt6M.

62 *"Ending Scene" into a microphone*: 방탄소년단 (@BTS_twt), "마지막에 혼동이와서 음이 나갔어요 . . . #이해좀 #이런엔딩," X, December 20, 2018, https://x.com/BTS_twt /status/1075551103809335296.

62 *"Through the Night" on a VLIVE livestream*: BTS, "꾸기 라이브," BTS, Weverse (live-stream), April 22, 2017, https://weverse.io/bts/live/0-105457252.

62 *The first song, fully recorded and produced in South Korea, was the national anthem in August 1947*: Lee Jun-hue, "Before K-Pop: Popular Music Since the Korean War; Tracks from War-Torn Years," *Koreana*, Korea Foundation, Summer 2020, https://www .koreana.or.kr/koreana/na/ntt/selectNttInfo.do?mi=1544&nttSn=52505&bb sId=1114&langTy=KOR.

62 *Melon contains data from as far back as 1955*: Melon Chart Finder, Melon, https:// www.melon.com/chart/index.htm.

62 *The first time that Koreans were tracked alongside global artists on Melon was 1964*: Ibid.

63 *From the 1950s . . . by Busker Busker*: Ibid.

63 *tens of thousands of noraebang that popped up across the country from the early nineties*: Ben McKechnie, "A Tour of Seoul's Five Best Karaoke Venues with Singer Neon Bunny," BBC, December 29, 2023, https://www.bbc.com/travel/article /20231228-a-tour-of-seouls-five-best-karaoke-venues-with-singer-neon-bunny.

63 *her debut performance on* Show! Music Core: "IU - Lost Child, 아이유 - 미아 @ First Debut Stage, Show Music Core Live," TV-People, YouTube, July 7, 2014, https:// www.youtube.com/watch?v=PgEuO7FEGuM.

64   *IU later called the first album a failure*: Lee Kyung-ran, "Singer IU Wins Fans by Going Her Own Way," *Korea JoongAng Daily*, January 5, 2011, https://koreajoon gangdaily.joins.com/2011/01/05/etc/Singer-IU-wins-fans-by-going-her-own-way /2930559.html.

64   *Superstar K2, earned an 18.1 percent rating during its live finale*: 김병규, "'슈퍼스타K 2' 최종회 시청률 18.1%," 연합뉴스, October 23, 2010, https://www.yna.co.kr/view /AKR20101023033400005.

64   *More than 130,000 text message votes were sent by viewers*: Sang-hee Han, "Pop Democracy: Viewers Vote Huh Winner of Superstar K 2," *The Korea Times*, October 24, 2010, https://www.koreatimes.co.kr/www/art/2025/02/688_75101 .html.

64   *of the nearly two million that reportedly auditioned . . .* : Mee-yoo Kwon, "'Superstar K3' Returns with Diverse Music," *The Korea Times*, August 16, 2011, https://www .koreatimes.co.kr/www/art/2025/02/688_92883.html.

65   *unearthed from a pile of two thousand preliminary auditions*: *New Yang Nam Show*, season 2, episode 1.

65   *wearing a white long-sleeve . . . he begins to sing "Lost Child"*: "New Yang Nam Show [방탄소년단편 비하인드] ★특종★ 방탄 정국 슈스케 지원 두번째 영상," Mnet TV, YouTube, February 23, 2017, https://www.youtube.com/watch?v=hUK5O1RSwhY.

65   *called to sing again, he chooses "This Song"*: *New Yang Nam Show*, season 2, episode 1.

65   *seven business cards from agencies*: *BTS Comeback Show—DNA*, aired September 21, 2017, on Mnet.

65   *it was pre-debut videos of RM that impressed him*: *New Yang Nam Show*, season 2, episode 1.

65   *his father had suggested Big Hit based on founder Bang Si-hyuk's appearances on* Star Audition: Myeongseok Kang, *Beyond the Story: 10-Year Record of BTS* (New York: Flatiron Books, 2023), 45.

65   *Hakdong Park to the third-floor apartment on an unremarkable street, Nonhyeon-ro 149-gil*: "Run BTS! 2022 Special Episode - Telepathy Part 2," BANGTANTV, YouTube, August 23, 2022, https://www.youtube.com/watch?v=nbRKyymm4Eg.

65   *the dorm was what J-Hope described as "a den of rap"*: Kang, *Beyond the Story*, 44.

65   *BTS originally planned to debut as a crew of rappers and producers*: *BTS Monuments: Beyond the Star*, directed by Park Jun-soo (Disney+, 2023).

66   *The arrival of Jungkook heralded a shift from a hip-hop crew to an idol group*: Kang, *Beyond the Story*, 45–46.

66   *They have spoken of hearing the other artists through their in-ear monitors*: Kang, *Beyond the Story*, 90–91.

67   *performed at the Tokyo Dome for more than 110,000 fans over two days*: "2 PM Attracts 110,000 Fans at Tokyo Dome," Yonhap News Agency, April 22, 2013, https:// en.yna.co.kr/view/PYH20130422009700341.

67   *"I was the main vocalist of BTS, but the main vocalists of other groups . . ."*: *You Quiz on the Block*, episode 99, aired March 24, 2021, on tvN.

67   *running in place for ten to twenty seconds before singing their parts to build stamina . . .* : "[슈취타] EP.12 SUGA with Jin #2023BTSFESTA," BANGTANTV YouTube, June 10, 2023, https://www.youtube.com/watch?v=tZscK8j5a5w.

67   *her delayed success gave her a greater appreciation for what she had achieved*: Lee, "Singer IU Wins Fans by Going Her Own Way."

67   *"I thought the only person who could change the way things were was myself . . .":* You Quiz on the Block, episode 99.

67   *From the moment he woke up . . . he would sing to himself:* "[슈취타] EP.15 SUGA with Jung Kook," BANGTANTV, YouTube, July 29, 2023, https://www.youtube.com/watch?v=ocDDLPLKe70.

68   *The panel described Jungkook's singing as sweet . . . :* King of Mask Singer, episode 72, aired August 14, 2016, on MBC.

70   *Jungkook and Suga agreed that it was from "Dynamite" . . . :* "[슈취타] EP.21 SUGA with 정국 II," BANGTANTV.

70   *Suga has said that Jungkook's live singing now sounds like it has been run through Auto-Tune:* Ibid.

70   *Jungkook replied that he wanted his name to become shorthand for singing . . . :* Myeongseok Kang, "Jung Kook: 'I Want to Prove Myself through My Music,'" Weverse Magazine, June 15, 2022, https://magazine.weverse.io/article/view/433?lang=en.

70   *"Even without subtitles or translations . . .":* BTS-Trans, interview by the author over email, October 29, 2024.

CHAPTER 4: THE WAY HE MOVES

71   *The first glimpse of Jungkook on BANGTANTV is a dance practice uploaded four months before his debut:* "Dance practice by 정국 of 방탄소년단," BANGTANTV, YouTube, February 4, 2013, https://www.youtube.com/watch?v=Q3lL7zQ7kkA.

72   *the dance fundamentals routine rehearsed by trainees at JYP Entertainment . . . :* Master in the House, episode 61, aired March 17, 2019, on SBS.

73   *moved into a nineteen-story, multimillion-dollar headquarters in Yongsan:* Lee Narin, "Big Hit Ent. Unveils Photos of Their New Headquarters; to Make a New Start as HYBE Corp.," SBS Star, March 22, 2021, https://sbsstar.net/article/N1006251317/big-hit-ent-unveils-photos-of-their-new-headquarters-to-make-a-new-start-as-hybe-corp.

73   *Jungkook filmed the practice video for "Standing Next to You . . .":* "[CHOREOGRA-PHY] 정국 (Jung Kook) 'Standing Next to You' Dance Practice," BANGTANTV, YouTube, November 11, 2023, https://www.youtube.com/watch?v=M_EpTvMOnT0.

73   *H.O.T.'s second album sold more than a million copies in ten days . . . :* "H.O.T 소개 - 엠넷닷컴," Mnet, February 2, 2018, https://web.archive.org/web/20180202012553/http://www.mnet.com/artist/77297/profile.

74   *whose collective revenue kept SM at the top of the Big Three for years . . . :* Andrew Salmon, "Korea's S.M. Entertainment: The Company That Created K-Pop," Forbes Asia, August 11, 2013, https://www.forbes.com/sites/forbesasia/2013/07/31/koreas-s-m-entertainment-the-company-that-created-k-pop/.

74   *SM accidentally posted footage of an "Only One" dance practice by Shinhwa:* "더쿠 - 요즘 아이돌 그룹 안무 영상의 시초," The Qoo, February 1, 2021, https://theqoo.net/hot/1829227140.

74 *"officially a decade later and we're still talking about taemin's shirt"*: J (@user-tj 3cy2sm5j), comment on "SHINee 샤이니 'Lucifer' Dance Practice," SMTOWN, YouTube, August 3, 2010, https://www.youtube.com/watch?v=ovztfpWPo5M.

74 *"me: tries to focus on other members / taemin's shirt: how about no"*: yanki (@yanki4120), comment on ibid.

76 *". . . Now it's shifted over there to K-pop . . ."*: Val "Ms. Vee" Ho, interview by the author, June 17, 2024.

77 *Infinite and BTS managed to rise to the top of their respective eras*: Chung Joo-won, "K-Pop Group INFINITE Continues to Push for 'Top Spot,'" Yonhap News Agency, September 19, 2016, https://en.yna.co.kr/view/AEN20160919011700315.

78 *"thousands and thousands and thousands of repetitions to really master"*: Val "Ms. Vee" Ho, interview.

78 *According to Jin, Bang Si-hyuk would pore over the footage frame by frame . . .* : Myeongseok Kang, *Beyond the Story: 10-Year Record of BTS* (New York: Flatiron Books, 2023), 56.

79 *As trainees, BTS rehearsed up to fourteen hours a day, some days dancing for twelve hours*: Ibid.

79 *the addition of V in 2018*: Sungdeuk Son (@sonsungdeuk), "태형이~ . #방탄소년단 #BTS #singularity #이제공식적으로댄라," Instagram, May 6, 2018, https://www.instagram.com/p/BiceFnUF3me/.

79 *"Specific to them, it's really great choreography . . ."*: Val "Ms. Vee" Ho, interview.

79 *"All the bad memories of my life are from that time"*: "It's Good to Eat Well?," 요정재형, YouTube, May 5, 2024, https://www.youtube.com/watch?v=SbvsTj1fnC8.

80 *at 3:30 a.m., remarking that the day's work wrapped up earlier than expected*: "130123 RAP MONSTER," BANGTANTV, YouTube, January 26, 2013, https://www.youtube.com/watch?v=RkCDOwVaBDc.

80 *RM was jokingly nicknamed "dance prodigy . . ."*: "[Spotlight] 방탄소년단 | ② 랩몬스터, 슈가, 제이홉's story," 아이즈 (*Ize*), July 18, 2013, https://www.ize.co.kr/news/articleView.html?idxno=30013.

80 *"Not everyone is a great dancer, but they practice hard to become one"*: "BTS Exclusive Interview #BTSonBBCR1," BBC Radio 1, YouTube, January 19, 2018, https://www.youtube.com/watch?v=oRSVrtKph_k.

80 *"I'm a thousand percent confident it's all the practice that they have to do . . ."*: Val "Ms. Vee" Ho, interview.

80 *"Sticking only with kalgunmu never helps you improve your dance ability"*: Choi Hyun-jung, "[인터뷰] 인피니트, 칼군무가 아닌 그래서 더 역대급인 '태풍,'" 스포츠동아 (*The Dong-A Ilbo*), September 24, 2016, https://sports.donga.com/ent/article/all/20160924/80433629/2.

81 *There is the pervasive Western perception that K-pop idols are manufactured*: John Seabrook, "Factory Girls," *The New Yorker*, October 8, 2012.

81 *"We used to create the image of* kalgunmu, *even though each member has a different body type and their own feeling. It is not the time for us to conceal our own style anymore"*: Choi, "[인터뷰] 인피니트, 칼군무가 아닌 그래서 더 역대급인 '태풍.'"

82 *choreography they had practiced for nearly two straight months, according to Jin*: Kang, *Beyond the Story*, 56.

82   *he dialed up his groove . . .* : Val "Ms. Vee" Ho, interview.

83   *. . . described the routine as physically taxing . . .* : "Dancer Breakdown: 정국 (Jung Kook) 'Standing Next to You' Dance Practice (Ft. Brian Puspos)," STEEZY, YouTube, July 28, 2024, https://www.youtube.com/watch?v=zhaid0uiH8A.

84   *"It feels like he directly output the feeling the choreographer wanted to express"*: comment by @JKYH00, "Perfect #JungKook Energy #BTS #정국 #LE_SSERAFIM #르세라핌 #Perfect_Night #shorts," LE SSERAFIM, YouTube, October 27, 2023, https://www.youtube.com/shorts/VedxoD6FRRw.

84   *"This doesn't seem like it's from memorizing the choreography . . ."*: Comment by @juice3145, ibid.

84   *stage was a true group effort. Each member contributed to the choreography*: "[EPISODE] BTS (방탄소년단) @ 64th GRAMMY Awards," BANGTANTV, YouTube, July 4, 2022, https://www.youtube.com/watch?v=Hr1OSHf3S2Q.

84   *J-Hope instructed the others to relax and groove*: Ibid.

84   *he was invited alone by organizers*: "[EPISODE] 정국 (Jung Kook) FIFA World Cup Qatar 2022 Opening Ceremony Sketch - BTS (방탄소년단)," BANGTANTV, YouTube, February 12, 2023, https://www.youtube.com/watch?v=6Cqe6NR2bzc.

85   *he went as Jungkook of BTS . . .* : *Jung Kook: I Am Still*, directed by Park Jun-soo (HYBE, 2024).

85   *The Qatar World Cup was marked by controversy*: Paul MacInnes, "Human Rights Abuses in Qatar 'Persist on Significant Scale', Says Amnesty Report | World Cup 2022," *The Guardian*, October 20, 2022, https://www.theguardian.com/football/2022/oct/20/fifa-world-cup-human-rights-abuses-qatar-amnesty-international.

85   *the horrors committed by the Korean government in the lead-up to the 1988 Seoul Olympics*: Kim Tong-hyung and Foster Klug, "AP: S. Korea Covered up Mass Abuse, Killings of 'Vagrants,'" AP News, April 20, 2016, https://apnews.com/general-news-c22de3a565fe4e85a0508bbbd72c3c1b.

85   *"It's the first time a World Cup song ever in the history, that does over a hundred countries, at number one in the first day . . ."*: "RedOne and BTS' Jung Kook Have a World Cup Hit Song with 'Dreamers,'" Associated Press, AP Archive, YouTube, November 25, 2022, https://www.youtube.com/watch?v=CWZgKcgRgyw.

85   *he . . . stayed up until six in the morning learning the steps*: "[EPISODE] 정국 (Jung Kook) FIFA World Cup Qatar 2022 Opening Ceremony Sketch - BTS (방탄소년단)," BANGTANTV.

85   *Jungkook began considering ways to improve the stage . . .* : Ibid.

86   *"It was one of the most beautiful experiences I've had . . ."*: William Mullally, "Fahad Al Kubaisi: 'Performing with Jung Kook Was the Best Moment of My Life,'" *Esquire Middle East*, April 5, 2023, https://www.esquireme.com/brief/fahad-al-kubaisi-performing-with-jung-kook-was-the-best-moment-of-my-life.

CHAPTER 5: THE WAY HE LOOKS

87   *"the most iconic billboard in the world"*: Cam Wolf, "'The Billboard of New York': How Calvin Klein Turned a Billboard into an Icon," *GQ*, July 21, 2021, https://www.gq.com/story/calvin-klein-billboard-history.

87   *"one of the world's most popular artists . . ."*: "Calvin Klein Announces BTS' Jung

Kook as Global Ambassador for Calvin Klein Jeans and Calvin Klein Underwear," PVH, March 28, 2023, https://www.pvh.com/news/jung-kook-calvin-klein.

88 *Jungkook's fall 2023 campaign for Calvin Klein Jeans generated $13.4 million in media impact value in forty-eight hours . . .*: Renan Botelho, "BTS Star Jung Kook Bested Jeremy Allen White's Viral Calvin Klein Underwear in Media Exposure," *WWD* (online), December 12, 2024, https://wwd.com/pop-culture/celebrity-news /jung-kook-jeremy-allen-white-calvin-klein-2024-campaigns-1236763188/.

88 *A 2017 YouTube compilation titled "Jungkook is still a baby . . ." has more than four-teen million views . . .*: "Jungkook Is Still a Baby . . . #HappyJungkookDay," Park Chim Chim, YouTube, September 1, 2017, https://www.youtube.com /watch?v=PNKohUryOsI.

89 *"Because Jungkook is cute . . .":* "Run BTS! 2021 EP. 129," RUN BTS!, YouTube, July 5, 2021, https://www.youtube.com/watch?v=xFh0y-gfFnI.

89 *"Lately there's a guy who I've been thinking, wow, he's so cool . . .":* "Who Wants to Have an Online Fan Signing with Jessi? 《Showterview with Jessi》 EP.42 by Mobidic," Mobidic, YouTube, March 17, 2021, https://www.youtube.com /watch?v=fUCx6yI74Ic.

89 *a fan posted a three-second clip of Jungkook walking backstage shirtless . . .*: jungkook admirer₇ (@dreamjeons), "jungkook :o," X, January 10, 2024, https://x.com /dreamjeons/status/1744996509505008127.

89 *In 2020, he was named* People *magazine's "Sexiest International Man":* People, Novem-ber 30, 2020, 99.

89 *"Sexy at Every Age" feature in the 2022 Sexiest Man Alive issue, representing age twenty-five:* Dana Rose Falcone, "Sexy at Every Age," *People,* November 21, 2022, 79.

90 *Jungkook acknowledged the similarity on a Weverse livestream:* JK, "똑똑 . . . ," BTS, Weverse (livestream), May 24, 2023, https://weverse.io/bts/live/1-119598161.

90 *"Wearing anything you like, regardless of gender":* Maggie Bullock, "The Vanity Fair Best-Dressed List," The Ensembles, *Vanity Fair,* October 2019.

90 *As far back as the 1800s . . . Asian American men have been subject to emasculating stereotypes . . .*: Park Michael, "Asian American Masculinity Eclipsed: A Legal and Historical Perspective of Emasculation through U.S. Immigration Practices," *The Modern American* 8, no. 1 (2013): 5–17.

91 *"I'm losing my mind IM LOSING MY MIND rolling on the floor kicking my feet screaming crying":* Rheinna (@Rheinna11), reply to jungkook admirer₇, X, January 10, 2024, https://x.com/Rheinna11/status/1745003620377170293.

91 *"Father master daddy sir lord":* sopy⁷ | hobi tour with LV bag (@theastrojin), reply to jungkook admirer₇, X, January 10, 2024, https://x.com/theastrojin/status /1744999850373218356.

91 *". . . uh, Jungkook is a very attractive human . . .":* "Charlie Puth Reveals Details on Jung Kook Collab and How Attractive the BTS Star Is," SiriusXM, YouTube, June 29, 2022, https://www.youtube.com/watch?v=MabRZws3hz0.

91 *"He is so hot":* "Dancer Breakdown: 정국 (Jung Kook) 'Standing Next to You' Dance Practice (Ft. Brian Puspos)," STEEZY, YouTube, July 28, 2024, https://www .youtube.com/watch?v=zhaid0uiH8A.

92 *the third-largest market in the world for online beauty sales in 2023, according to*

Euromonitor: Kim Geumie, "Beauty Sales Surge through E-Commerce Expansion of K-beauty's Overseas Expansion Channels," 매일경제 (*Maeil Business Newspaper*), August 8, 2024, https://www.mk.co.kr/en/business/11088036.

94   *Jin called it the "eternal ingredient"*: "고빠닭진," *Bangtan Blog*, April 28, 2013, https://bangtan.tistory.com/m/151.

94   *In 2013, IU revealed the now-infamous diet . . .* : Eom Da-sol, "Shocking Diet Plans of Female Korean Celebs," *The Korea Times*, April 13, 2017, https://www.koreatimes.co.kr/www/art/2025/02/688_227532.html.

94   *an audience member called her a pig at her debut*: Cho Yunjung, "'You Look Like a Pig!' IU Recalls Her Debut Stage When She Was Booed & Insulted by the Audience," *SBS Star*, January 30, 2024, https://sbsstar.net/article/N1007518419/34you-look-like-a-pig34-iu-recalls-her-debut-stage-when-she-was-booed-insulted-by-the-audience.

94   *she began to struggle with eating disorders and poor body image*: "140회 힐링캠프," SBS, July 7, 2014, https://programs.sbs.co.kr/enter/healingcamp/vod/3213/22000107242.

94   *. . . after losing about forty-four pounds in forty days, he returned and was accepted*: Kang Bo-min, "[결정적장면]YG 양현석, 빅뱅 탑에 '데뷔하려면 살빼와' 지시에 20kg 감량," Newsen, May 19, 2015, https://www.newsen.com/news_view.php?uid=201505190029085810.

95   *that year, approximately twelve thousand men had their hair cut against their will by the police*: Kang Hyun-kyung, "'Ridiculous' 1970s," *The Korea Times*, February 22, 2019, https://www.koreatimes.co.kr/www/culture/2024/12/135_264236.html.

96   *Minho from SHINee, who upstaged Melania Trump at the 2018 PyeongChang Olympics*: "Melania 'Upstaged' by Korean Pop Star - BBC News," BBC News, YouTube, November 9, 2017, https://www.youtube.com/watch?v=EkiWMWdf02A.

96   *"I noticed that this man's face is perfect . . ."*: Charles S. Lee, MD, FACS (@drlee90210), TikTok, November 21, 2020, https://www.tiktok.com/@drlee90210/video/6897412085030997253?lang=en.

97   *He once shared that he was discovered on the street in middle school by SM Entertainment*: koya⁷ +ㅅ-) (@sugasjoonie), "jin actually went to the sm audition once but never returned," Jin radio interview, X, https://x.com/sugasjoonie/status/1411467875609714694.

97   *. . . he was allegedly discovered by a Big Hit casting director who spotted him getting off the bus*: *You Quiz on the Block*, episode 99, aired March 24, 2021, on tvN.

97   *He wanted to get a tattoo, he said*: BTS American Hustle Life, aired in 2014, on Mnet.

98   *in 2021, celebrity tattoo artist Doy was fined five million won . . .* : Lee Hae-rin, "Court Rules against Tattooing by Unlicensed Practitioners," *The Korea Times*, July 21, 2022, https://www.koreatimes.co.kr/www/nation/2025/01/113_333149.html.

98   *his body with tattoos, some he considered meaningful and others meaningless*: JK, "잘 지내셨습니까," BTS, Weverse (livestream), February 1, 2023, https://weverse.io/bts/live/2-113198481.

99   *"There might be ARMY that hate it but . . . I'm sorry, I really wanted to do it"*: JK, "후후후 . . ." BTS, Weverse (livestream), June 30, 2023, https://weverse.io/bts/live/4-123235750.

99   *Actress Han So-hee, for instance, removed the bulk of her tattoos* . . . : Lee Narin, "'I Didn't Want to Get Rid of Them' Han So-Hee Says It Was Not Her Choice to Remove Her Tattoos," *SBS Star*, January 16, 2024, https://news.sbs.co.kr/news/endPage.do?news_id=N1007500852.

99   *"Our mom and dad gave birth to us . . ."*: JK, "잘 지내셨습니까," Weverse.

100   *"Finding Jung Kook by Jimin PD," where Jimin went searching for Jungkook* . . . : "[BANGTAN BOMB] Finding Jung Kook by Jimin PD," BANGTANTV, YouTube, June 28, 2014, https://www.youtube.com/watch?v=mn6JrXmLdsU.

101   *13.5 cosmetic procedures were performed per every 1,000 individuals circa 2011*: SAPS (2011) ISAPS global statistics. International Society of Aesthetic Plastic Surgery, Hanover.

102   *more than 600,000 international patients visited Korea in 2023* . . . : "More Than 600,000 International Patients Visited Korea in 2023," Ministry of Health and Welfare press release, May 1, 2024, https://www.mohw.go.kr/board.es?mid=a20401000000&bid=0032&act=view&list_no=1481263&tag=&nPage=1.

102   *"A slant-eyed Korean interpreter speaking excellent English . . ."*: D. R. Millard, Jr. MD, "Oriental Peregrinations," *Plastic and Reconstructive Surgery* 16, no. 5 (November 1955), https://journals.lww.com/plasreconsurg/citation/1955/11000/oriental_peregrinations.1.aspx.

CHAPTER 6: HIS AUTHENTICITY

105   *A textbook pop song in the style of Katy Perry's "Firework . . ."*: Gil Kaufman, "Jessica Agombar, Co-Writer of BTS' 'Dynamite,' Says Goal for the Song Was 'A Positive, Huge Ball of Energy,'" *Billboard* (online), September 17, 2020, https://www.billboard.com/music/pop/bts-dynamite-jessica-agombar-writer-interview-9448606/.

106   *When discussing the origins of Korean hip-hop, witnesses and historians traced it back to Seoul in the 1980s*: "Episode 4: Itaewon Moon Night," Archive-K, YouTube, January 24, 2021, originally aired on SBS in 2021, https://www.youtube.com/watch?v=mI-TSMomeAI.

107   *"The seventies and eighties, Korean TV at the time was not only boring, but there was a curfew . . ."*: Dr. Kyung Hyun Kim, interview by author, June 14, 2024.

107   *grew up watching Alfred Hitchcock* . . . : Lee Seo-hyun, "American Genre Movies Are in My Blood, Says Bong Joon-Ho," *The Dong-A Ilbo*, February 15, 2020, https://www.donga.com/en/article/all/20200215/1979610/1.

107   *"From the moment I saw [Michael Jackson], my eyes were blinded . . ."*: "Episode 4: Itaewon Moon Night," Archive-K.

107   *Solid Gold, an eighties American pop music program, was also influential*: Ibid.

107   *"We knew exactly when Soul Train was coming on"*: Dr. Kyung Hyun Kim, interview.

108   *Moon Night was run by a man named Seo Chi Hoon*: "이태원 문나이트 사장님이자 이태원 카우보이 서치훈씨 그리운 우리 작은아빠," 네이버 블로그 | 포차도 해보고 밥집도 해보고 아이도 키우며 깨알잡식, May 23, 2023, https://blog.naver.com/yumi770808/223109113304.

108   *having witnessed racial discrimination against Black soldiers* . . . : "흑인들의 천국<솔트레인>,"*Ilgan Sports*, September 18, 1991.

108 *With Moon Night, Seo opened the doors to all club-goers* . . . : "Episode 4: Itaewon Moon Night," Archive-K.

108 *Artists like Run DMC, Public Enemy, and 2 Live Crew could only be heard at Moon Night* . . . : Ibid.

108 *Photographs captured Yang Hyun-suk* . . . : Ibid.

108 *"They would be the ones who would hang out there all of the time . . ."*: Dr. Kyung Hyun Kim, interview.

108 . . . *the only Korean allowed into the Soul Train club to learn dance* . . . : "Episode 4: Itaewon Moon Night," Archive-K.

109 *Their first three albums sold more than 1.6 million copies*: Fred Varcoe, "Seoul Music: Hot Rockin' In Korea," *Billboard*, April 20, 1996, 18.

109 *"godfather of Korean rock, the most important Korean musician of all time"*: Dr. Kyung Hyun Kim, interview.

110 *Seo Taiji and Boys released songs that rallied against the country's education system* . . . : Jiwon Choi, "K-Pop Pioneer Seo Taiji's 30 Years Remembered in 30 Hits," *The Korea Herald*, May 31, 2022, https://m.koreaherald.com/article/2875923.

110 *". . . we've often been subjugated even in that land that we call ours . . ."*: Dr. Kyung Hyun Kim, interview.

111 *he planned to model the group after the American R&B boy band B2K* . . . : Lee Eun-jung, "YG 양현석 'B2K 같은 아이돌그룹 육성중,'" Yonhap News, Naver, May 16, 2005, https://m.entertain.naver.com/article/001/0001003383.

111 *"Hip-hop, as a genre, places great importance on the rapper's values and worldview . . ."*: Ibid.

111 *". . . Truthfully, it's not something people will acknowledge"*: "[아이돌 메이커] 피독 프로듀서 | 무대에 맞춘 음악을 만드는 것," *Weiv*, November 29, 2013, https://www.weiv.co.kr/archives/6410.

112 . . . *he was composing poems about despair and loneliness, comparing himself to a fallen leaf*: Shim Jeong Hee, "램몬스터의 진짜 이야기," *Singles*, April 2015, 586–87.

112 *By age thirteen, he was active in the underground rap community* . . . : Ibid.

112 *"In Korea, Epik High and Garion, in overseas, Nas and Eminem . . ."*: Ibid.

112 *Though he flubbed it, forgetting most of the lyrics, RM's performance impressed Sleepy*: Myeongseok Kang, *Beyond the Story: 10-Year Record of BTS* (New York: Flatiron Books, 2023).

112 *One night over drinks, Sleepy shared RM's work with his friend Pdogg* . . . : "[아이돌 메이커] 피독 프로듀서 | 무대에 맞춘 음악을 만드는 것," *Weiv*.

112 *There were around thirty in total, as Pdogg said in a 2013 interview with* Weiv: Ibid.

112 *In a 2011 video advertising Hit It the Second Audition, Bang called for trainees who could sing and dance* . . . : "'hitman'bang Hit It Audition Ment," HYBE Labels, YouTube, July 12, 2011, https://www.youtube.com/watch?v=8XKDXHdj95s.

113 *At the time, BTS received criticism in Korea for acting too similar to groups like H.O.T.* . . . : Kim Bong-hyun, "램몬스터 | '욕하기 위해서라도 믹스테잎을 꼭 들어주시면 좋겠다,'" *Hiphopplaya*, March 24, 2015, https://hiphopplaya.com/g2/bbs/board.php?bo_table=interview&wr_id=782&sca=&sf1=wr_subject&stx=+%EB%9E%A9%EB%AA%AC%EC%8A%A4%ED%84%B0+&sop=and&scrap_mode=&mode=.

113 *"That's why we're just trying to plainly express the reality of now . . ."*: Ibid.

114 *"... We know you'll get hate for it, but if you want to do it, just do it"*: "[슈취타] EP.19 SUGA with 김종완," BANGTANTV, YouTube, October 17, 2023, https://www.youtube.com/watch?v=0FH-NPFe2So.

115 *Hit, who had sunk its resources into debuting the girl group Glam to low returns*: Kang, *Beyond the Story*, 53.

115 *As a trainee, RM curated a playlist of fifty-some tracks, from Nas and Biggie and Tupac*: Ibid.

115 *he and Suga and J-Hope taught the others everything they knew about hip-hop . . .*: Ibid., 54.

115 *The lyrics to "No More Dream" were written by RM, Suga, and J-Hope . . .*: Ibid., 78.

115 *Jimin recalls that the rap trio had asked him to describe his classmates . . .*: Ibid., 80.

116 *beyond family trips and four months studying in New Zealand at age twelve*: Kim Jae-Ha, "BTS's Rap Monster Talks Travel," *Chicago Tribune* (online), May 30, 2017, https://www.chicagotribune.com/2017/05/30/btss-rap-monster-talks-travel/.

117 *on the SimSimTaPa radio program in June 2013, he said his individual talent was speaking as a "heug hyung" or "Black bro"*: "신동의 심심타파 - BTS individual, 방탄소년단 개인기 20130625," MBCkpop, YouTube, June 25, 2013, originally aired on *SimSimTaPa* on MBC, https://www.youtube.com/watch?v=tMBGlvygT8w.

117 *In the introduction to the 1999 single "T.O.P.," RM said the N-word, as written in the original lyrics*: "BTS - This Love & T.O.P (SHINHWA), 방탄소년단 - 디스러브 & 티오피 (신화), Show Champion 20140319," MBCkpop, YouTube, March 21, 2014, https://www.youtube.com/watch?v=MHP6d-nGA14.

117 *"Bang Si Hyuk was absolutely more respectful of Black culture . . ."*: Dr. Kyung Hyun Kim, interview.

117 *The series begins with a staged kidnapping . . .*: *BTS American Hustle Life*, aired in 2014, on Mnet.

117 *"The show had serious problems with racial representation . . ."*: Dr. Kyung Hyun Kim, interview.

118 *RM spoke of collaborating with Warren G . . .*: Shim, "랩몬스터의 진짜 이야기."

118 *He spoke of learning from Warren G that negative stereotypes . . .*: Kim, "랩몬스터 | '욕하기 위해서라도 믹스테잎을 꼭 들어주시면 좋겠다.'"

119 *"I thought I need to hold responsibility for that . . ."*: BTS, "RM's Hello 2017!," BTS, Weverse (livestream), originally posted on VLIVE, January 3, 2017, https://weverse.io/bts/live/2-105470545.

119 *Suga later revealed that at the time, he had felt sure the album would be their last*: "[슈취타] EP.20 SUGA with 태민," BANGTANTV, YouTube, October 30, 2023, https://www.youtube.com/watch?v=_SEuehZqEXs.

120 *"Defining hip-hop is the same as trying to define love . . ."*: Shim, "랩몬스터의 진짜 이야기."

CHAPTER 7: HIS HUMILITY

121 *a lit cigarette between his lips*: Elaine Lui, "JK in LA," *Lainey Gossip*, September 7, 2023, https://www.laineygossip.com/does-jungkooks-appearance-in-la-mean-hes-heading-to-mtv-vmas/74714.

122 *"Dua was really smart . . ."*: Rhian Jones, "'Artists Have the Best Chance of Success When They Get Things Rolling Themselves,'" *Music Business Worldwide*, June 22,

2018, https://www.musicbusinessworldwide.com/artists-have-the-best-chance-of
-success-when-they-get-things-rolling-themselves/.

122   *Bang explained his desire to bring K-pop's "modularized" infrastructure* . . . : "The K-Pop
Mogul Behind BTS Is Building the Next BTS in LA," Bloomberg Television, You-
Tube, October 13, 2023, https://www.youtube.com/watch?v=wAd0LRkts8M.

123   *. . . it combines both culture and technology in a "logically formulized" way* . . . : Kim-
berley Kao, "Man behind the Korean Wave Talks about the Future of K-Pop
and What Aspiring Artistes Can Do," CNBC, December 5, 2022, https://www
.cnbc.com/2022/12/05/sm-entertainment-founder-lee-soo-man-on-k-pop-future
-running-business.html.

124   *. . . when he realized the potential of K-pop's particular fandom culture* . . . : Alex Barasch, "The K-Pop King," *The New Yorker*, October 14, 2024.

125   *Jungkook speaks in a very simple and clear manner*: BTS, "Jungkook 'Golden' Live On
Stage," BTS, Weverse (livestream), November 25, 2023, https://weverse.io/bts
/live/3-140559061.

126   *he spoke atypically as a child, not knowing how to properly use* jondaenmal . . . :
Myeongseok Kang, *Beyond the Story: 10-Year Record of BTS* (New York: Flatiron
Books, 2023), 61.

126   *he quickly noticed how others reacted to his informal style of speech* . . . : Ibid.

127   *"I knew they would succeed when I met them"*: "[INT.] Best Choreographer: 'BTS Destined for Success' (PART.2)," KOREA NOW, YouTube, October 9, 2023, https://
www.youtube.com/watch?v=GOWXMft9HYY.

127   *"Jungkook, if I like other male idols . . ."*: JK, "잘 지내셨습니까," BTS, Weverse (livestream), February 2, 2023, https://weverse.io/bts/live/2-113198481.

127   *The Ministry of Culture, Sports and Tourism was given funding to promote K-pop* . . . :
Kang Hyun-kyung, "Hallyu Boom Triggers Bureaucratic Turf War," *The Korea
Times*, March 12, 2012, https://www.koreatimes.co.kr/www/nation/2025/02
/113_106750.html.

128   *"I think he's become the most open-minded of all of us"*: "[2019 FESTA] BTS (방탄소년
단) '방탄다락'," BANGTANTV, YouTube, June 13, 2019, https://www.youtube.com
/watch?v=CPW2PCPYzEE.

128   *"It's about us being against racism and violence . . ."*: Rebecca Davis, "BTS on the
Decision to Donate to Black Lives Matter: 'Prejudice Should Not Be Tolerated,'"
Variety (online), October 2, 2020, https://variety.com/2020/music/news/bts
-black-lives-matter-donation-1234789434/.

128   *President Moon Jae-in brought BTS to the UN General Assembly* . . . : "[EPISODE] BTS
(방탄소년단) @ UNGA | SDG Moment 2021," BANGTANTV, YouTube, October 28,
2021, https://www.youtube.com/watch?v=3APNtu6gzLQ.

129   *"We live in uncertainty, but really, nothing's changed . . ."*: "BTS (방탄소년단) Speech at
the 75th UN General Assembly," BANGTANTV, YouTube, September 23, 2020,
https://www.youtube.com/watch?v=5aPe9Uy10n4.

CHAPTER 8: ARMY

131   *"Not like the other fans. #BTSArmy"*: The Simpsons (@TheSimpsons), X, April 24,
2023, https://x.com/TheSimpsons/status/1650290147353608204.

132   *uniting with other K-pop fandoms in 2020 to fight white supremacy* . . . : "K-Pop Fans Drown Out #WhiteLivesMatter Hashtag," BBC, June 4, 2020, https://www.bbc .com/news/technology-52922035.

132   *Jungkook became the face of a meme that remixed three stills from* Lord of the Rings: Return of the King: Jungkook SNS (@Jungkook_SNS), "Throwback to the most iconic 'stan jungkook' meme & #jungkook used by locals to call K-Pop fans for help during BLM movement," X, February 27, 2023, https://x.com/Jungkook _SNS/status/1630236527849779200.

134   *With a large team working together across time zones* . . . : BTS-Trans, interview by the author over email, October 29, 2024.

134   *The shortest videos can be done in a few hours* . . . : Ibid.

135   *"I like to think of Bangtansubs/BTS-Trans (and translators in general) as the 'glue' of the fandom* . . .": Ibid.

136   *Videos like "jungkooks duality being a threat to humanity for 8 minutes* . . .": "jungkooks duality being a threat to humanity for 8 minutes," KOOKIESTAETAS, YouTube, July 25, 2021, https://www.youtube.com/watch?v=EnkUTo0dPbE.

136   *"Jungkook hates losing at anything | 'you always have to let jk win' - Hobi" by SugArmyy, which has more than 5.8 million views* . . . : "Jungkook hates losing at anything | 'you always have to let jk win' - Hobi," SugArmyy, YouTube, January 2, 2022, https:// www.youtube.com/watch?v=zwrAg8nlAPI.

137   *"That was actually almost our last performance* . . .": Lee Narin, "EXID Hani Talks About Being 'Saved' by 'Up & Down' Fancam," *SBS Star*, December 31, 2020, https://sbsstar.net/article/N1006150639/exid-hani-talks-about-being-34saved34 -by-up-down-fancam.

138   *fancam of "Boy With Luv" on M Countdown (more than sixty-two million views)*: "[입덕직캠] 방탄소년단 정국 직캠 4K '작은 것들을 위한 시 (Boy With Luv)' (BTS JUNG-KOOK FanCam) | @MCOUNTDOWN_2019.4.25," M2, YouTube, April 27, 2019, https://www.youtube.com/watch?v=w5XxXWJrARU.

138   *an unofficial fancam of BTS's performance of "Idol" at the Lotte Family Concert* . . . : "190811 롯데패밀리콘서트 - IDOL / BTS JUNGKOOK fancam 방탄소년단 정국 직캠," JUST KEEP GOING, YouTube, September 3, 2019, https://www.youtube.com /watch?v=D87u-gkemxc.

138   *A May 25 streaming party for "Butter" attracted more than 400,000 listeners* . . . : Tatiana Cirisano, "This Social Audio App Is Driving Millions of Streams With Unofficial Listening Parties," *Billboard* (online), June 3, 2021, https://www.billboard.com /pro/stationhead-social-audio-streams-listening-parties/.

139   *Livestreams used to be supervised by a staff member, according to BTS*: Myeongseok Kang, *Beyond the Story: 10-Year Record of BTS* (New York: Flatiron Books, 2023), 153.

139   *On February 1, 2023, he turned on an impromptu live* . . . : JK, "잘 지내셨습니까," BTS, Weverse (livestream), February 1, 2023, https://weverse.io/bts/live/2-113198481.

140   *In June 2023, Jungkook fell asleep on Weverse in front of more than six million viewers* . . . : JK, "잘 거임," BTS, Weverse (livestream), June 12, 2023, https://weverse.io/bts/live /4-121390952.

140   *"You go on this livestream sometimes* . . .": "BTS' Jung Kook Talks New Single Going Platinum and Teaches Jimmy His 'Standing Next to You' Dance," The Tonight

Show Starring Jimmy Fallon, YouTube, November 7, 2023, https://www.youtube.com/watch?v=yY5wZemtXHI.

141 *"BTS's ability to capture hearts through their honest experiences . . .":* BTS-Trans, interview.

141 *Jungkook remarked, with light frustration, that sasaengs were still outside his house*: JK, "어," BTS, Weverse (livestream), December 8, 2023, https://weverse.io/bts/live/3-142418350.

141 *Jaejoong of TVXQ once woke up to a sasaeng fan in his bed*: "We were destined to meet｜Jaefriends Ep.32｜The Boyz Kim Jaejoong," Jae friends｜ST7, YouTube, March 21, 2024, https://www.youtube.com/watch?v=szZ5GxDu8xk.

141 *There are accounts online dedicated to selling idols' personal information . . .* : Pyo Kyung-min, "HYBE Exposes Illegal Sale of Artists' Personal Information," *The Korea Times*, June 19, 2024, https://www.koreatimes.co.kr/www/art/2025/02/732_376985.html.

142 *Jungkook putting on a fuzzy hood shaped like Cinnamoroll, the Sanrio mascot*: "190425 PERSONA 팬싸인회 N번 변신하는 정구기/방탄소년단 정국 직캠 BTS JUNGKOOK FOCUS FANCAM," Headliner, YouTube, April 26, 2019, https://www.youtube.com/watch?v=2_9AUk94RsU.

143 *a compilation of fan calls Jungkook conducted for Golden*: "[ENG SUB] Jungkook Fancall Compilation 231118," BTS BORA WORLD, YouTube, November 20, 2023, https://www.youtube.com/watch?v=JOJ5EXXqEGc.

143 *"The thing we're really digging into is the psychological mechanism of falling in love"*: Elizabeth de Luna, "The Fandom Business Is Booming. Can Weverse Capture Its Growth?," *Mashable*, April 25, 2023, https://mashable.com/article/weverse-app-president-joon-choi-interview.

143 *"shining and special existence"*:*I-Land*, episode 1, aired June 26, 2020, on Mnet.

144 *. . . sharing series like Nichijou . . .* : hitman (@hitmanb), Twitter, August 26, 2018, https://x.com/hitmanb/status/1033601489153867777.

144 *. . . idols like Akina Nakamori . . .* : hitman (@hitmanb), Twitter, February 17, 2014, https://x.com/hitmanb/status/435080918823206913.

145 *in 2024, they revealed that Aespa's Karina and actor Lee Jae-wook were dating*: "[단독] '서로, 첫눈에 반했다' . . . 카리나♥이재욱, 밀라노 연인｜디스패치｜뉴스는 팩트다!," *Dispatch*, February 27, 2024, https://www.dispatch.co.kr/2282864.

145 *Karina issued a handwritten apology*: Dong Sun-hwa, "Does Aespa Member Karina Really Have Anything to Apologize For?," *The Korea Times*, March 6, 2024, https://www.koreatimes.co.kr/www/art/2025/02/732_370151.html.

145 *there were hundreds of fans waiting at Incheon Airport's international arrivals . . .* : "BTS JungKook｜Humble Prince｜Airport Arrival," Korean First Class, YouTube, June 22, 2023, https://www.youtube.com/watch?v=txepyG8qpBI.

146 *A cover of "Rainism," performed at the 2016 MBC Gayo Daejejeon show*: "방탄소년단 – 레이니즘 BTS - Rainism @2016 가요대제전," TV-People, YouTube, January 6, 2017, https://www.youtube.com/watch?v=8WOxFTrFw70.

147 *"I believe a lot of hate and discrimination in this world is born out of ignorance and fear of the unfamiliar . . ."*: BTS-Trans, interview.

147 *"My main motivation is for the fandom . . ."*: Ibid.

148   . . . *gift for the 180 fans who won the lottery to attend. A bottle of Golden perfume . . .* : 꾸무•ˎₓ•´(@KooMu_twt), "꺄아아아아 정국이 엠카 조공 '골든향수'!!!!!!! 향수 안에 '금가루' 이씨!!", X, November 15, 2023, https://x.com/KooMu_twt/status/1724674797685407777.

148   *"Blooming splendidly in a resplendent display . . ."*: Ibid.

148   *"I'm happy that you all can listen to my song. Thank you. -JK-"*: Ibid.

148   . . . *began an impromptu Weverse livestream titled "Oh I missed you, a lot"*: JK, "보고 싶었 네 많이," BTS, Weverse (livestream), December 18, 2024, https://weverse.io/bts/ live/4-187961598.

CHAPTER 9: HIS SOLO CAREER

151   *He stayed up as late as he wanted . . .* : JK, "배고파요 . . . 첫찌 . . . 불금 . . . ," BTS, Weverse (livestream), March 24, 2023, https://weverse.io/bts/live/3-115684831.

152   *He played music on the speakers . . .* : JK, "3," BTS, Weverse (livestream), March 14, 2023, https://weverse.io/bts/live/1-115864714.

152   *He boiled buckwheat noodles . . . stirring it well*: JK, "모두 아프지말고 편안한 하루 되 세요," BTS, Weverse (livestream), April 25, 2023, https://weverse.io/bts/live /3-117661738.

152   . . . *watching YouTubers like YOOXICMAN . . .* : BTS, "What's going on," BTS, Weverse, originally posted on VLIVE, June 16, 2022, https://weverse.io/bts/live /0-105457354.

152   *"While I'm still young, I have to enjoy it . . ."*: JK, "3," Weverse.

152   *"Ah, our Jungkook has a talent for this and is good at it"*: "SUGA의 화양연화 pt.1 Album review," BANGTANTV, YouTube, October 4, 2015, https://www.youtube.com /watch?v=d5liS0Ah_W8.

152   *The night before the interview for the* Wings *concept book in 2017, he stayed up until seven . . .* : *BTS Wings Concept Book* (Big Hit Entertainment, 2017).

153   *"Besides, the kind of music and emotions I like are different from what the other members like . . ."*: Ibid.

153   *"When I see you smile in the screen, you're good at everything, you're just perfect / Feels like I've never been you"*: "BTS Jungkook – Decalcomania (Demo) Lyrics," Jaeguchi, YouTube, September 1, 2019, https://www.youtube.com/watch?v=DkGH 5lA9QXY.

153   *when fans inquired about its release two years later, he said he had deleted the files*: 페르 (@pere_bts), "정국이 머릿속에는 남아있는 데칼코마니," X, August 10, 2021, https://x .com/pere_bts/status/1424783319791587328.

153   *he had written many songs and sat on them . . .* : Myeongseok Kang, "Jung Kook: 'I've Been Changing a Bit,'" *Weverse Magazine*, July 20, 2023, https://magazine .weverse.io/article/view/825?ref=&lang=en.

154   . . . *he had come to "an all-stop," comparing his lifestyle to that of a rock*: JK, "잘 지내셨 습니까," BTS, Weverse (livestream), February 1, 2023, https://weverse.io/bts/live /2-113198481.

154   *The track, which was originally written for Bieber*: Alex Barasch, "The K-Pop King," *The New Yorker*, October 14, 2024.

154   *finalized over a year before its debut, according to an interview with* Forbes . . . : Hugh McIntyre, "The Producers of Jung Kook's 'Seven' Share the Behind-the-Scenes

Story of the No. 1 Smash," *Forbes*, July 28, 2023, accessed February 4, 2025, https://www.forbes.com/sites/hughmcintyre/2023/07/28/the-producers-behind-jung-kooks-seven-share-the-behind-the-scenes-story-of-the-no-1-smash/.

154 *Watt played the song for his manager Scooter Braun*: Ibid.

155 *He saw that the Southeast Asian K-pop market was stagnating and there was potential for growth in America*: "The K-Pop Mogul Behind BTS Is Building the Next BTS in LA," Bloomberg TV, October 12, 2023, https://www.bloomberg.com/news/videos/2023-10-13/k-pop-mogul-bang-si-hyuk-is-building-the-next-bts-video.

155 *"Scooter was the one that actually said this could be the biggest song in the world if Jung Kook sings it"*: McIntyre, "The Producers of Jung Kook's 'Seven.'"

155 *Braun took the song straight to Bang . . .*: Barasch, "The K-Pop King."

155 *Bang then personally took it to Jungkook . . .*: "The K-Pop Mogul Behind BTS," Bloomberg TV.

155 *"Upon hearing 'Seven,' I thought, 'This is it . . .'"*: Chris Willman, "Jung Kook of BTS Launches Solo Single, 'Seven,' With a Surprise Latto Feature: 'I Want to Show a More Mature and Grown Version of Myself,'" *Variety* (online), July 14, 2023, https://variety.com/2023/music/asia/jung-kook-bts-solo-single-seven-latto-feature-surprise-mature-1235669878/.

156 *"I only have one, big goal, and it's to be a giant pop star"*: Kang, "Jung Kook: 'I've Been Changing a Bit.'"

156 *On April 8, 2023, fans had lined up by 7 p.m. at Incheon Airport Terminal 2 . . .*: *Jung Kook: I Am Still*, directed by Park Jun-soo (HYBE, 2024).

156 *On April 10 at 1 p.m., he headed to the studio, seeming slightly anxious . . .*: Ibid.

156 *Accompanied by Bang Si-hyuk, a testament to the importance of this project to HYBE . . .*: Ibid.

157 *the pride he carried as a Korean artist and the desire to represent his nation on the stage of Western pop*: "[슈취타] EP.21 SUGA with 정국 II," BANGTANTV, YouTube, November 4, 2023, https://www.youtube.com/watch?v=0RKnjVL2kWA.

157 *"This kid is perfect, baby"*: *Jung Kook: I Am Still*.

157 *"I'm Korean, but I'd like to be the one and only singer who can cross back and forth between K-pop and pop songs . . ."*: Ibid.

158 *". . . it's pretty clear how massive of a run this guy is about to go on . . ."*: Ibid.

158 *Watt played two demos for Jungkook*: Ibid.

158 *Jungkook left and spent the evening with the demo track and lyrics . . .*: Ibid.

158 *"This is what all the hard work of being in BTS was for, ostensibly . . ."*: Jon Caramanica, "NewJeans' Ultimatum Casts K-Pop's Displays of Labor in a New Light," Arts, *The New York Times*, September 25, 2024, https://www.nytimes.com/2024/09/25/arts/music/newjeans-kpop-hybe.html.

159 *Jungkook said his solo schedules, though jam-packed and stressful, had been far more fun than he expected*: JK, "Golden," BTS, Weverse (livestream), November 3, 2023, https://weverse.io/bts/live/0-128993548.

159 *Jungkook realized that he was the type of person who preferred to be active . . .*: Ibid.

159 *"Because, in the end, I want it . . ."*: Myeongseok Kang, "Jung Kook: 'I Want to Prove Myself through My Music,'" *Weverse Magazine*, June 15, 2022, https://magazine.weverse.io/article/view/433?lang=en.

160   *Watt said he sounded like Michael Jackson: Jung Kook: I Am Still.*

160   *Would he receive recognition from others, he fretted to himself often:* Ibid.

160   *Jungkook had always dreamed of being a "U.S. pop star":* Barasch, "The K-Pop King."

160   *Originally, he had planned for a small EP . . . :* "[슈취타] EP.21 SUGA with 정국 II," BANGTANTV.

160   *Once, he stumbled over a tongue twister of a phrase . . . : Jung Kook: I Am Still.*

160   *Jungkook decided to proceed with an album fully in English:* Ibid.

161   *he shared on a VLIVE livestream that he wanted to help RM . . .":* BTS, "감사합니다앙!," BTS, Weverse (livestream), originally posted on VLIVE, April 14, 2019, https://weverse.io/bts/live/1-105471133.

161   *Jungkook capably fielded a few questions in English:* "BTS on First Impressions, Secret Career Dreams and Map of the Soul: 7 Meanings," The Tonight Show Starring Jimmy Fallon, YouTube, February 25, 2020, https://www.youtube.com/watch?v=v_9vgidPJ8g.

161   *he had a long way to go to reach RM's level of fluency and continued to practice . . . :* Kang, "Jung Kook: 'I Want to Prove Myself through My Music.'"

161   *"This album was prepared for the overseas music market, so we chose all English songs":* Suh Jung-min, "Jungkook of BTS Shares 'Golden Moments' with World in All-English Solo Album," *Hankyoreh*, November 6, 2023, https://english.hani.co.kr/arti/english_edition/e_entertainment/1115138.html.

161   *"I wasn't working on an album, but after listening to 'Seven,' I came out of a break . . .":* Rania Aniftos, "Jung Kook Enjoys Korean Treats off His Spotify Billion Streams Plate," *Billboard*, December 18, 2023, https://www.billboard.com/music/music-news/jung-kook-eats-korean-food-spotify-billion-streams-plate-1235561480/.

161   *he went to a doctor's office to have his throat examined . . . : Jung Kook: I Am Still.*

162   *Seconds after he left the stage, the rain began to fall . . . :* Ibid.

162   *"Isn't this too much?" he said. "I'm so sad . . .":* Ibid.

162   *Jungkook was backstage at* The One Show *in London, warming up his body . . . :* Ibid.

162   *he had recorded in Seoul in July, taking notes and a video call with the producer David Stewart:* Ibid.

162   *Jungkook pulled up the lyrics to "Hate You," rehearsing them in the quiet darkness:* Ibid.

162   *"Before I go to the military . . . I'll release the singles . . .":* Ibid.

163   *"I received approval as Jung Kook of BTS. I received lots of it . . .":* Ibid.

163   *Pdogg . . . noticed that as a solo artist . . . Jungkook was free to delve into different sounds:* Ibid.

163   *Stewart . . . noted that Jungkook's accent and Western pop vocals had grown more natural . . . :* Ibid.

163   *Braun advised Jungkook to follow the lead of Justin Timberlake:* Barasch, "The K-Pop King."

164   *he himself became a fanboy, seeing Jungkook reach a new level of skill: Jung Kook: I Am Still.*

164   *"I think the fans will really love it . . .":* Ibid.

164   *"I really like his songs and his videos. MJ is coming through all of the moves. I just think he's great!":* "Jungkook: Standing Next to You," Diana Ross website, February 21, 2024, https://www.dianaross.com/my-favorites/jungkook-standing-next-to-you.

164   "'Standing Next to You' was obviously a smash when Jungkook put it out . . .": Usher, interview with iHeartRadio, February 9, 2024.

165   he smiled as he signed a copy of Golden to give to Usher . . . : "정국 (Jung Kook), USHER 'Standing Next to You - USHER Remix' Official Performance Video Sketch," BANGTANTV, YouTube, February 3, 2024, https://www.youtube.com/watch?v=wb17xbM5LhU.

165   he later invited him to perform at the 2024 Super Bowl halftime show: Barasch, "The K-Pop King."

166   Jungkook went live on Weverse to discuss Golden's successful release . . . : JK, "Golden," Weverse.

166   he considered his voice an instrument . . . : Ibid.

167   "I think it was a year where I showed who I am . . .": Ibid.

CHAPTER 10: HIS LOYALTY

169   Jungkook sat down . . . with his hairdresser Park Naejoo: Jung Kook: I Am Still, directed by Park Jun-soo (HYBE, 2024).

169   "Please never forget that whenever or wherever I am, I am always with all of you": BTS, "Jungkook 'Golden' Live On Stage," BTS, Weverse (livestream), November 25, 2023, https://weverse.io/bts/live/3-140559061.

170   "It was fun, right . . .": Jung Kook: I Am Still.

173   their sunshiny Hobi had also "become a man": BTS, "잘 다녀오겠습니다!," BTS, Weverse (livestream), December 5, 2023, https://weverse.io/bts/live/2-130707485.

173   Jungkook announced that it was officially his last schedule . . . : "정국 (Jung Kook), USHER 'Standing Next to You - USHER Remix' Official Performance Video Sketch," BANGTANTV, YouTube, February 3, 2024, https://www.youtube.com/watch?v=wb17xbM5LhU.

174   ". . . you would probably feel melancholy by the time you watch this video . . .": Ibid.

175   he resolved to cut his hair slowly, bit by bit, like "mobal-lighting": JK, "똑똑 . . . ," BTS, Weverse (livestream), May 24, 2023, https://weverse.io/bts/live/1-119598161.

175   . . . their last group live broadcast before they enlisted in the military . . . : BTS, "잘 다녀오겠습니다!," Weverse.

176   The matter of gendered conscription was brought to the constitutional court once in 2014 and once in 2023 . . . : Park Boram, "Constitutional Court Upholds Male-Only Conscription," Yonhap News Agency, October 4, 2023, https://en.yna.co.kr/view/AEN20231004004200315.

176   "It's unfortunate, but it's time to go," Jimin said . . . : BTS, "잘 다녀오겠습니다!" Weverse.

177   The singer MC Mong was sentenced in 2011 . . . : Jee-ho Yoo, "(LEAD) Singer MC Mong Gets Suspended Jail Term over Draft Dodging," Yonhap News Agency, April 11, 2011, https://en.yna.co.kr/view/AEN20110411009800315.

177   In 2023, Ravi of VIXX left the group after his suspected involvement . . . : Kim Rahn, "K-Pop Star Ravi under Probe for Involvement in Draft Dodging Scandal," The Korea Times, January 13, 2023, https://www.koreatimes.co.kr/www/art/2025/01/398_343533.html.

177   his most recent and third attempt to receive a visa was denied in September 2024: Ji-won Woo, "Singer Steve Yoo Files Lawsuit Following Third Korean Visa Rejection,"

Korea JoongAng Daily, September 30, 2024, https://koreajoongangdaily.joins.com/news/2024-09-30/entertainment/kpop/Singer-Steve-Yoo-files-lawsuit-following-third-Korean-visa-rejection/2144773.

177   *the second-fastest-rising income inequality rate as of 2023*: Ryu Yi-geun, "Income Inequality in S. Korea Is Widening at Second-Fastest Rate in OECD," *Hankyoreh*, April 10, 2023, https://english.hani.co.kr/arti/english_edition/e_national/1087257.html.

177   *campaigned on a promise to restore "fairness and common sense"*: Lee Seung-jun, "After 2 Years in Office, Yoon's Promises of Fairness, Common Sense Ring Hollow," *Hankyoreh*, May 7, 2024, https://english.hani.co.kr/arti/english_edition/e_national/1139560.html.

179   *"Whilst these young pop stars are contributing to the image of Korea as much as people in traditional arts and sports . . .":* Chung Esther, "Law May Be Changed to Give BTS Military Extension," *Korea JoongAng Daily*, November 22, 2020, https://korea joongangdaily.joins.com/2020/11/22/national/socialAffairs/BTS-military-service-amendment/20201122172308969.html.

179   *"[We've] been on track to reduce cases of military exemptions until now . . .":* Lee Michael and Kim Jee-Hee, "[WHY] BTS and the War on Korea's Military Exemptions," *Korea JoongAng Daily*, June 4, 2022, https://koreajoongangdaily.joins.com/2022/06/04/why/BTS-military-duty-korea/20220604070019881.html.

180   *As fans commented that they were sad, he remarked thoughtfully that he was sad too . . .* : JK, "어," BTS, Weverse (livestream), December 8, 2023, https://weverse.io/bts/live/3-142418350.

180   *"To me, BTS is more important than my solo work":* JK, "Golden," BTS, Weverse (livestream), November 3, 2023, https://weverse.io/bts/live/0-128993548.

180   *he looked sentimental as he spoke of how much he missed the noise . . .* : BTS, "잘 다녀오 겠습니다!" Weverse.

181   *". . . we also want to see BTS as a full group sooner than later . . .":* Ibid.

181   *At under eight minutes, the live was brief, the mood sober . . .* : JK, "자르 다녀오겠습니다," BTS, Weverse (livestream), December 11, 2023, https://weverse.io/bts/live/3-142889334.

182   *"I always think that I stopped growing up mentally at age fifteen":* *BTS: Burn the Stage*, episode 3, "Just Give Me a Smile," directed by Park Jun-soo, aired April 5, 2018, on YouTube, https://www.youtube.com/watch?v=RmZ3DPJQo2k.

182   *"The guys filled me in one by one . . .":* Ibid.

183   *Jin declared that he wanted to give "light hugs" to a thousand fans . . .* : Fan Wang, "BTS' Jin to Hug 1,000 Fans As He Returns from Military Service," BBC, June 12, 2024, https://www.bbc.com/news/articles/cglle5x8pgdo.

183   *the alleged "six-month post-discharge plan":* "[슈취타] EP.14 SUGA with J-Hope," BANGTANTV, YouTube, July 19, 2023, https://www.youtube.com/watch?v=5x fosKUglZw.

183   *the company was in talks with BTS to resume their group activities in 2026*: Pyo Kyung-min, "Will BTS' Reunion Be Delayed to 2026?," *The Korea Times*, November 7, 2024, https://www.koreatimes.co.kr/www/art/2025/02/732_385902.html.

184   *"We were BTS!":* BTS, "잘 다녀오겠습니다!" Weverse.

185 *opened an exhibition dedicated to his solo career.* Golden: The Moments *was:* "Jung Kook Exhibition 'Golden: The Moments' Ticket Opening Information," HYBE Insight notice, Weverse, July 29, 2024, https://weverse.io/bts/notice/21096.

186 *"jeon jungkook the whole world loves you, i love you, jeon jungkook kpop legend . . .":* BTS EXHIBITION (@bighit_exhibition), "[HYBE INSIGHT] Jung Kook Exhibition 'GOLDEN: The Moments' IN SEOUL 0901 Congratulations! Heartfelt messages from the exhibition visitors," Instagram, September 1, 2024, https://www.instagram.com/p/C_Wy2wmBTcN/?img_index=2.

187 *Tens of thousands of guests reportedly visited the Seoul exhibition:* BTS EXHIBITION (@bighit_exhibition), "[HYBE INSIGHT] Jung Kook Exhibition 'GOLDEN : The Moments' IN SEOUL The [HYBE INSIGHT] Jung Kook exhibition 'GOLDEN : The Moments' in Seoul, which has been visited by tens of thousands of guests, is coming to a close tomorrow," Instagram, September 21, 2024, https://www.instagram.com/p/DAKWJKRhjki/.

187 *"Why am I so popular? . . .":* Myeongseok Kang, "Jung Kook: 'I've Been Changing a Bit,'" *Weverse Magazine,* July 20, 2023, https://magazine.weverse.io/article/view/825?ref=&lang=en.

188 *"BTS Jung Kook shines brightly, but Jungkook is shabby . . .":* "[2019 FESTA] BTS (방탄소년단) '방탄다락,'" BANGTANTV, YouTube, June 13, 2019, https://www.youtube.com/watch?v=CPW2PCPYzEE.

189 *he and Jimin both entered the army's 5th Infantry Division:* Shim Sunah, "(2nd LD) Jimin, Jungkook Join Army; All BTS Members Now on Hiatus," Yonhap News Agency, December 12, 2023, https://en.yna.co.kr/view/AEN20231211008652315.

189 *he began his duties as a cook:* Kang Kyung-min, "Peek into Jungkook's Military Life with 'Workman' Cooking Show," *K-en News,* April 23, 2024, https://www.k-ennews.com/news/articleView.html?idxno=736.

189 *"ARMY are you doing well?:* JK, Weverse, March 16, 2024, https://weverse.io/bts/artist/4-156420956.

190 *one reason he did not participate in the songwriting was because of his personality . . . :* JK, "Golden," BTS, Weverse (livestream), November 3, 2023, https://weverse.io/bts/live/0-128993548.

191 *As he wondered aloud what he would have been doing if he had never become an idol . . . :* BTS, "Jungkook 'Golden' Live On Stage," BTS, Weverse (livestream), November 25, 2023, https://weverse.io/bts/live/3-140559061.

191 *Jungkook went to visit a Barnes & Noble in the city . . . : Jung Kook: I Am Still,* directed by Park Jun-soo (HYBE, 2024).

191 *he wondered, if he wasn't a singer, if he would come to buy someone's album . . . :* Ibid.

192 *"I'm in good condition, and it's a good day to wrap up . . .":* Ibid.

192 *"You've got 30min New York. Jung Kook is performing LIVE on the TSX Stage. 5:30 p.m. See you soon":* TSX Entertainment (@tsxentertainment), Instagram, November 10, 2023, https://www.instagram.com/tsxentertainment/p/CzcPaxMxi0D/.

192 *He could hear their cheers from the hotel room above the square . . . : Jung Kook: I Am Still.*

192 *"Hey, New York City! I'm Jungkook of BTS, let's have fun":* "Jung Kook Live at TSX,

Times Square," BANGTANTV, YouTube, November 10, 2023, https://www
.youtube.com/watch?v=geHuX7E3NX8.

193 *Jungkook walked along the sidewalk in Los Angeles, clutching a simple white paper
flyer . . .* : *BTS American Hustle Life*, aired in 2014, on Mnet.

193 *"Most of all, when I engage in solo activities, I deeply miss the moments we shared
together . . ."* : Gladys Yeo, "Jungkook Says He 'Misses' Performing with His BTS
Bandmates," *NME* (online), September 18, 2023, https://www.nme.com/news
/music/jungkook-says-he-misses-performing-with-bts-bandmates-3499514.

193 *Jungkook wanted to write his own lyrics . . ."* : BTS, "BTS Live : WINGS Behind story
by RM," BTS, Weverse (livestream), originally posted to VLIVE, October 20, 2015,
https://weverse.io/bts/live/0-105457236.

193 *Around January 2016, the seven members of BTS had gathered together to cry . . .* : Ibid.

ABOUT THE AUTHOR

MONICA KIM is a writer, known primarily for her work at American *Vogue*, where she was an editor for five years. A former stylist and brand consultant, she splits her time between Seoul and New York. *The Meaning of Jungkook* is her first book.